Für Ingrid,
mit herzlichen Grüssen und Wünschen für
ein gesundes und gutes neues Jahr.

Din
1-13-94

Edition Axel Menges

Dirk Lohan

**Buildings and Projects of Lohan Associates
1978–1993**

edited by
Cheryl Kent

with a preface by
Franz Schulze

Wasmuth

© 1993 Ernst Wasmuth Verlag, Tübingen/Berlin
ISBN 3-8030-2809-4

All rights reserved, especiallly those of translation
into other languages.

Design: Axel Menges

Printed in Korea.

Contents

7	Franz Schulze: A Work in Progress
13	Cheryl Kent: An Interview with Dirk Lohan
20	McDonald's Office Campus, Oak Brook, Illinois
39	TRW World Headquarters, Lyndhurst, Ohio
50	Frito-Lay National Headquarters, Plano, Texas
56	The Oceanarium, Chicago, Illinois
66	Museum Campus, Chicago, Illinois
68	Cityfront Center, Chicago, Illinois
74	Market Tower, Indianapolis, Indiana
78	Dean Witter Financial Services Headquarters, Riverwoods, Illinois
82	Rockwell International Graphic Systems Headquarters, Westmont, Illinois
84	Lakefront Lagoon, Chicago, Illinois
86	One-Fifty North Dearborn Office Tower, Chicago, Illinois
88	Ameritech Center, Hoffman Estates, Illinois
100	Illinois State Toll Highway Authority Headquarters, Downers Grove, Illinois
106	Devon House, Ada, Michigan
110	Harold Washington Library Center, Chicago, Illinois
114	Amerika-Gedenkbibliothek, Berlin, Germany
118	Steelcase/Stow & Davis Showroom, Chicago, Illinois
122	Dain Bosworth Tower, Minneapolis, Minnesota
126	Village of Old Mill Creek, Old Mill Creek, Illinois
128	Safety-Kleen Corporate Headquarters, Elgin, Illinois
130	Eli Lilly and Company Interiors, Indianapolis, Indiana
134	University of Chicago Graduate School of Business, Chicago, Illinois
138	University of Illinois at Chicago Molecular Biology Research Facility, Chicago, Illinois
140	Lincoln Park Residence, Chicago, Illinois
144	Harris Trust and Savings Bank Operations Center, Chicago, Illinois
148	Olympiaquartier 2000, Berlin, Germany
150	American Business Center, Berlin, Germany
152	Mies van der Rohe Glass Tower at Bahnhof Friedrichstraße, Berlin, Germany
158	Credits for Illustrated Buildings and Projects
160	Photo Credits

Acknowledgments

This book represents a collective effort and I can only begin to name the people who deserve thanks. Dirk Lohan, and his partners, John Bowman, Joseph Caprile, and James Goettsch have been unfailingly supportive of the book and the considerable demands I have made on the office for its sake. I am particularly grateful to Dirk Lohan for all the time he gave to our conversations. There are many others who have been similarly generous, who took time to discuss specific projects in detail with me, among them: Edwin Denson, George Halik, Michael Heider, Perry Janke, John LaMotte, Karen Lindblad, Algis Novickas, Matthias Royal-Hedinger, Thomas Shafer and Basil Souder. David Fleener is to be thanked for the high level of drawings that prevails throughout. David did many of the most beautiful drawings himself and directed the preparation of all the rest. He was assisted by Boonlert Chutkrich, Brad Erdy, Masachika Hisatake, Perry Janke, Jason Kerwin, James Lee, Keith McLemore, Shirley Moy, Martin Newton, Phuong Nguyen, Camilo Oquendo and Edwin Witkowski. Jane Powell compiled the photography, and, with seemingly boundless professionalism and patience, found the answers to countless questions.

Cheryl Kent

Franz Schulze
A Work in Progress

In the revolt against Modernism that began in the late 1960s, Chicago undertook a serious reassessment of its architectural past. Proud of the legacy of John Wellborn Root, Louis Sullivan, Frank Lloyd Wright and Ludwig Mies van der Rohe – builders traditionally identified with both Chicago and Modernism in one way or another – the city nonetheless came to recognize that these artists were as different from one another as they were similar, and that the architecture of Chicago consisted of substantially more than what they and their disciples had produced.

During the last generation, local observers have learned to respect much that was formerly scorned or ignored. The 1893 World's Columbian Exposition, once deplored as a gargantuan exercise in stylistic regression, is now appreciated for the unity and logic of its planning. Comparably, the ornamented office buildings of the 1910s and 1920s are no longer dismissed as throwbacks to nineteenth-century historicism and are, instead, widely admired for their scale and probity as well as the manner in which their deference to tradition enhances their civic presence. Chicago Art Moderne has been reevaluated upward, whether in the form of the commercial structures of Holabird and Root, Graham, Anderson, Probst & White, the daring light and color effects achieved in the 1933 Century of Progress Exposition, or the suburban houses of William and George Fred Keck. Other independents – Howard Van Doren Shaw, Andrew Rebori, Howard Fisher and David Adler – lead a growing list of designers esteemed today who were little more than textbook footnotes 30 years ago.

Moreover, as the city has acknowledged a greater complexity in the forces contributing to its architectural history, its current architectural practice admits a widened range of philosophical and stylistic approaches. The Postmodernism of Hammond, Beeby and Babka and the high-tech efforts of Murphy/Jahn are evidence enough of this, but no better proof of a freer and more open climate may be cited than that Modernism has sustained a vital place in Chicago. It is, to be sure, a modified Modernism, one that has learned much from the lessons of the last quarter century.

Thus to Lohan Associates, whose singular place in Chicago architecture derives from the working synthesis it has made of Modernism and its latter-day alternatives. The firm's fidelity to the former is less surprising than its exploration of the latter. Originally Lohan Associates was the office of Ludwig Mies van der Rohe, one of the most illustrious representatives of the early Modernist movement and, by far, the most influential Chicago architect in the decades following World War II. A central figure among European vanguardists of the l920s, who sought to create a revolutionary architecture out of what they perceived as an irresistible new technology, Mies abstracted his buildings into almost purely structural configurations of steel and glass. Hence their lean undecorated rectilinearity, their freedom from the presumably corrupting burden of traditional historical styles. Hence too, by extension, the dissimilarity between Modernist buildings and the environments they invaded, which were regarded as less deserving of accommodation than replacement.

As an artist, Mies was great enough to survive the failure of Modernism's dogmas. Ultimately, the urban landscape proved too vast to be conquered by any single architecture and too unruly even to be kept in check. Moreover, the Modernists found themselves victimized by a double irony: in those instances where messy ancient neighborhoods were replaced with their new visions, the Modernists often showed how cold and uncommunicative a heaping of their »purity« could be while demonstrating how much warmth and sociableness had been immanent in the old cityscape after all.

What followed was a recognition throughout the profession that any new architecture might profitably work its way into the existing urban frame rather than strain imperiously against it. Forms might also be cultivated that would convey meaning to a public long unmoved by a vocabulary of reductivist abstraction. This gradual shift of intention developed even in Chicago, where some of the best and most defensible Modernist work had been produced by Mies and his gifted disciples, chiefly Skidmore, Owings & Merrill (SOM) and C.F. Murphy Associates. Thus the city was a fitting place to recall the triumphs of Modernism even as its shortcomings revealed themselves.

The period in which the change occurred coincided with the coming of age of Dirk Lohan, Mies's grandson and the central figure in the firm that now bears his name. Lohan was born in 1938 in Rathenow, a small town near Berlin. Among the clear images of his youth are the modestly scaled houses and civic buildings of German towns, their rootedness in tradition, their intimacy with the natural environment. These recollections have little to do with the tenets of Modernist architecture in which Lohan was formally trained, first at the Illinois Institute of Technology in Chicago (the school whose architecture department had been shaped by Mies following his emigration to the U.S. in the year Lohan was born), later at the Technische Hochschule in Munich.

In 1962, when Lohan graduated from the Technische Hochschule and took a place in the office of his grandfather, Modernism was at its international crest. Lohan's first major assignment was to assist Mies in the design and execution of the master's last great work, the New National Gallery in Berlin. By the time that building was completed in 1968, Mies's health was in decline and Lohan, personally closer to him than anyone else in Chicago, persuaded the old man to ensure the continuity of the firm by establishing a partnership. At Mies's passing in 1969, the Office of Mies van der Rohe was formally created, with control shared by Lohan and two devoted former students of Mies, Joseph Fujikawa and Bruno Conterato. The name of the firm was changed in 1975 to Fujikawa, Conterato, Lohan and Associates and shortened to FCL Associates in 1982 when Joseph Fujikawa formed his own firm, Fujikawa Johnson and Associates. Four years later, following the retirement of Bruno Conterato, the office was renamed Lohan Associates.

Both surviving businesses could claim to have inherited the Miesian mantle, although, prior to the division, differences in approach among the partners could already be discerned. Fujikawa, long entrusted with supervision of the high-rise structures that were a hallmark of Mies's architecture in the 1960s continued to specialize in that building type during the three-man phase of the firm while Conterato spent some of his time designing but more of it overseeing administrative matters in the office.

Meanwhile Lohan, youngest of the three, was put in charge of a large project in 1978 that was to be a significant marker in his career. It was also a job representing a building type with far-reaching consequences for the American landscape. This was the corporate headquarters of McDonald's, the most famous and successful purveyor of fast food to a world market and, when Lohan began his design, one of the largest corporations in America.

Such huge businesses once housed themselves in big-city downtowns. But, with the automobile's conquest of the countryside since World War II, corporations have progressively moved into suburban areas. The results of the shift include some of the most execrable architecture of the twentieth century. The worst and most common examples take the form of hulking speculative office buildings, hastily conceived, cheaply built and dropped aimlessly like Brobdingnagian children's blocks along metropolitan freeways. They surround nearly every big city in the United States. During the 1970s the Kennedy Expressway northwest of Chicago was devastated by such objects, which were put up close enough to draw upon the city's resources but at sufficient distance to lighten or escape the burden of its tax rolls. Not only did they desert established communities, they composed themselves into solipsistic packages so limited in services that the possibility of forming any new communities was foreclosed.

Happily, these structures are not the only examples of the genre. Some thoughtfully designed corporate headquarters buildings were produced during the last several decades, perhaps most often by SOM. It may suffice to recall the Emhart Corporation Headquarters in Bloomfield, Connecticut (1963), and the American Can Company Headquarters in Greenwich, Connecticut (1967–70), both by Gordon Bunshaft of the SOM New York office, and the Weyerhaeuser Headquarters in Tacoma, Washington (1972), by Edward C. Bassett of the SOM San Francisco office. In each case the architects worked in the established Modernist manner of clean, structurally oriented lines learned mostly from the Miesian example.

While Lohan knew these works, he had a special and deeper attachment to the John Deere Administration Center in Moline, Illinois (1957 to 1963). The architect, Eero Saarinen, had established his own record of devotion to Mies, most obviously in his General Motors Technical Center in Warren, Michigan (1948–56). Moreover, in the Deere headquarters Saarinen made daring use, for the first time on a large scale, of the technologically innovative Cor-Ten steel. In short, he had certifiable Modernist credentials. Yet, in the interiors at Deere, he added substantially to the Cor-Ten such time-honored materials as brick and wood and generous amounts of judiciously arranged greenery with the result that the building was embellished without being ornamented. An equally manifest Modernism on the exterior was also qualified by a landscaping program that softened and enriched rather than conflicted with the steel façade.

Indeed it was the perceptible warmth of the Saarinen design that was most on Lohan's mind as he began work on McDonald's. That and the recognition that the corporate headquarters building was destined ineluctably for a location at the edge or outside of the city. That fact was given. In an automobile age there was too little incentive to stay in town and too much to leave. The principal question was how to create an architectural work that would not only respect the countryside but provide a civilized working environment in an artificial, virtually self-sufficient construct removed from existing communities.

The solution common to SOM, Saarinen and Lohan has been the campus, a large tract of land the company would take to itself to build its mini-city. This is the genre in which Lohan Associates has made its most distinctive mark on recent American architecture.

The McDonald's campus stands on 80 acres of land in Oak Brook, a western Chicago suburb. While Lohan left most of the indigenous heavy woods undisturbed, he has added a pair of lakes and a network of roadways that run casually among the trees and around an informally sited group of buildings. All three structures, an office building, a lodge and a training center, are low and ground-hugging, as asymmetrical in their plans as the campus is as a whole. None of them rises higher than the trees.

The outward reach of the office building is searching and unimpeded, lending it a faint resemblance to the pinwheel plan of Mies's famous Concrete Country House (1923) and the Bauhaus in Dessau (1925/26) by Walter Gropius and Adolf Meyer. These are the first of a number of associations Lohan appears to have drawn, consciously or unconsciously, from the work of the early masters of Modernism. As he designed it, however, Lohan was fully aware of the quotation evident in the spacious three-story central atrium at the entry. It is lined in emphatic horizontal courses of red brick with glass brick and rusticated limestone accents, the whole articulated by a double staircase and strikingly reminiscent of the foyer of Frank Lloyd Wright's Johnson Wax Administration Building in Racine, Wisconsin (1936–39), itself one of the classic pieces of corporate headquarters design.

Indeed the autumnal palette and use of brick so powerfully identified with Wright are perhaps the most memorable marks and among the most winning features of the McDonald's campus. Elsewhere, and again gratifyingly, the interiors of the building are illuminated by natural light issuing through either windowed walls or crowning skylights. The arms of the building are flanked by balconies with details of brick, lime-

stone and ship's railings that are also reminiscent of Johnson Wax.

The exterior is less pronounced in its indebtedness to any single architectural source. The rectilinear modularities of the elevations are generically Modernistic and enlivened by the bold three-dimensional rhythm of brick stanchions and wide overhanging eaves. Low, curving, fieldstone walls mediate between the geometry of the elevation's proportions and the almost dreamy play of the landscape as it drifts toward the lakes and into the trees. There was a marked effort by the architect to create a psychically inviting atmosphere by uniting work areas with recreation facilities. That is most dramatically expressed in the footbridge arching in a sensuous S-curve over one of the ponds and joining the training center, with its classrooms and offices, to the lodge, with its guest rooms and exercise complex.

McDonald's is only the first of several campuses Lohan constructed during the 1980s and early 1990s. The three other principal examples are: Frito Lay in Plano, Texas, TRW in Lyndhurst, Ohio, and Ameritech in Hoffman Estates, Illinois. All share features with McDonald's in their acknowledgment of and capitalization on the openness of their exurban sites. Parking areas are, in each case, either masked or absorbed within the building. The long arms of the structures are narrow to permit natural light to reach the center. To augment a sense of community among employees, restaurants, lounge areas, and recreational centers are taken to be vital supplements to these corporate campuses.

While Lohan makes next to no effort to invoke historicist allusions common to orthodox Postmodern architecture, he is not averse to using tradition in his own way. Among the first responses to Ameritech, especially as one sees it at a distance from the interstate highway, is that it has the profile of a Baroque palace. A central pavilion is joined by two great arms to wings that extend forward in a plan akin to Balthasar Neumann's Residenz in Würzburg (begun in 1719) or to François Mansart's Chateau de Maisons near Paris (1642–50). Moreover, the entrance is reached by a circular driveway that rises a full story and looks and functions as a kind of *cour d'honneur*. By contrast with McDonald's, which took a rich natural surround as the context to which it adapted itself, Ameritech is built on a large empty prairie that it has almost totally to itself. Appropriately, it projects a countenance that is as stately, formal and self-aware as McDonald's plan is rambling and casual. For all its formality, Ameritech is anything but cold, largely on account of a vigorous and colorful decorative program that – typical of Lohan – communicates through a Modernist rather than historical iconography. Glass brick, the dominant device of the interior, is used to spectacular effect in the grand two-story foyer. Indeed, the square is the module of the entire program. The shape is repeated throughout the building in plan and in a profusion of patterns and hues that enliven the interior wall surfaces and punctuate the exterior granite spandrels.

Lohan has lately made the traditional city office tower one of the office's principal concerns, with Market Tower in Indianapolis his first major effort in the genre. The building stands within a stone's throw of Monument Circle, the ceremonial center of the city. Early in the twentieth century this became the site of a handsomely integrated group of low-rise buildings focused on the Soldiers' and Sailors' Monument. That harmony was violated in intervening years as some of the older buildings were demolished and replaced with less sensitive structures. How, then, to put up a high-rise building that would serve the needs of a contemporary business district without doing further violence to the historic elements remaining there: this became the chief design task.

The solution is a 32-story tower that looks every inch a modern building, with enough variations, however, to suggest resonances with older structures in the vicinity. Pink granite sheathing the base is, by itself, a more traditional material than steel or aluminum and its use, most conspicuously in the lowest four floors of the façade, relates to the cornice line of the ad-

1. Skidmore, Owings & Merrill, Headquarters of the American Can Company, Greenwich, Connecticut, 1967–70.
2. Eero Saarinen and Associates, John Deere Administrative Center, Moline, Illinois, 1957–63.
3. Lohan Associates, McDonald's Office Campus, Oak Brook, Illinois, 1978–.
4. Frank Lloyd Wright, S. C. Johnson & Son Administration Building, Racine, Wisconsin, 1936–39.

jacent building. Green-tinted glass reflects both the statuary of Monument Circle and some of the copper roofs of the surrounding buildings, just as the arched entry of Market Tower echoes similar uses elsewhere in the immediate area. Even its more candidly contemporary qualities distinguish the tower from the standard prismatic slab of Modernist high rises. The north and south façades feature 15-foot cantilevered walls that create a vigorous notched effect in the elevation and several setbacks that rise above level 22 to a quasi-mansard roof – the latter referring to a neighboring building – to produce a distinctive profile.

The setback feature is even more pronounced in the Dain Bosworth Building. At the base of this tower – one of the most prominent high rises in Minneapolis – is a retail center containing a galleria, artificially lit to create an atrium effect. While this four-story block extends outward from the main mass of the building, its rear is slipped under the tower. The effect is an asymmetry that is reflected in the profile of the whole building. The tower's core is set off center to accommodate the retail block occupying the tower's base. The 33-story shaft is a gleaming study in glass, the reflectivity of which is heightened by the complex series of setbacks that animate it volumetrically and assist in effecting the transition to the retail block. This complex surface has inspired the addition of lights at several levels of the tower producing a lively play of effects on the tall walls. Dain Bosworth is not reductivist architecture in either content or form.

The Oceanarium of the John G. Shedd Aquarium in Chicago is probably the most dramatic work produced by Lohan Associates during the firm's seven-year existence. It is a large facility with a physically challenging function: the accommodation of a collection of fascinating marine mammals, like whales, dolphins, seals and sea otters. The architects' solution was a space and structure that do justice to the manifold and complex program.

The old John G. Shedd Aquarium, to which the Oceanarium has been added, is one of the main components in the renowned ensemble of museum buildings standing near Lake Michigan and flanking Lake Shore Drive just south of the Loop. The Shedd, which was designed by Graham, Anderson, Probst & White and completed in 1929, stands near the Field Museum of Natural History. The two buildings are clearly related in their white marble dress and neoclassical manners – the Field in the Corinthian order, the Shedd in the Doric – and they command their site with stunning authority. (At a slight remove but allied functionally is the domed Adler Planetarium with Art Déco ornament drawn from classical sources.) The integrity of the group is such that any addition risked discordance.

If the new element repeated the classical manner of the old, it might look like so much architectural archaeology; if it took a contemporary identity, it risked looking out of place among its neighbors.

The Oceanarium is frankly Modernist and avoids potential failings by the adroitness of its siting below and behind the main building. Conceived as an arc embracing the back of the aquarium, it is built on landfill extending well into the lake. The visitor, guided along a newly created route through the old aquarium, is ushered into the column-free space of the Oceanarium, where he enjoys a view eastward toward a great glass wall that discloses the lake beyond it. The waters of the several pools, where the animals disport themselves, appear to merge with the surface of the lake, producing an uncannily seamless effect of endless distance. The roof's space-frame support is exposed overhead and its massive dimensions are in keeping with the vastness of the space. Auditorium seating at the pools' edge is bordered by a convincing array of artificial flora appropriate to the Pacific northwest coast habitat of the animals. Nearby are subsidiary display spaces for penguins and otters. The addition is flanked by a meeting hall and a restaurant that offers a panoramic view of the Chicago skyline.

The Oceanarium has purposely been made difficult to see from Lake Shore Drive, but it is visible enough from the causeway road that leads

5. Lohan Associates, The Oceanarium, Chicago, Illinois, 1983–91.
6. Lohan Associates, TRW World Headquarters, Lyndhurst, Ohio, 1981–85.
7. Lohan Associates, Devon House, Ada, Michigan, 1987–92.
8. Lohan Associates, Harold Washington Library Center, Chicago, Illinois, 1988. Competition entry.
9. Leo von Klenze, Alte Pinakothek, Munich, Germany, 1826–36. The stairs were added by Hans Döllgast in 1956.

eastward. Here one can see that the Oceanarium is faithful to the Miesian tradition in structure and in its realization of unitary space. Indeed the airiness that is the most memorable feature of the new addition could have been achieved only by steel and glass technology and in no better manner than straightforward Modernism. Nonetheless, Lohan has been mindful of the original aquarium's classicism, expressing the great glass wall of the Oceanarium as a trabeated temple front with its long white architrave supported by abstracted capitals.

Equal in stature to the Shedd among Chicago's cultural institutions is the Chicago Public Library whose traditional home, a building completed in 1894 by the Boston firm of Shepley, Rutan and Coolidge, had been outgrown by the 1970s. In 1975 the library was obliged to move the overflow of its collections to another space, and then another, while local authorities wrangled over a new facility. In 1988 a design competition was held for a new central library on a site south of the Loop.

Lohan Associates was among the five competitors for the Harold Washington Library Center (named for the city's deceased mayor). The firm did not win the commission, but its proposal was of sufficient thoughtfulness to qualify among its most ambitious works.

Lohan's design exhibits a strong commitment to a declarative structuralism that is apparent at a glance: first in the steel frame of indented bays on the east front; second, in the modular rectangular fenestration used throughout the building. This perception is reinforced by the clean geometric components of the interior, especially in the grand foyer where huge sheets of glass admit light, and in the system of supports that emphasize the frame.

Yet, as a whole, the building has next to none of the self-referentiality associated with strict Modernism. Located with its main entrance facing State Street, it follows the scale and proportion of the great old buildings lining the street and, in its end pavilions, there is even a reminder of the »Chicago window« so commonplace up the street to the north. Louis Sullivan's Carson Pirie Scott Building (1899–1904) comes to mind, as do the old Davis Store (1912) and the former Wieboldt's Store (1905), both by Holabird & Roche, and the Reliance Building (1894/95) by D.H. Burnham & Co.

But a context of time as well as of space is observed: the building conveys a monumentality identified with institutional edifices of the past. The recessed façade's hung columns dramatize the main entrance, which leads to an imposing foyer dominated by one of history's most dependable symbols of public authority, the staircase. The source here is the great stair added by Hans Döllgast in 1956 to Leo von Klenze's Alte Pinakothek, the museum of old master painting in Munich, well known to Lohan from his student days. Lohan volunteers his debt to the stair and, no less, to the Pinakothek's façade, from which he took the idea of a pair of strong ends flanking an indented center. These various elements stress the monumentality of a design that is ambitious and provocative enough to have retained its interest to students of architecture and urban planning.

Earlier in his career, when his office still bore Mies's name, Lohan was assigned the repair and renovation of the Farnsworth House in Plano, Illinois (1946–50), one of Mies van der Rohe's masterpieces and the only major residential design he completed in the United States. Lohan came to know the building so intimately that it intensified his desire to produce a house on his own.

The commission for the Devon House provided the opportunity to satisfy his wish. The contour of the house, which was completed in 1992 in Ada, Michigan, describes a pure 42-foot cube. Yet that simple geometric solid has been subjected to a remarkably complex treatment in plan and elevation. While it is technically three-floors high, more than one floor per story issues from a staircase rising the height of the building, adding up to more than one plane per story. The complicated interior space is reflected in the exterior surfaces, expressed differently on each face of the cube. The plan itself, ambiguous and asymmetrical, is anchored by a fireplace and the main stair, around which spaces develop in an arhytmic pattern. The kitchen and dining room are raised higher than the living room, which – with a two-story height – is the dominant interior space. All three rooms constitute the second floor, which is in the nature of a *piano nobile* on two planes. The similarly multi-leveled third floor is given over to bedrooms. A Corbusian image is invoked by the garage on the ground floor and garden on the roof – one recollects the Villa Savoye – but the elevation, in its rigorously linear framing, turns this association toward Mondrian and De Stijl. Even the Farnsworth House comes to mind. The Devon House is a cunning marriage of freedom and compelling order, not precisely indebted to any one of the masters it recalls, but rather to all of them.

Lohan Associates is comparatively young by the standards of the profession. The record of the firm's passage from stern orthodoxy to probing eclecticism reflects the searchings of late-twentieth century architecture. The Lohan catalog is bound to look very different ten years hence. Just as no one could have foreseen that a firm once belonging to Mies van der Rohe would produce works as disparate as Ameritech and the Devon House, it seems safe to say that still more unpredictable forms responding to yet-unencountered requirements are waiting to emerge from the office's drawing boards. Certifiably among the major firms active in one of the world's most architecturally important cities, Lohan Associates has reached a point in its fortunes where it can anticipate the widening of its international audience.

DL: I think so. It's a search for that. Life is change. That is not to say you have to change for change's sake, but if you don't drive yourself, you will fossilize and dogmatize.

CK: When you say change for change's sake, I think of Postmodernism. The word suggests a reaction against rather than a movement towards something.

DL: Yes, I've never been too enamored with it. At the same time, I am grateful for what it has brought us.

CK: Freedom?

DL: Yes, and the ability to look into history again and consider how to visualize the lessons of the past. My criticism of Postmodernism is that there are too many practitioners willing to adopt formal solutions for today's problems. That is a meaningless transportation of a style from one period to another. But the debate over the last 15 years has been healthy. It has exposed the 1950s and 1960s as a monolithic period. What we have now is diversification in architecture. I'm not sure that we will ever go back to a dominant movement. I think it will be much more pluralistic from now on.

CK: And that's more desirable to your mind?

DL: I think it is inevitable. It's part of modern society and its technology. The state of communications technology means everything is thrown at you wherever in the world it is done. When you look at our work the projects appear quite different from one another, but we believe that each building, and each situation should have its own solution. Now that we are back in Europe again [Lohan Associates opened a Berlin office in 1991], we will have solutions that are quite different from those we had here in Chicago. That is not to say there aren't some underlying principles: you can elevate structural concerns as a way of guiding expression. That is valid. But not for me. I think it is too limited. There are other factors, like context, technology, economy: in considering different parameters, the issue is to strike a balance among them.

CK: Let's talk about another area of work in the office – the corporate campus. This is a uniquely American, uniquely suburban building type. They are like immense skyscrapers laid on their sides.

DL: In architectural literature there is so much more attention given to high-rise design even though, for the last 50 years, almost all the important development in terms of size and money has gone into the suburbs. Probably half or more of all Americans live and work in the suburbs. So these corporate campus projects are certainly very important.

CK: They reflect the decentralizing dynamics of the United States. McDonald's was your first such commission?

DL: Yes, McDonald's was the first. I was 35 years old and flabbergasted that I got the job. Then I wondered if I wanted it. McDonald's was not exactly a purveyor of good taste so I was a little leery. What we finally designed and built had nothing to do with our original competition design.

CK: That was a more Modern scheme?

DL: Yes, it was a much more rigid, rectilinear, Modern scheme.

CK: McDonald's is out in the countryside.

DL: Yes. The site is beautiful by Illinois standards. It is subtly rolling with nice stands of oak trees, and one magnificent and rare, big Ohio Buckeye tree. We made that the central focus in the Lodge courtyard.

CK: Another issue was the identity of the corporation.

DL: McDonald's has an innate sense for bringing people together and fostering a sense of belonging. They succeed in this extremely well. Fred Turner [McDonald's senior chairman] always stressed creating environments that would be conducive to that kind of interaction.

CK: How did your design support that?

DL: First of all – even though there is a structure – it is informal and appears unstructured. It is very open and accessible, and the materials are warm and rich. There is a lot of red brick and wood.

CK: Wasn't one of the influences on this design Frank Lloyd Wright's Johnson Wax buildings in Racine, Wisconsin?

DL: There is a tradition in the Midwest and Frank Lloyd Wright's work is very much a part of that. John Deere [John Deere and Company Administration Center in Moline, Illinois, by Eero Saarinen] is another outstanding Midwestern design of a similar building type. So, perhaps, both of these played indirect roles. Everyone who worked on this project certainly was aware of these first-rate examples of architecture done for corporations in the flatlands.

CK: You told me McDonald's was the first building you ever put a curve in.

DL: That's true. And since then I like curves.

CK: So it has more sensuous forms.

DL: Yes.

CK: Well, TRW is another corporate campus – quite different from McDonald's though.

DL: Yes, it came after McDonald's. It is much more structured, more ordered and systematic than McDonald's – less free.

CK: Expressive of another kind of culture?

DL: Yes, a more traditional, hierarchical one. Therefore, the architecture is more structured and formal. I was very influenced by Saarinen's John Deere when I was designing TRW. It's evident in the long spans and the window walls that are recessed from the perimeter. Mies was another influence. He was meticulous in his detailing and TRW is very finely detailed, particularly in the curtain wall and exterior cladding.

CK: In some ways, Ameritech is the most formal of your corporate campuses.

DL: Yes, the plan is formal and axial. It makes the organizational principle of the whole site plan immediately understandable. We did that partly as a reaction to the disorganized development in the suburbs where buildings and road systems have no apparent logic. The building is formal for the same reason. When you have 1.3 million square feet on four floor plates, you get a typical floor of over 250,000 square feet. Each floor is the size of an entire building. Making it formal organizes it. At the same time formality often brings with it monumentality.

CK: Intimidating?

DL: Imposing. But when you are inside the building the rigidity of the plan is broken. We rotated the two atriums so there is a surprising twist in the whole building system that relieves the plan.

CK: One of the problems that runs throughout the corporate campus plans is what to do with the car.

DL: In the suburbs, where these projects are located, the car is even more important than it is in the city. You must provide a parking space for every person at work. The challenge is to arrange the parking in such a way that it doesn't take over the whole site so it looks like a shopping mall surrounded by a sea of parking. We've gone to great lengths in each of these projects to either put the cars underground, if the owner is willing to pay that expense, or to do some limited structural parking. At Frito-Lay we put parking on the high ground and the building is in a valley. Almost all the views to the outside overlook the landscape, not parking lots. We think a lot about trying to make the car work functionally without letting it dominate the project.

CK: The car creates another problem, how do you deal with the entry of the building when employees are arriving by car and parking in remote lots?

DL: All the buildings have strongly expressed entries. Ideally, we'd like to have employees walk through the front door. But that might mean parking in front of the entry – not the best spot. At McDonald's and TRW employees actually arrive in the main lobby of the building from parking inside the building. That way they still come through the front door, so to speak. We didn't want them to take some back stair, the sense of arrival and departure in the building is too important. At Ameritech and Frito-Lay there is outdoor parking and a vast amount of it. So it wasn't possible to have all the employees come through the front door. We developed employee side entrances. They are treated as secondary entrance lobbies. They are not just back doors, they celebrate the arrival. In those two cases the front door is for visitors, and those few fortunate people who arrive by taxi or limousine.

CK: You've said the corporate campus is the American version of the chateau.

DL: Literally, they are like chateaux because they are large grand structures built in the land-

Cheryl Kent

scape and surrounded by gardens. These buildings are oases. The landscaping and views as one approaches the building and looks out from it are all very important.

CK: Another concern running consistently through the corporate campus projects is bringing light into the building.

DL: We work hard to give everybody daylight – secretaries, clerical people, and executives. Sometimes that means executives don't get perimeter offices. Or if they do, we might have clerestory or glass walls inside, so the inner spaces also receive daylight. [In Lohan's corporate campus buildings, wings – where work areas are located – extend from a central hub. The wings are narrow, permitting light to penetrate into the center. Generally, enclosed offices are placed in the center instead of on the perimeter where they would block light.]

CK: That's not the traditional order. Has that been a tough sell to some of your clients?

DL: Everybody agrees with the principle but sometimes the implementation becomes a problem. It means doing away with perks that upper management cherishes, such as private offices on the window wall. But human beings, secretaries as well as executives, need natural light to orient themselves during the day. Without that you might as well live in a bunker. And who would think that is humane? You want to know if the sun is shining or if it's raining.

CK: In Ameritech you kept the size of the offices uniform.

DL: The managers, directors and higher-ups are on the inside. Their offices have glass walls overlooking the clerical work stations on the perimeter of the building, a reversal of the usual arrangement. Ameritech's management wants the company to become more entrepreneurial. Managers used to be rewarded with bigger offices and special furniture. But they are restructuring their culture and a part of that is eliminating some of the old-fashioned rewards.

CK: And making the middle manager offices the same size, the same 150 square feet, also helps people to be moved within the building more easily.

DL: Yes. We've just been hired to do the German consulate here in Chicago. The space plan they brought us is terribly antiquated. They have a dozen different office sizes for different ranks. Can you imagine: somebody retires, or quits, or dies and suddenly they have an office that can't legitimately be occupied by somebody of a different rank. That makes no sense at all.

CK: You have an office in Germany now. Let's talk about the work there. Is it different?

DL: I've always felt if Berlin could be whole it would be an important city again. Then came the events of two years ago: the Wall came down, the East opened, Communist regimes collapsed and Berlin became one city. This is one place in the world where there are great challenges for architects and planners. You're not just filling in a parking lot with a new building in an otherwise complete city. There are vast areas that are undeveloped, that have been ruined either by bombing in World War II or by replanning. They want to rebuild that city and knit it back together. We are in the final rounds for Olympiaquartier 2000, a large development on public land near where the Wall used to be. It will be built by the private sector and partially used by the city.

CK: What does the project include?

DL: It includes an enclosed sports hall for 20,000 people, for gymnastics, boxing, equestrian events and so on. It's right in the middle of the city about five minutes from Unter den Linden, which is like Fifth Avenue or Michigan Avenue. It also involves a large amount of office, residential, hotel and retail development. So it is not just an Olympic hall. It is the large-scale planning that is fascinating.

CK: You could not put up a stadium of that size in this country and have anything but acres of parking lots. It couldn't be in the city, it would have to be outside.

DL: That's true.

CK: This is a different sensibility.

DL: The city wanted only limited parking, about 1,200 cars, and all of it will be underground. Madison Square Garden is the only comparable case in this country where you have a performance arena in the middle of the city, but no parking around it. They are forcing people to take public transportation but they will provide a good subway connection. That's how Berlin city officials are thinking about these things. I think that's very positive.

CK: It's also the only possible way that you could have a stadium with residences and offices in the area. The scale and density of the buildings is not like anything you would find in a comparable American city.

DL: Almost nothing in Berlin goes higher than the official cornice height, which is 22 meters. That allows just about six floors, maybe seven, depending on how you do it. High rises will be permitted only in very special situations. There has been a lot of pressure from the private sector to permit higher buildings, but planners have allowed very few. Berlin has been a latecomer to reconstruction after World War II. The city has never really been fully rebuilt. But it has learned a lot from other examples. A lot of mistakes were made after the War throughout Europe. Berlin doesn't want to become another Frankfurt. I do think, however, that the city will have to identify areas where high-rise development can occur.

CK: Even the configuration of contemporary buildings is influenced by old models. They have to be a certain depth to permit natural light inside.

DL: German regulations require every office worker to have daylight. There is no way you can put a secretary on the inner part of an office building without a view.

CK: It's very humane.

DL: Yes, it's very humane. But it's also a very costly way to build because you have to make the buildings very slender and you pay a lot for more enclosure.

CK: We're talking about contextualism again.

DL: It is contextualism. It is another culture. It is another way of thinking of the workplace. Germans, for instance, are very sensitive about acoustical privacy, much more so than Americans. Americans accept hissing sounds from air conditioning systems, motors running, and fans overhead without complaining. If there is even the smallest noise from a machine, Germans won't accept it.

CK: Now that you are back in Germany. What are you bringing with you that's American?

DL: Well, I'm discovering there seem to be more regulations in Germany than I thought, and certainly more than there are in the United States. As a good American, I'm sometimes really annoyed at all the things Germans tell you how to do. In the American tradition I've become independent, entrepreneurial, and aggressive.

CK: The office in Germany brings us full circle. You are returning to your roots and the roots of the office. I would like to talk about the history of the office, its evolution, and the changing nature of the work over time. We should begin, I think, by talking about Mies, and your arrival at the firm when you finished school.

DL: I first came in 1957 after graduation from the Gymnasium [preparatory school] in Germany, and I enrolled at IIT. I was a freshman. The first time I worked in Mies's office was during the Christmas vacation. They were designing the Bacardi Building in Santiago, Cuba. This was before Castro had come down from the mountains. [Bacardi abandoned the project after Fidel Castro came to power.] I worked in the shop on a model presentation for the project.

CK: Were you a committed Modernist then? You were just 19 years old.

DL: There was no alternative. Everything, anywhere in the Western world, was Modernist. That included Germany where I returned for four years to the Technische Hochschule in Munich to get my degree in architecture. After I graduated I came back to Chicago in 1962 to enter Mies's office. I worked with him until his death in 1969. Personally, I worked on a number of things in those seven years including the Chicago Federal Center and the Toronto Dominion Center. But the major project I was involved in was the National Gallery in Berlin. Speaking the language, I had a natural ability for handling the job. Every young architect has some project he looks back on as a major learning experience. This one was mine. I worked directly with my grandfather on this project unlike those where other senior people were the designers.

CK: This was also a very important building for Mies wasn't it?

DL: He had tried several times to get a building like it done. It began with Bacardi, which was this great roof plate supported by eight perimeter columns. Bacardi was to be done in concrete because there was no steel in Cuba. Concrete was available and labor was relatively cheap so the form work could be done. Then later, when I was a student in Germany, my father-in-law [industrialist and art collector Georg Schäfer] hired Mies to design a museum to be given by him to his city, Schweinfurt. I was married to my first wife, Heidemarie Schäfer, which was another reason I wanted to go back to Germany for school. The Schäfer museum commission was the first time this idea was converted to steel. It was a scheme long before Berlin came along. But then the City of Berlin came and asked Mies to design a museum. He was nearly 80 years old but he said, »This is really the appropriate city for this design, not a smaller town in Germany.« He wanted to do this concept in Berlin. He knew his design was historically related to Schinkel and he wanted it in the same city as Schinkel's major works. So, it became my task to persuade my father-in-law to give up the Schäfer design which he ultimately and graciously did having already paid the fee for it. That's how this design got to Berlin.

CK: And your role?

DL: I was really put in charge of it in 1965 or so and I worked directly with Mies on it for several years. I travelled to Berlin a lot, to oversee construction.

CK: Will you describe the topping-out day?

DL: The whole steel roof had been welded together on the ground, and there were steel towers erected to raise the roof hydraulically. It was all done in an eight-hour day. It was timed by the steel construction company to coincide with the annual convention for the German concrete institute which was meeting in an auditorium across the street from our site. When the concrete people went into their morning meetings there was nothing on our site. When they came out in the evening the entire building was there. It was instant architecture. Of course you can't do that in concrete.

CK: And the columns were attached by pin hinges?

DL: Yes, as the roof was raised the columns gradually became vertical and eventually were hanging free so they could be set onto their foundations. That was an exciting day. Mies was there. When the roof was about eight feet off the ground he insisted on walking under it even though that was forbidden for safety reasons. If something failed the whole roof could crash down. I always made sure I was not standing directly under a beam. But he didn't care. He was old, you know.

CK: To help Mies realize his last project when he was too ill to fly to Germany very often must have deepened your relationship with him.

DL: He couldn't go to the opening ceremony and he asked me to deliver a speech on his behalf which I did. But over all those years he and I had a *jour fixe* every week on Thursday nights. I would go after work and we would have a couple of martinis, smoke some cigars, and have dinner which was prepared by his Hungarian cook. For seven years I spent an evening every week alone with him. We talked about architecture, his life, everything.

CK: Tell me about the McCormick Place commission.

DL: Mies may have been 80 then. A great fire burned down the old McCormick Place. And Richard Daley, the mayor, called his old friend, Charlie Murphy, Sr. [of C.F. Murphy, later to become Murphy/Jahn], and supposedly said, »Charlie, start drawing, we need a new one in a hurry.« Well, the Murphy people didn't really have a very good designer in their office for that kind of assignment. They hired Gene Summers for the job. And Gene, who had been a head designer in Mies's office, felt this was a job Mies should do. So they all came and met with Mies to ask him if he would collaborate with the Mur-

phy firm. But he said, »No, gentlemen, I'm too old. I'm too old to count all those columns, you can do it.«
CK: Did you want to give him an elbow?
DL: Yes.
CK: Where would you say that Mies's legacy is evident in the office now?
DL: Well it is less evident today than it was ten years ago. Which is only natural, things change. But his legacy is greater than the visual appearance of buildings. It is deeper than that and concerns a commitment to designing honest buildings that are true to their time.
CK: What do you mean by honest?
DL: I mean an honest search for the proper expression of the problem. It is one of the great misunderstandings about Mies that he demanded and expected every building done by his students and colleagues to look like one of his buildings. Absolutely not. He was perfectly willing to recognize a good building that looked different. To me the essence of Mies's legacy – one that I'm still committed to – is the question: What are the essential factors that shape our life? He asked himself that question in his time. I have come to slightly different answers than he did, but that is only natural because things have changed. The concerns, for instance, about contextualism, ecology and energy efficiency are new. Those were not things he was concerned about or even aware of.
CK: So, the continuity is in asking the same set of questions?
DL: I'll give you an example. Europeans came and asked him: »Why do you have only one pane of glass in the 860 Lake Shore Drive apartment windows?« His answer was: »This is America. Energy is cheap. You just fire up a little more, and you have the heat you need to overcome the cold.« That was unthinkable in Europe then and now. Only recently has it become unthinkable in America too. There has been a complete change in attitude. He was right then. And improved insulation technology has had an impact on what you can do and what you can't do. This is a technological development, but energy efficiency is also a new attitude that we all have developed.
CK: Let's talk about the Devon House. This may be an example of Mies's enduring influence. The client wanted another Farnsworth House. And your answer was?
DL: »No way.« This client had discovered Mies and read about Philip Johnson's involvement with him. He called Philip and asked him to design a Mies house for him. Philip said he didn't do Mies houses anymore, but told him to call me. I said, I don't do Mies van der Rohe houses anymore either. But I offered to do a Dirk Lohan house for him. The Devon House is a Modern house. It is based on an idea I've had for some time, a notion of contiguous flowing space divided by freestanding partitions and walls over several stories. Rather than being confined between two planes – the floor and ceiling – this house is more volumetric. It is four stories tall so its development is more three-dimensional. It is the idea of the Farnsworth House developed vertically. That's why the whole house is a perfect 42-foot cube. Space is completely fluid.

CK: This is a big one, Dirk: What did Mies mean to you?
DL: It's hard for people who never met him to understand his incredible – I can only think of the German word – *Ausstrahlung* [the force with which his personality emanated from him]. His personality affected you strongly even though he said very little. You were immediately impressed by the power of his authority. Maybe someone like Churchill had that radiance. I cherish my discussions with him. Perhaps the most important thing he taught me is that architecture raises philosophical questions, that it isn't just a matter of nuts and bolts. In its finest expression it reaches into fine art as well as philosophy. Mies was able to achieve that in his work. There wasn't anything frivolous about his pursuit. Nothing light and superficial. He is the great master from whom I learned, whom I admire, but with whom I also feel free to disagree now. If he were sitting here I would love to have a good argument with him about some of the things he stood for that I don't think were right.
CK: What were they?
DL: Well, the idea that his style of Modern building could be built anywhere in the world without regard for the context.
CK: There is a very good example of that in the contrast between Cityfront Center and Illinois Center.
DL: Yes.
CK: Two huge developments on opposite sides of the Chicago River and two very, very different sensibilities.
DL: Yes.
CK: One very Modern, rather aloof from the city.
DL: Correct.
CK: And one that is trying to bring the city out to an isolated spot.
DL: You said it very well. I cannot really blame Mies. In the latter part of his life when things like Illinois Center were designed they were largely done by his disciples, his co-workers, or his employees who developed a dogma about his work. Their work distorted the true intention of Mies van der Rohe.
CK: It's interesting, Mies gave you a double-edged sword. He is your mentor, and he gave you so much, at the same time you inherited this legacy, this…
DL: This burdensome legacy, you mean.
CK: You had to become an architect in your own right.
DL: That's true. It is never easy for the descendant of a great person to establish his identity, because you live in the shadow of a giant. I waslucky to be two generations removed. I am the grandson. After working for him and finishing my responsibilities to him I felt free to seek my own bearings. I began to question some things he taught me but other things endure.
CK: What are those?
DL: Architecture must be the expression of its time. That's one of the principles that I absolutely subscribe to. The question is, of course, what is the essential expression of our time. It is how you answer that question that guides you.

Buildings and Projects

McDonald's Office Campus, Oak Brook, Illinois
1978–

In a competition among six architects Lohan Associates was chosen to design McDonald's corporate headquarters on an 80-acre wooded site in Oak Brook, a suburb of Chicago. The ongoing project thus far includes three buildings containing corporate offices, a research and development center, a training and meeting center, a lodge, and parking. The buildings are clad in brick and stone, materials that blend with the natural landscape.

The training center, where McDonald's franchise owners and managers go for intensive two-week training sessions, was the first building completed on the campus. The 109,000-square-foot facility has seminar rooms, classrooms and eight auditoriums arrayed in three interlocking wings radiating from a two-story entryway with a grand stair. The building has a deliberately relaxed air that is intended to encourage communication among the visiting trainees. Stone and wood are used as complements to a warm color scheme.

The 225-room lodge was designed to resemble a resort. It provides accommodations for those attending training sessions and for corporate visitors. Its U-shaped plan was conceived to wrap around a rare 200-year-old Ohio Buckeye tree that stands in the forecourt. The building has several restaurants, a lounge with a rustic stone fireplace, a swimming pool and fitness center.

The office building is a four-story, 255,000-square-foot structure for approximately 800 McDonald's employees, senior managers and executives. Offices are laid out in an open plan. No offices are fully enclosed, leaving everyone's work habits visible. The boardroom is circular and partially glass-enclosed to underscore openness and the company's non-hierarchical approach to management. Natural light is brought into the center of the building through skylights and light wells. The four-story lobby is topped with a glazed skylight and is surrounded on three sides with balconies. Presently, the office building has three wings and is roughly T-shaped. Second- and third-phase additions are planned that will eventually bring the building to a total of 710,000 square feet. In addition to offices, the building contains 25,000 square feet in laboratories and test kitchens on the top floor. At grade and below are three levels of parking.

McDonald's landscaped grounds are open to the public with paths for walking and biking throughout. Two retention lakes were created out of flood plains. To help preserve the site's beauty, surface parking has been kept to a minimum.

1. View from the training center to the lodge across the man-made lake.

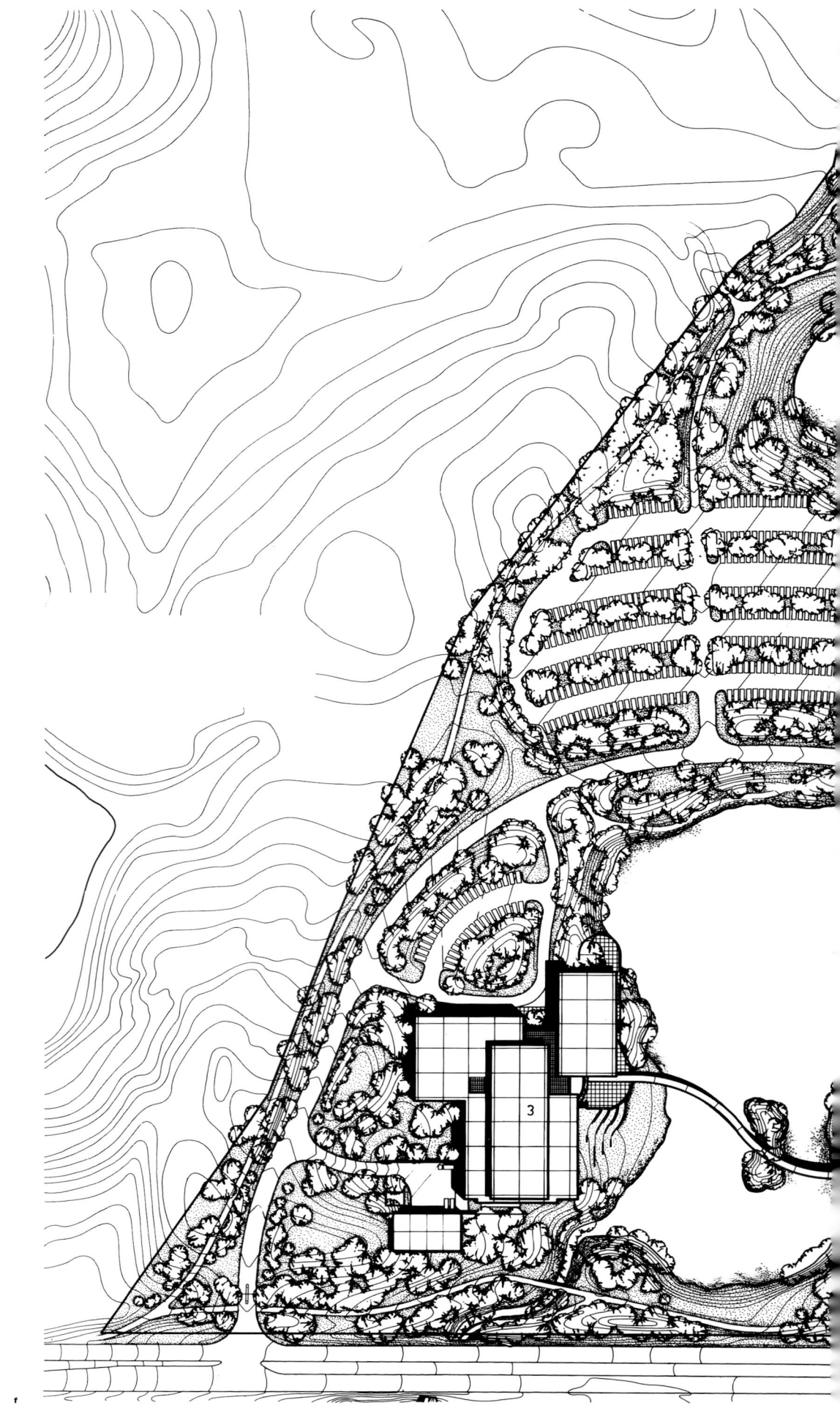

2. Site plan. Key: 1 office building and proposed expansion, 2 lodge, 3 training center.

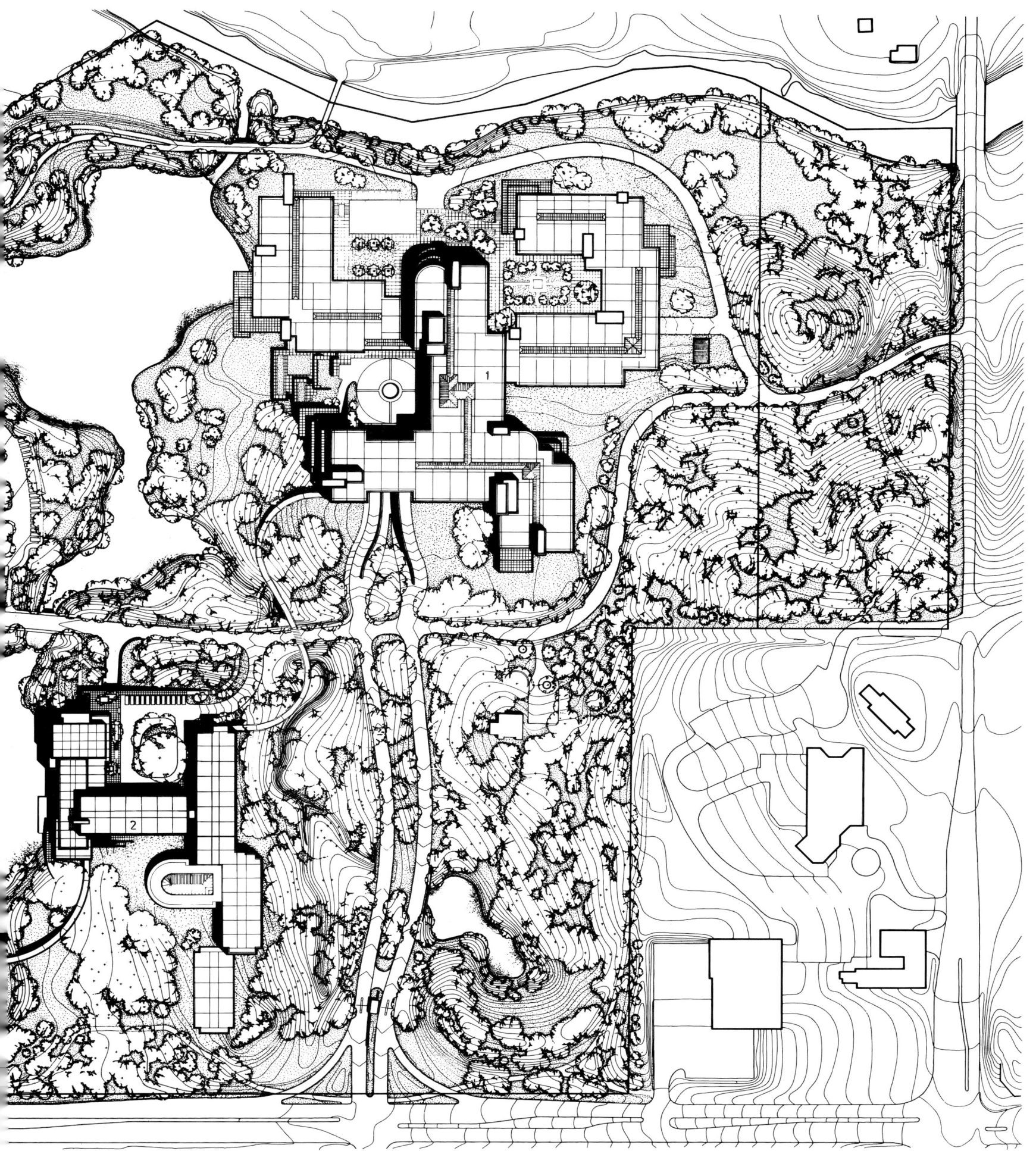

3. Office building plan (2nd floor). Key: 1 atrium, 2 light well.
4. The approach to the office building from the west is along a wooded path.

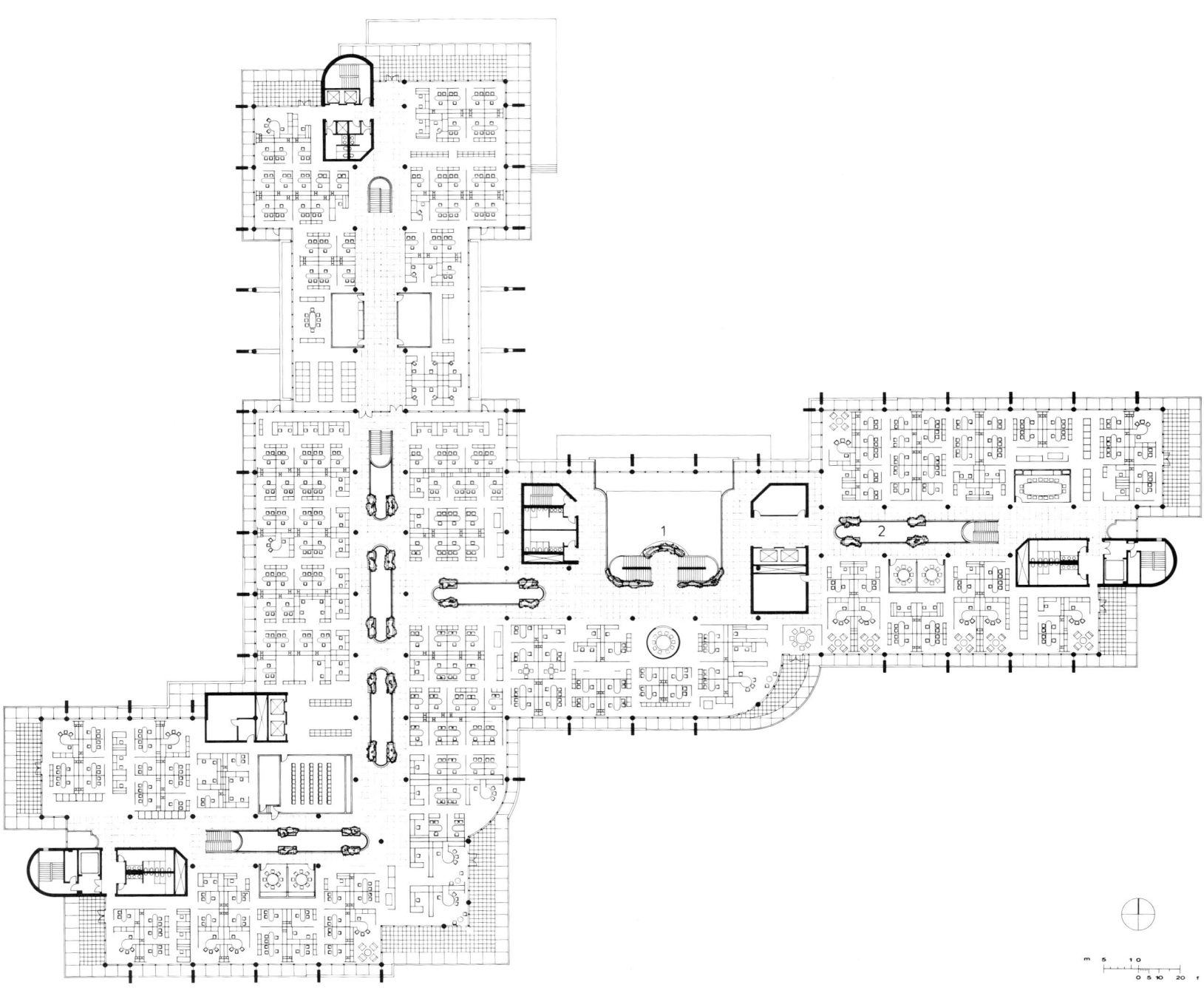

5, 6. Views of the office building lobby atrium.
7. Lobby stair detail.

8. View of a light well in the office building.
9. Offices have access to natural light.
10. Management and executive work areas are open to view.

11. Partial view of the training center.
12. Training center plan (site and ground floor).
Key: 1 pedestrian bridge, 2 lobby, 3 auditorium,
4 informal meeting area, 5 classroom.

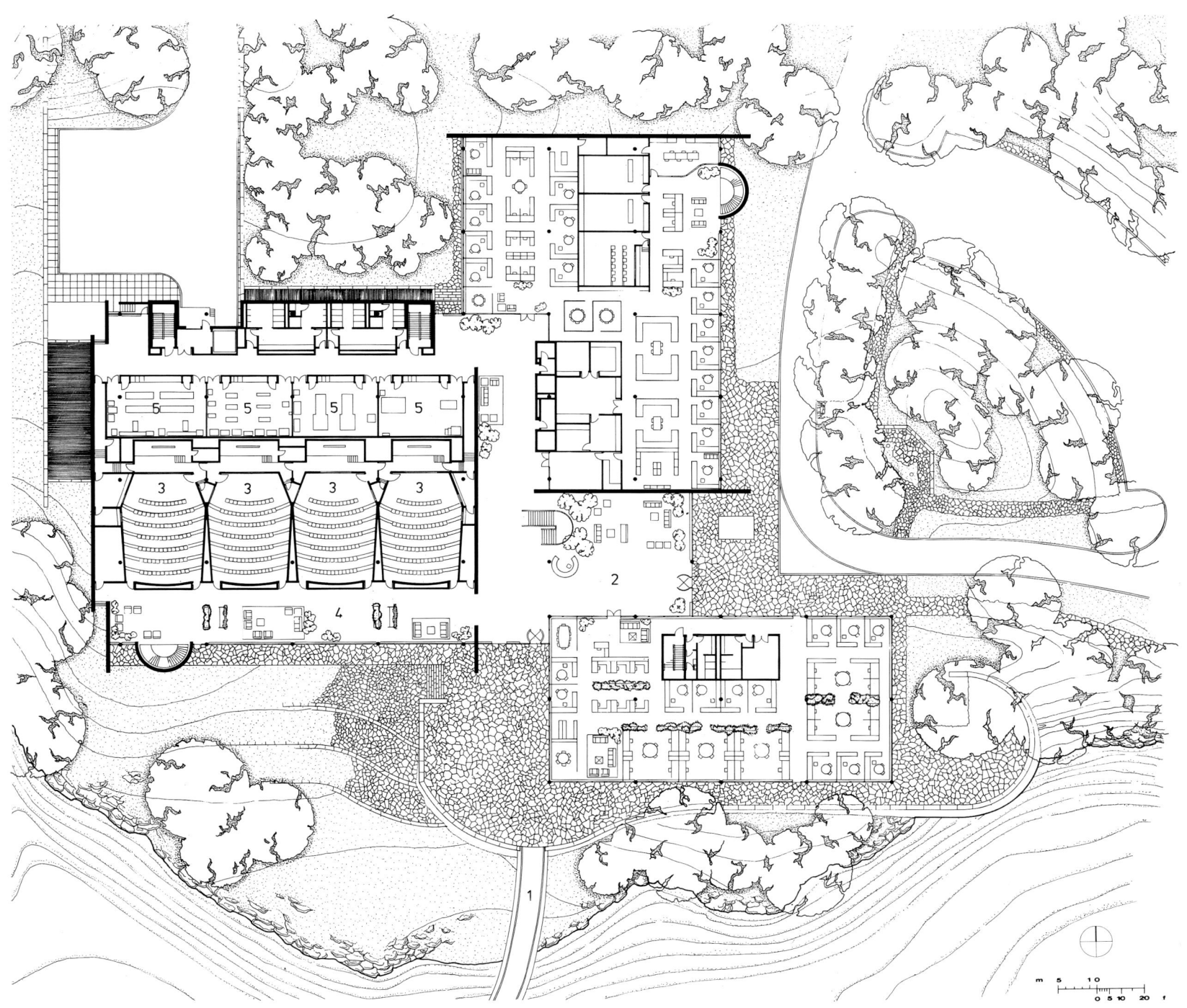

13. The training center lobby and stair.
14. An informal meeting area is adjacent to the auditorium classrooms.
15. Brickwork detail in an auditorium classroom.

16. Lodge plan (ground floor). Key: 1 lobby, 2 swimming pool, 3 ballroom.
17. View of the lodge from the north.

p. 36/37
18. Partial view of the lodge with a covered walkway in the foreground.

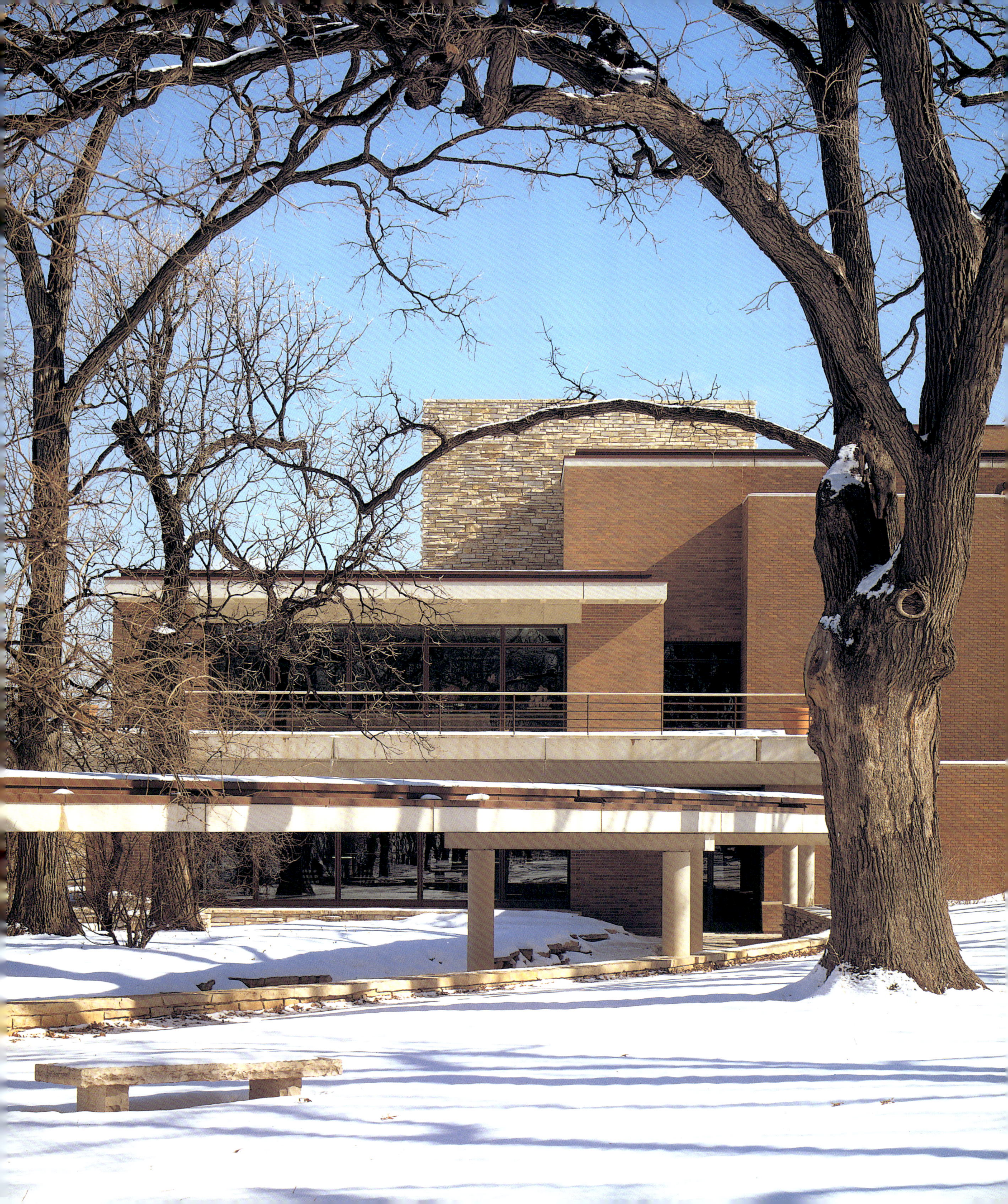

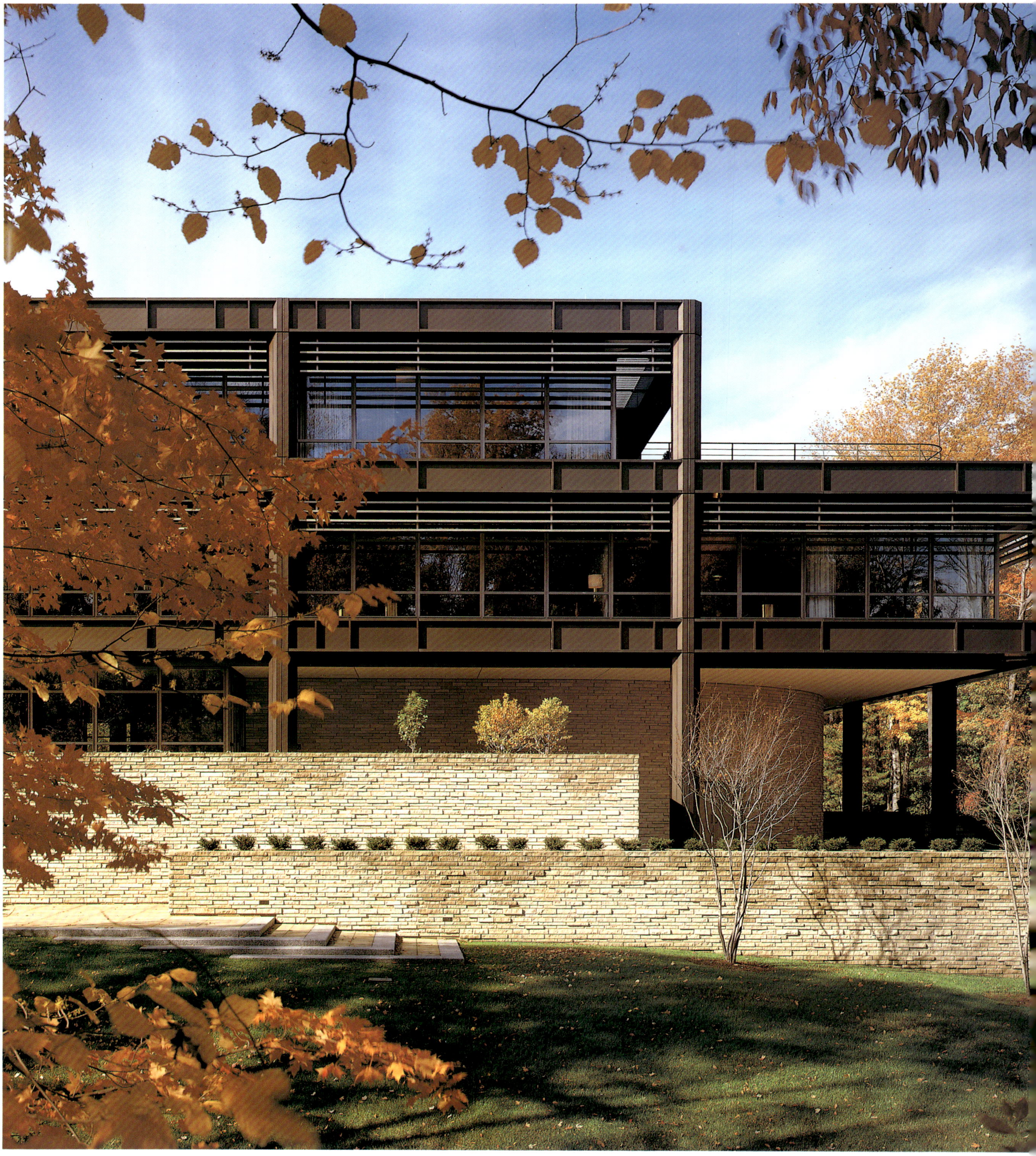

TRW World Headquarters, Lyndhurst, Ohio
1981–1985

The TRW corporate headquarters in Lyndhurst, Ohio, appear as a series of airy pavilions set lightly in the landscape. At its highest point, the building is four stories tall. It appears to hug the contours of the site as it steps down to three stories.
With 450,000 square feet of office space the size of the building is considerable, but TRW has been configured to visually minimize its mass. The plan rotates around a central atrium that serves as a meeting and socializing space, a circulation hub and as a means of bringing natural light into the center of the building. Four narrow pavilions, where the work spaces are located, radiate from the atrium. In a reversal of the normal order, work stations are on the perimeter and private offices are in the center of the pavilions. This arrangement permits sunlight to pass over the low walls of the stations and penetrate deep into the pavilion so that all workers may enjoy natural light and a view.
Exterior walls are recessed six feet from the structural frame to shade windows from direct light. This shading allowed the architects to use a clear glass that gives the building a rare transparency. Fixed aluminum louvers set into the structural frame provide further protection from the sun.
Materials compatible with the country setting were used throughout TRW. The steel-frame structure is clad with bronze-anodized aluminum. Verde Antique marble walls conceal fire stairs on the outside of the building. Both the green of the marble and the brown aluminum blend into the natural 137-acre headquarters' site. Ohio sandstone is used for the building base and substructure as well as for site amenities like bridges and retaining walls.
A mansion on the grounds, which was occupied by the former owners of TRW's site, has been renovated as a corporate guest house under the supervision of Lohan Associates. Formally planted grounds surrounding the house have been restored and stand in agreeable contrast to the natural landscaping around the headquarters.
Great effort went into preserving the landscape around the headquarters. The road leading to the building is narrow and carefully masked so that it is difficult to see. All parking is concealed below the building.

1. The building's massing and materials blend into the landscape.

p. 40/41
2. General view.

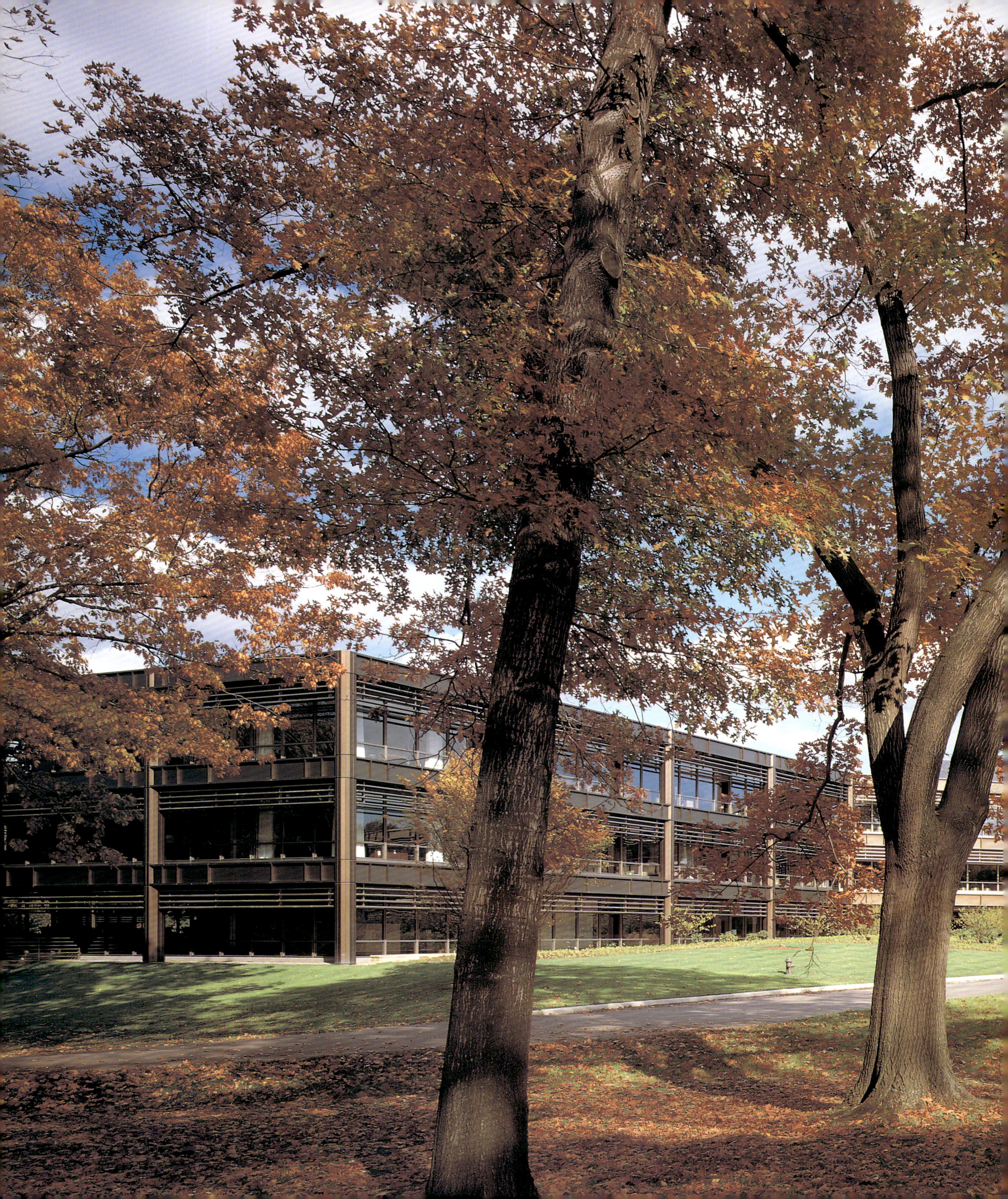

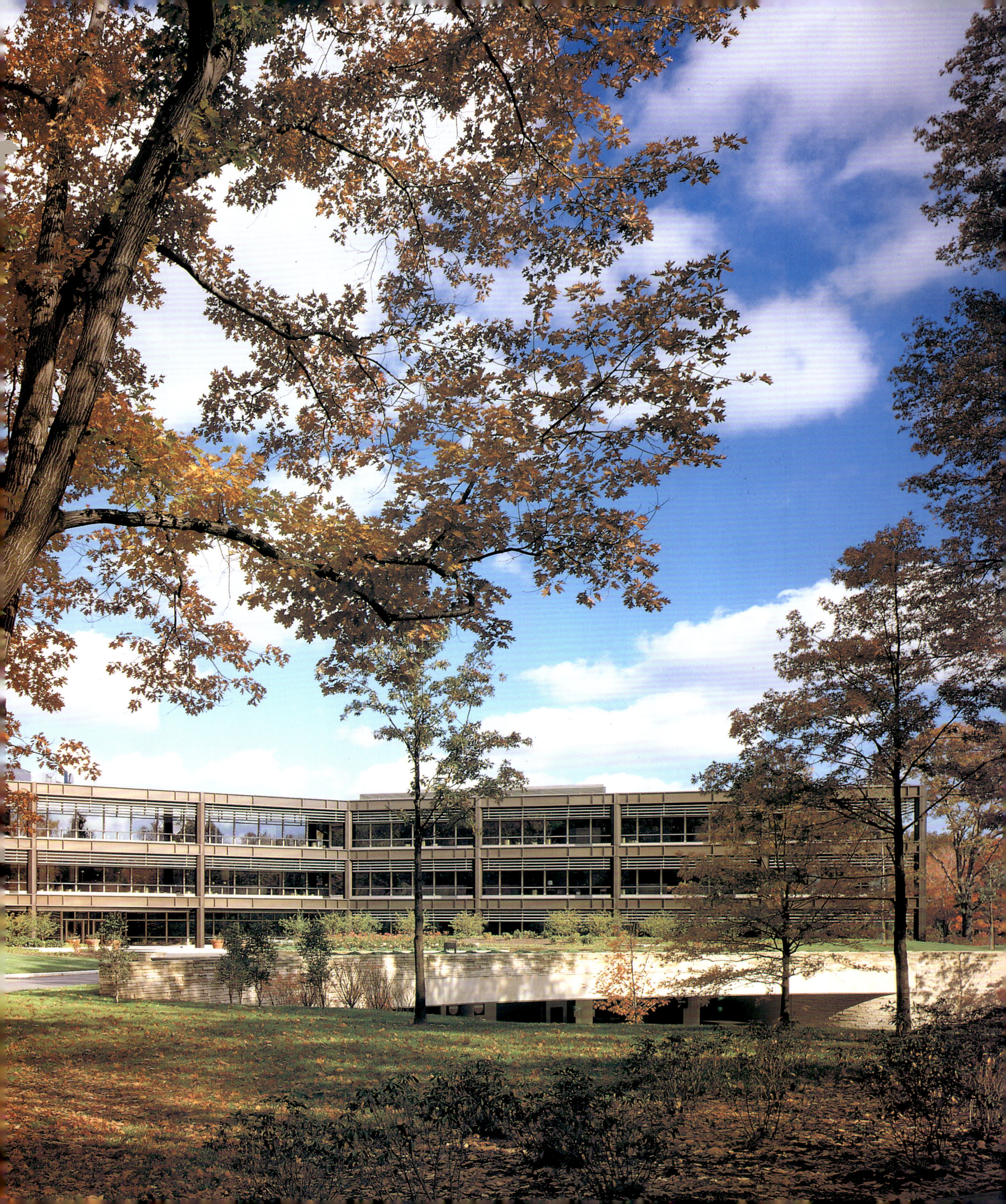

3. Site plan. Key: 1 headquarters building, 2 parking entry, 3 guest house.

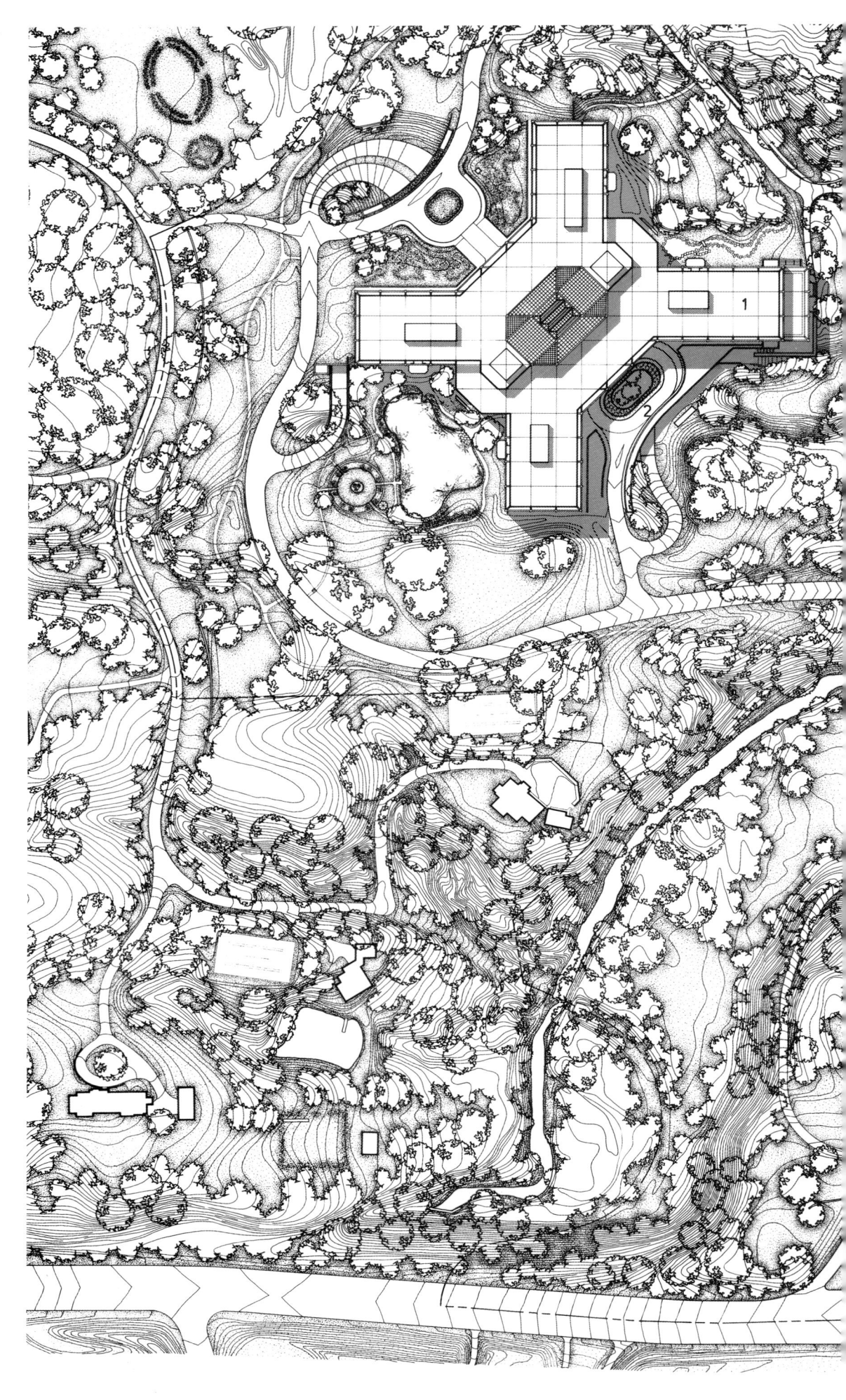

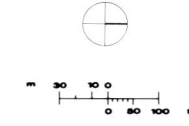

43

44

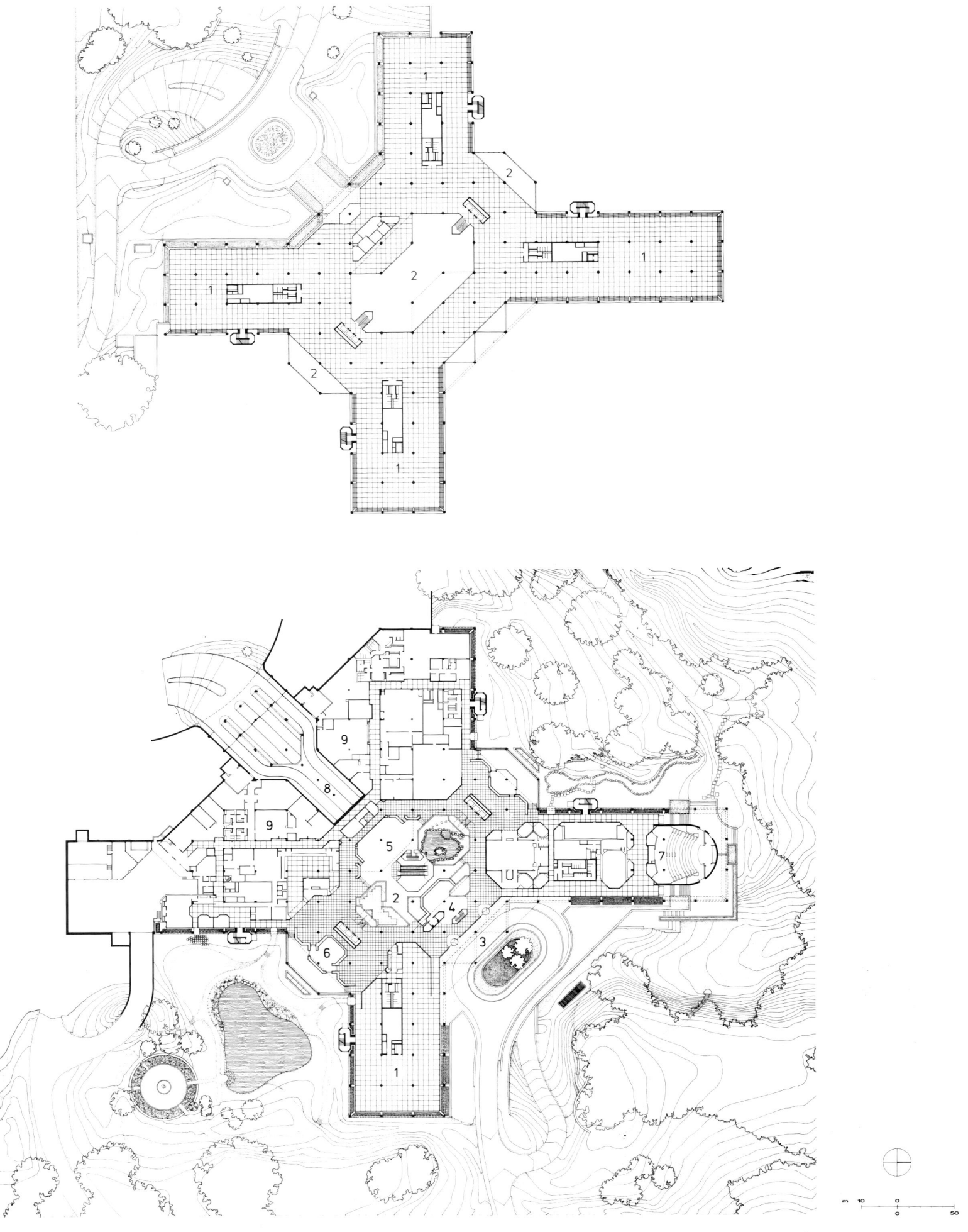

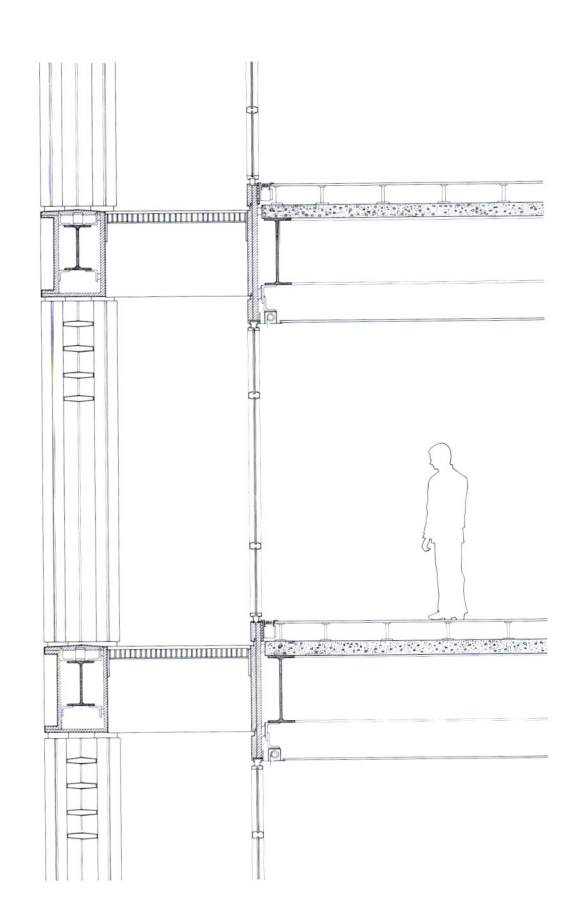

4. Plans (ground floor and 3rd floor). Key: 1 office area, 2 atrium, 3 visitors' entry, 4 reception, 5 exhibition, 6 dining, 7 auditorium, 8 ramps to parking, 9 service areas.
5. Wall section.
6. The curtain wall is recessed from the structural frame.
7. View of the south pavilion.

8. Employees enter the atrium by stairs from parking areas below the building.
9. A view of the atrium.
10. Section.

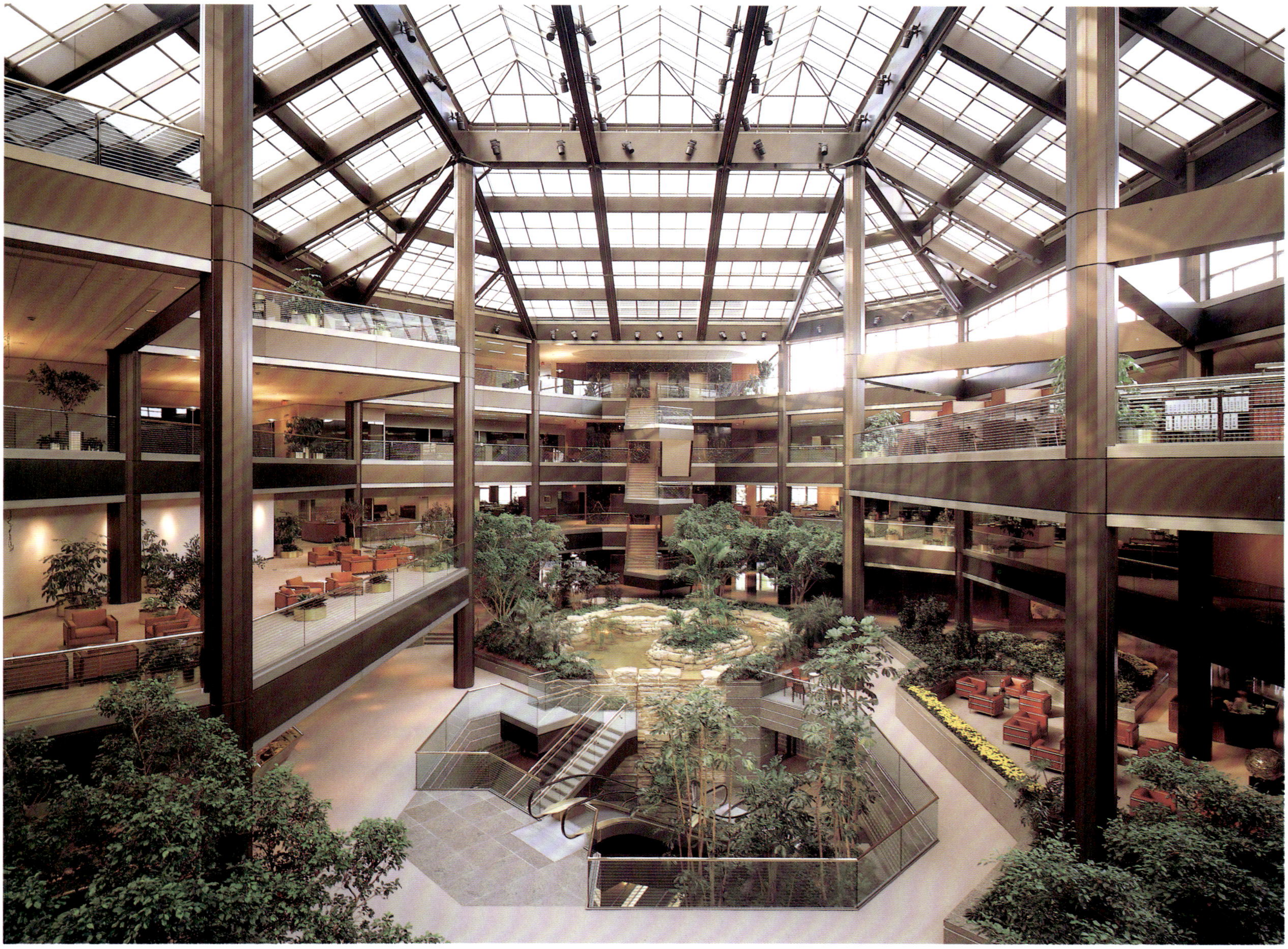

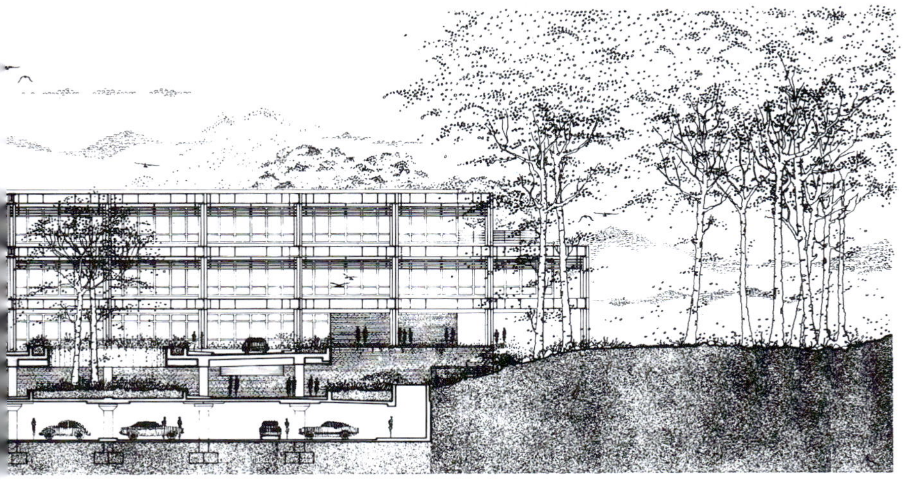

11. A sculpture created by the architect and made from the actual steel beams of the building.
12. Corner detail.

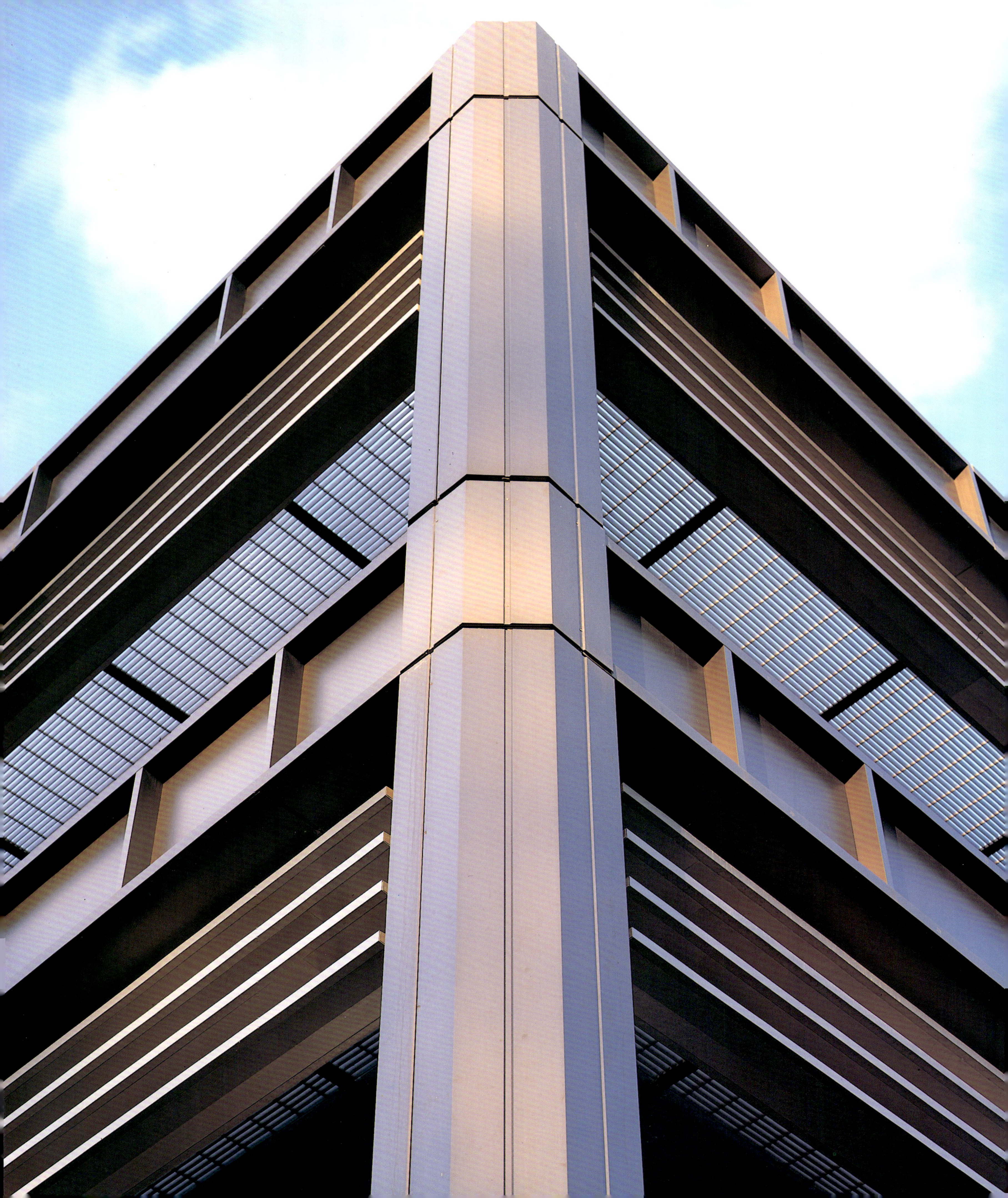

Frito-Lay National Headquarters, Plano, Texas
1982–1985

The Frito-Lay National Headquarters, Plano, is part contradiction, part conciliation. The building accommodates itself to its site outside Dallas even as it asserts its place in the landscape.

The structure emerges from opposing slopes on a base of split-faced granite cut in randomly varied thicknesses and lengths. As the structure rises from its base, it becomes more apparently man-made, a geometrically precise expression of the stone- and aluminum-clad frame.

The building is composed of three wings joined together leaving a triangular courtyard at the center. An artificially channeled stream flows beneath the building and through the courtyard to a seven-acre lake in front of the building. The south wing of the building which spans the lake is supported by a 120-foot bridge structure.

The courtyard has been landscaped with Texas limestone, indigenous plants and a waterfall. It is the central organizing space with the principal interior circulation for the building occurring on its perimeter.

In addition to the headquarters building commission, the architects were asked to do the space planning and interiors, allowing them to complete their concept for the building.

The integration of materials, interiors and architecture is apparent in the four-story lobby which looks out, on one side, to the Frito-Lay grounds and, on the opposite side, to the courtyard. A cantilevered stair mounts the height of the lobby joining bridges at each floor that connect office areas in adjacent wings. The geometric pattern of the lobby's custom carpet reiterates the building's overall triangular form.

Custom-designed cherry-veneer work stations are arranged in clusters in an open office plan. Work station sizes are standardized so employees may be moved instead of furniture.

Managers' enclosed offices are placed in the center of the wings, thus offering privacy to their occupants without blocking natural light coming through the windows.

Executive offices are on the second level, at the height of the treetops and offer the best view of the company grounds. Highly detailed and finished custom-designed secretary stations stand in the common area outside the offices. The conference room is furnished with a wood horeshoe-shaped table inlaid with marble.

The headquarters function like a small town with a range of support facilities contained within the building. There is a conference center, a barber, a company store and a fitness center. Jogging paths wind around the site. Four different dining areas, including an outdoor terrace, are located within the food service facility.

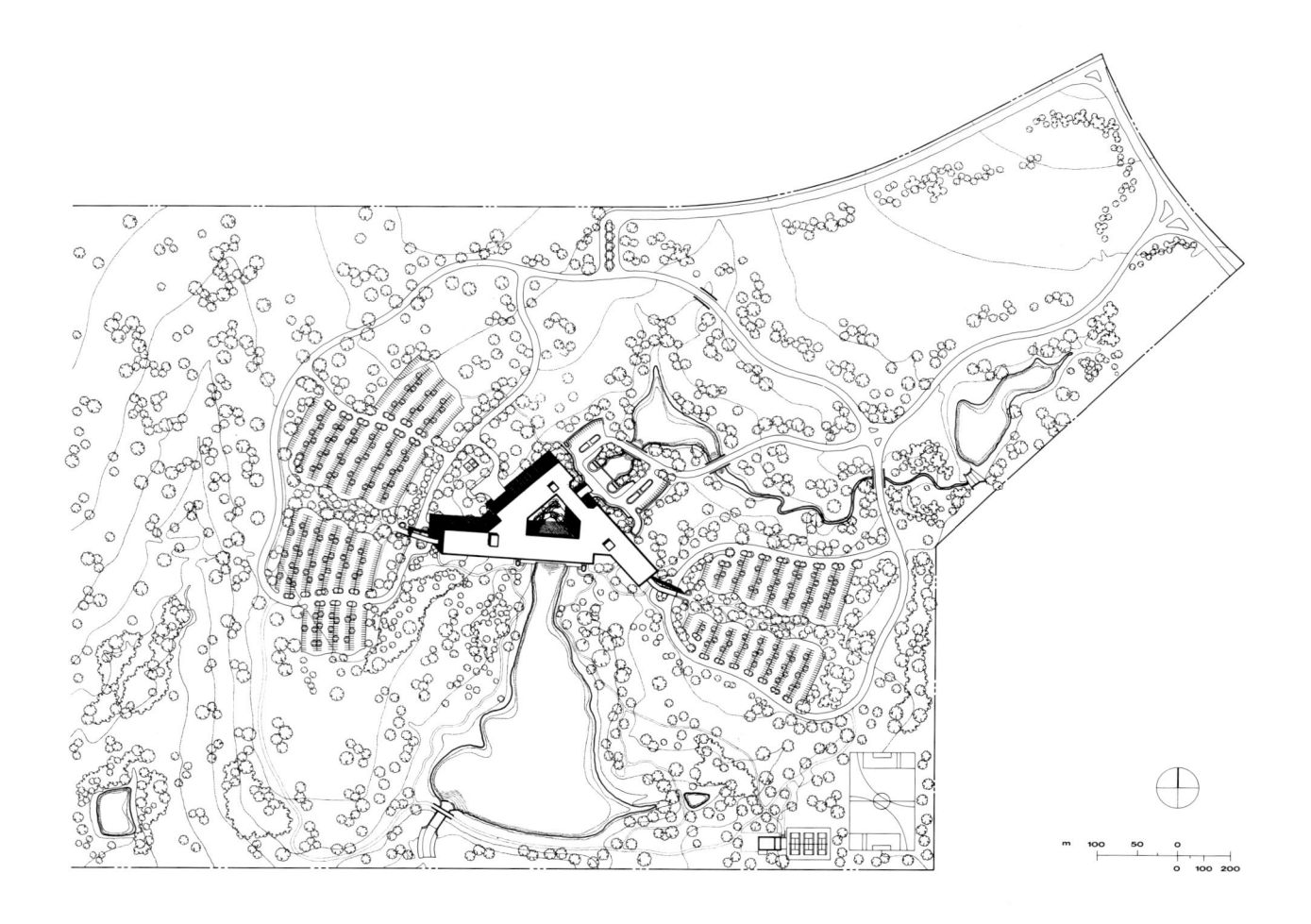

1. Site plan.
2. View of the façade.

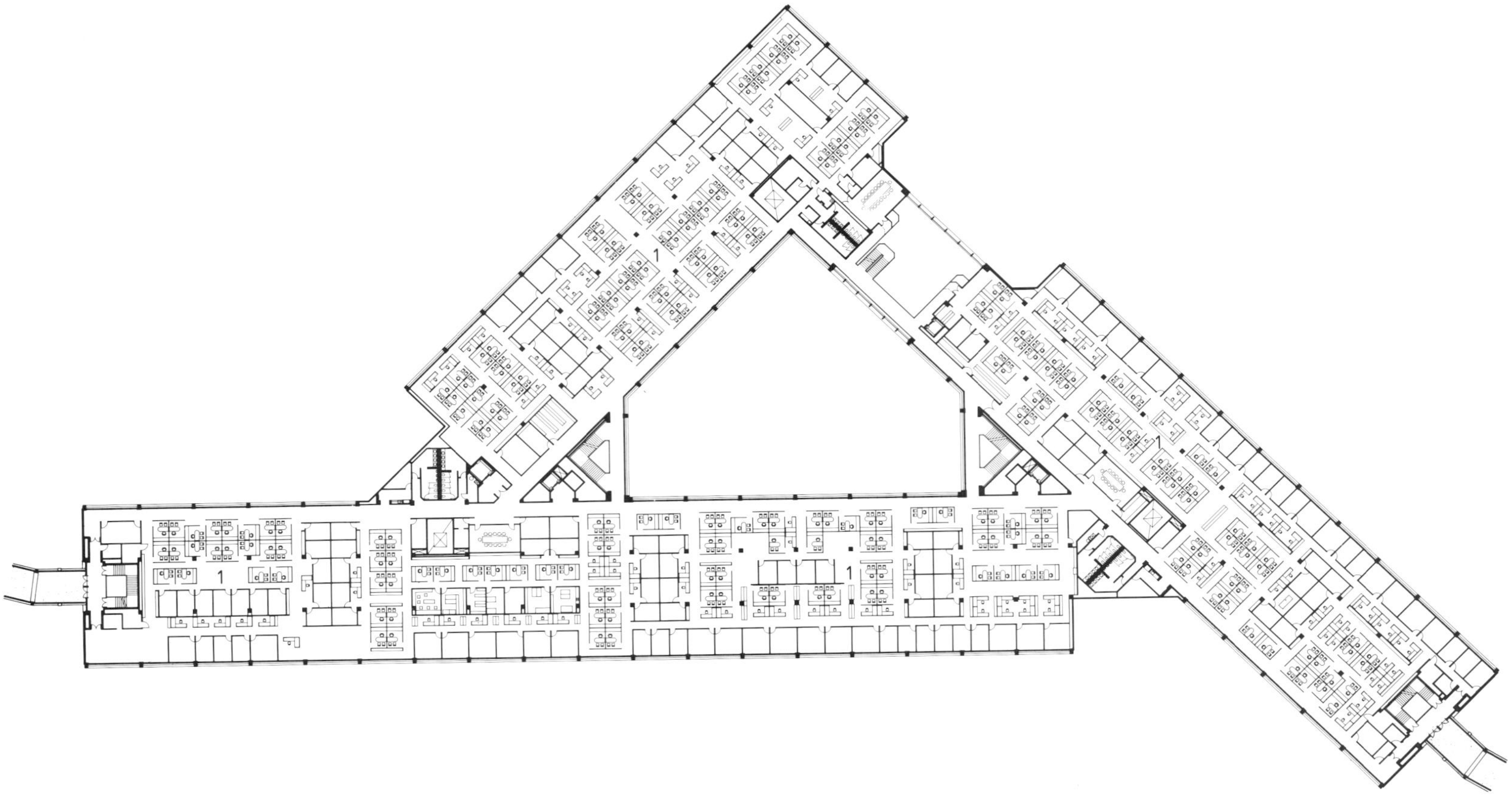

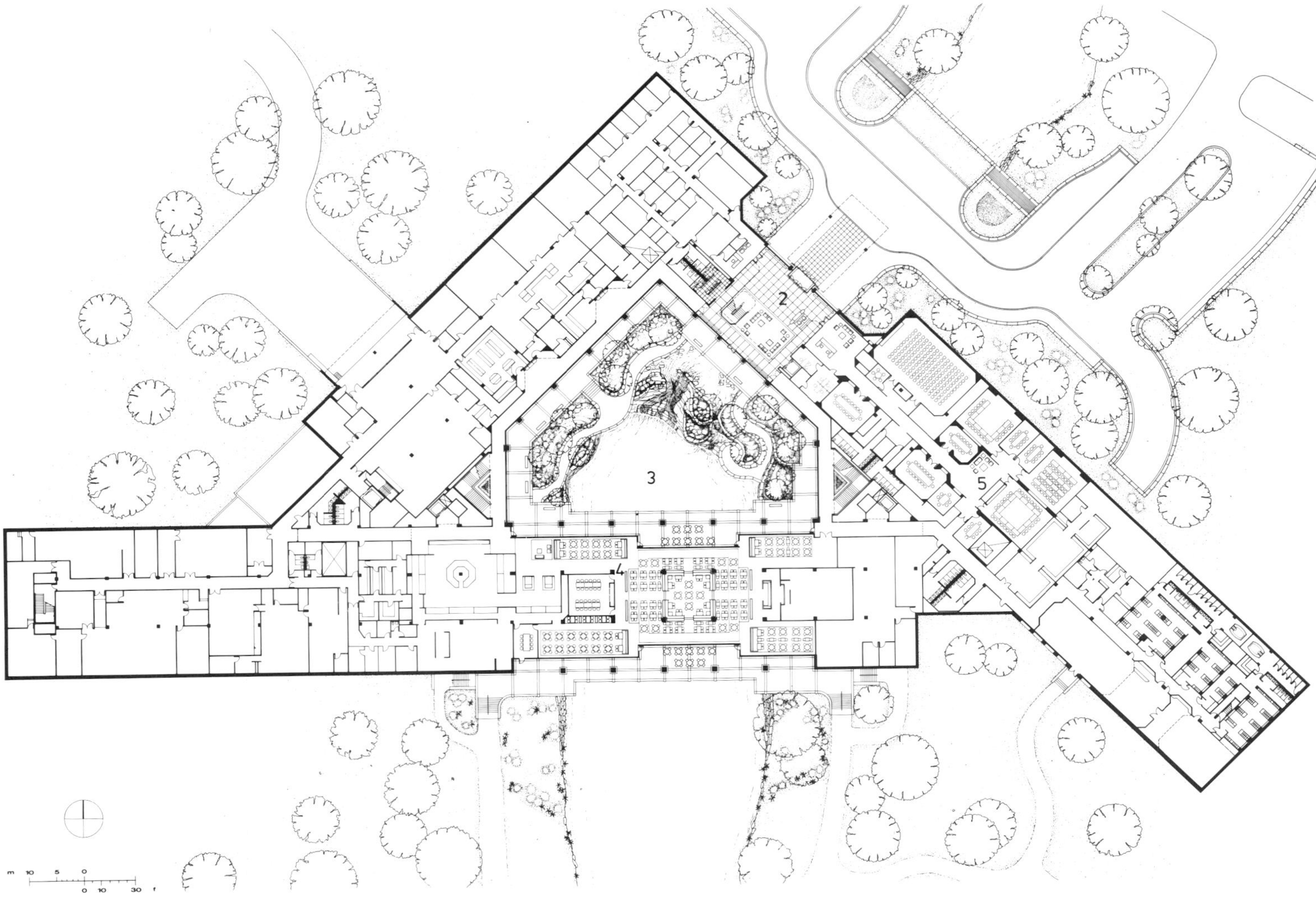

3. Plans (ground floor and 2nd floor). Key: 1 office area, 2 lobby, 3 courtyard, 4 dining area, 5 conference center.
4. The dining area has a view to the courtyard.
5. The south wing spans a stream and is supported by a bridge structure.

6. View of the lobby.
7. The cantilevered stair rises through the atrium.

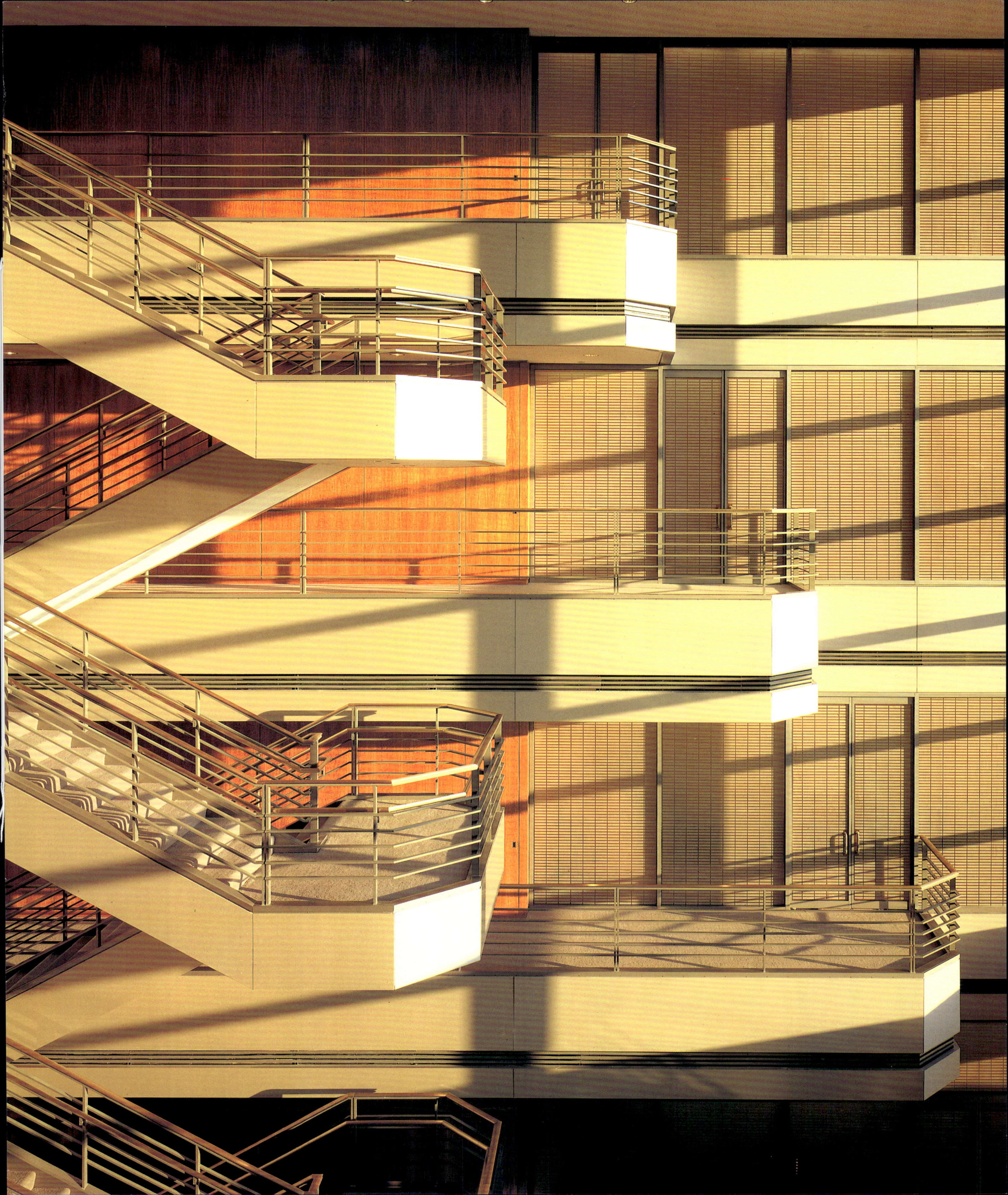

The Oceanarium, Chicago, Illinois
1983–1991

Unlike many American cities where waterfronts are knotted with rail lines and industrial buildings, Chicago's Lake Michigan shore has been preserved for public parks and cultural institutions. Placed in one of these parks is the John G. Shedd Aquarium, a landmark building designed in the Beaux-Arts style by Graham, Anderson, Probst & White and completed in 1929.

In 1983 Lohan Associates was asked to design the Oceanarium, an addition to the Shedd that would house an exhibition of marine mammals. Initially, the unorthodox octagonal massing of the Shedd seemed to preclude addition. The challenge was compounded by the size of the addition (175,000 square feet) and the architectural importance of the original building.

The architects' solution was to wrap the new construction around the back, or lakeside, of the Shedd. The chief signal of the Oceanarium's presence is a low-profile curving glass and metal wall. It stands well below the Shedd's rotunda leaving the building's distinctive silhouette and façade intact. On either side of the curtain wall are new pavilions that serve as transitions from the Shedd to the Oceanarium. These are clad in marble retrieved from the back of the original building.

Circulation was a key concern. In the Shedd a rotunda crowns a circulation hub from which the exhibition wings radiate. To maintain that logic, two stairways were carved through existing mechanical space to connect the rotunda with the Oceanarium.

While the Oceanarium is deferential to the original building, the addition is plainly a contemporary structure. Classical themes are borrowed but the interpretation is not literal. For example, the entablature above the lakeside curtain wall is supported by a series of white metal columns with standing vertical seams obliquely suggesting the fluting of classical columns.

Behind the curtain wall is the vast exhibition hall that is the heart of the addition. Sea otters, seals, and two types of whales reside there in an environment simulating their natural Pacific Northwest habitat. From stepped seating where visitors watch demonstrations, the pools and the lake appear as one continuous body of water stretching to the horizon. The view is unimpeded by support columns. Instead, an internally exposed long-span truss system supports the roof.

The addition is vast and much of it cannot be seen from the outside. Two acres of landfill were required to build the addition, nearly one acre was left as parkland. Below grade is the complex water filtration apparatus. The addition also contains offices, an auditorium, an arcade, a gift shop, a library and two restaurants.

1. The Shedd Aquarium and Oceanarium complex stand in a park near the city center.

p. 58/59
2. General view from the south.

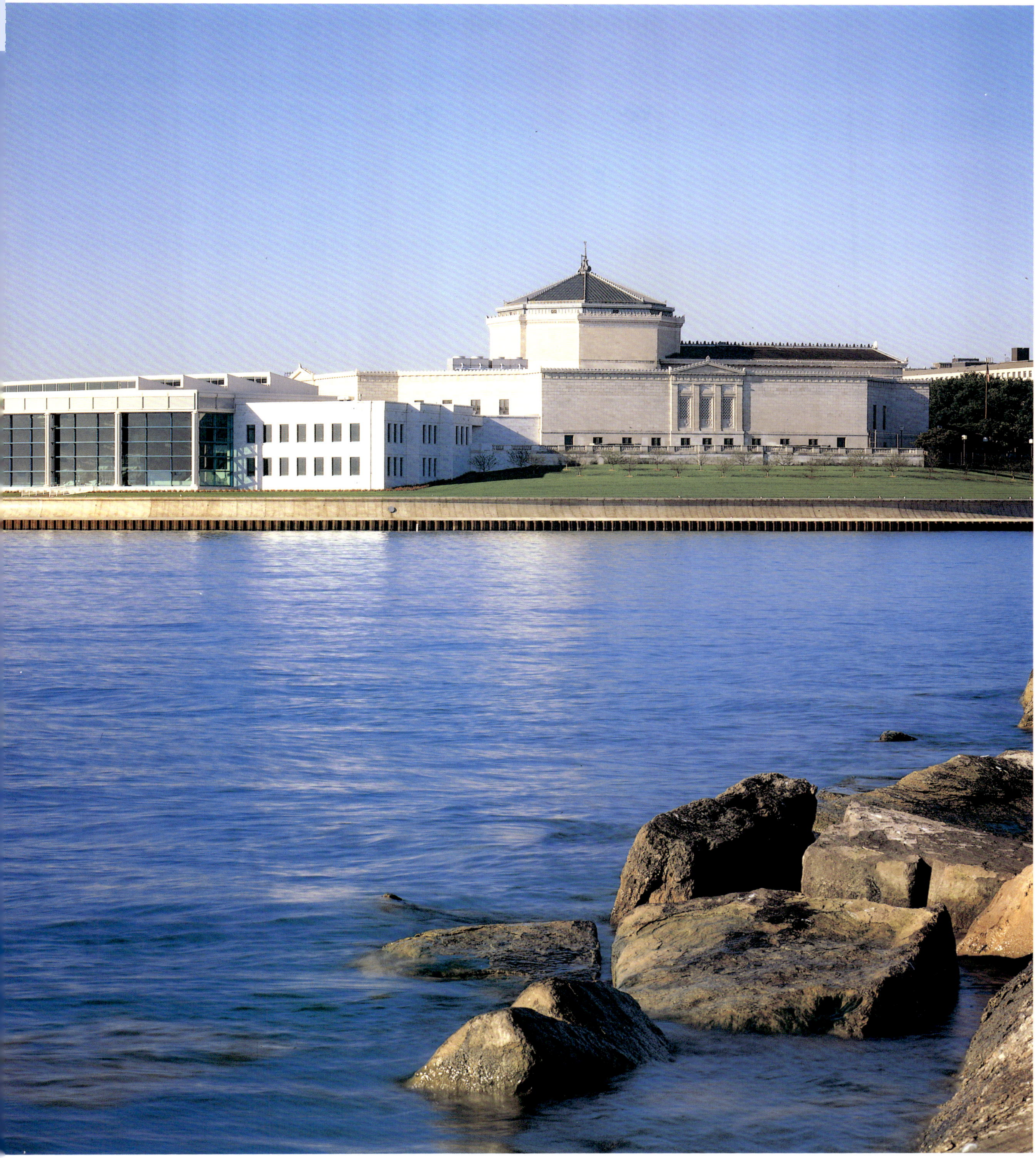

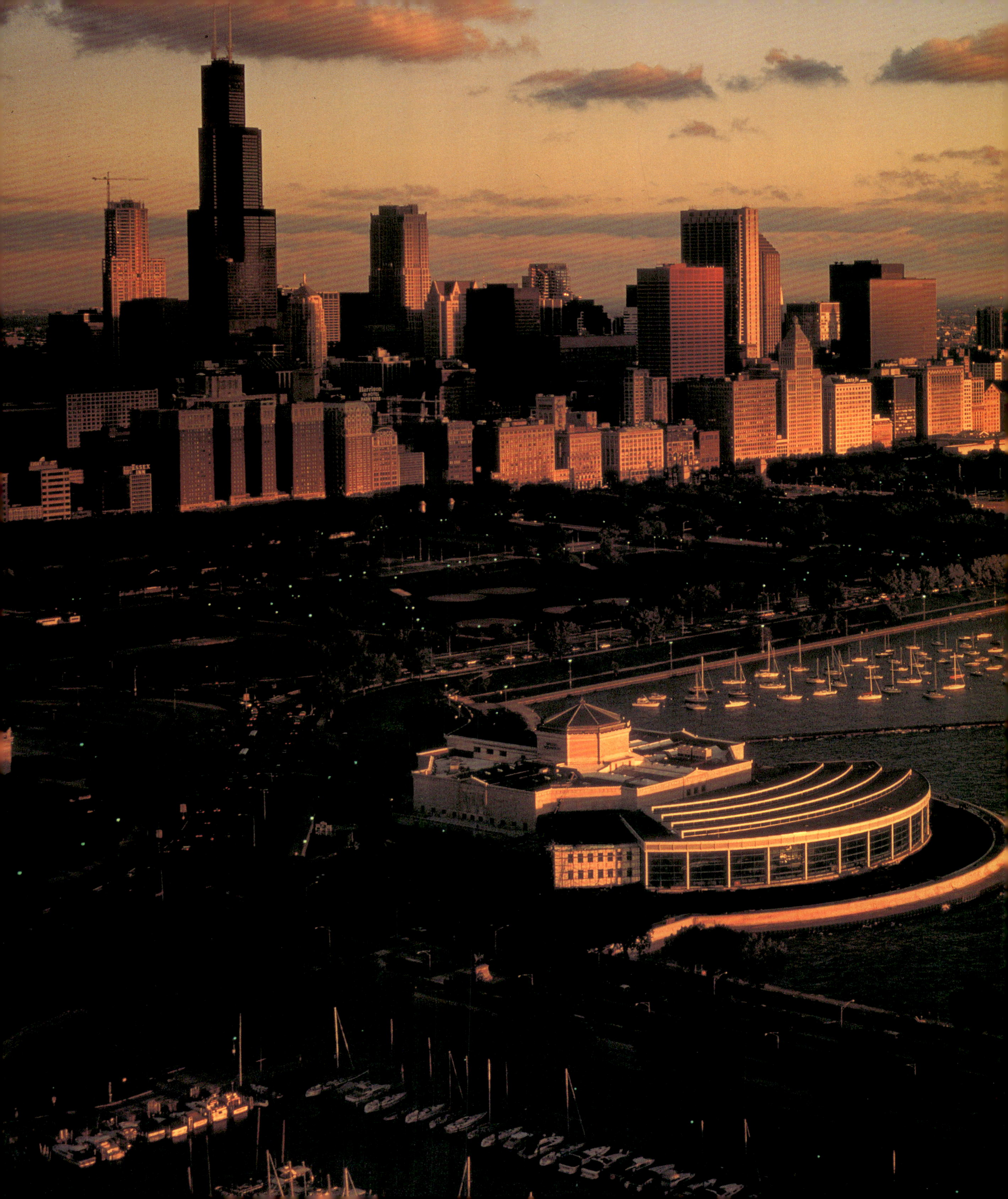
Harrison
HOTEL
PARK FREE
ESSEX
INN

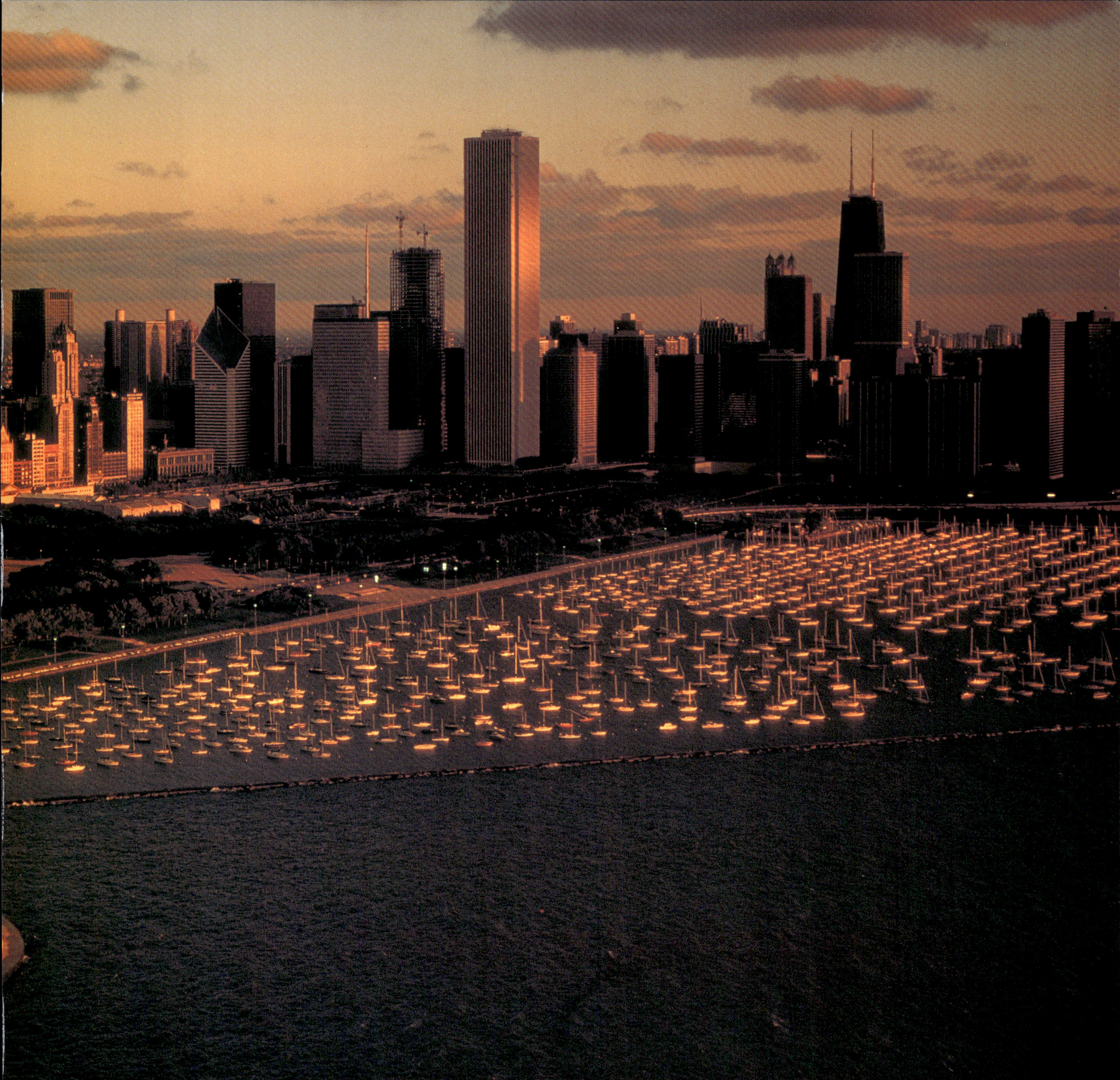

3. Rendering.
4. Curtain wall detail.
5. Site plan. Key: 1 entrance, 2 existing building, 3 Oceanarium, 4 promenade, 5 Lake Michigan, 6 Lake Shore Drive, 7 Field Museum of Natural History.
6. Mezzanine plan. Key: 1 entrance, 2 existing aquarium exhibits, 3 connecting stairs, 4 Oceanarium lobby, 5 dining pavilion, 6 sea otter habitat, 7 large whale habitat, 8 seating, 9 seal cove, 10 small whale habitat, 11 changing exhibits, 12 auditorium pavilion, 13 gift shop, 14 coastal walkway, 15 shared habitat.

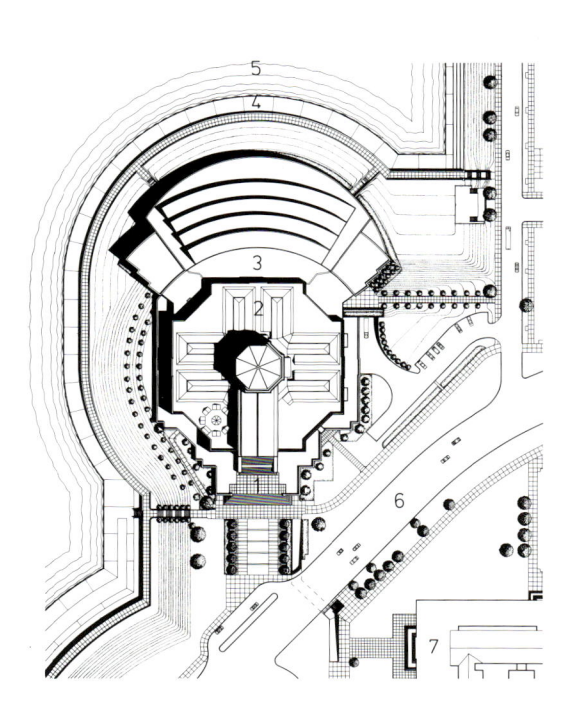

61

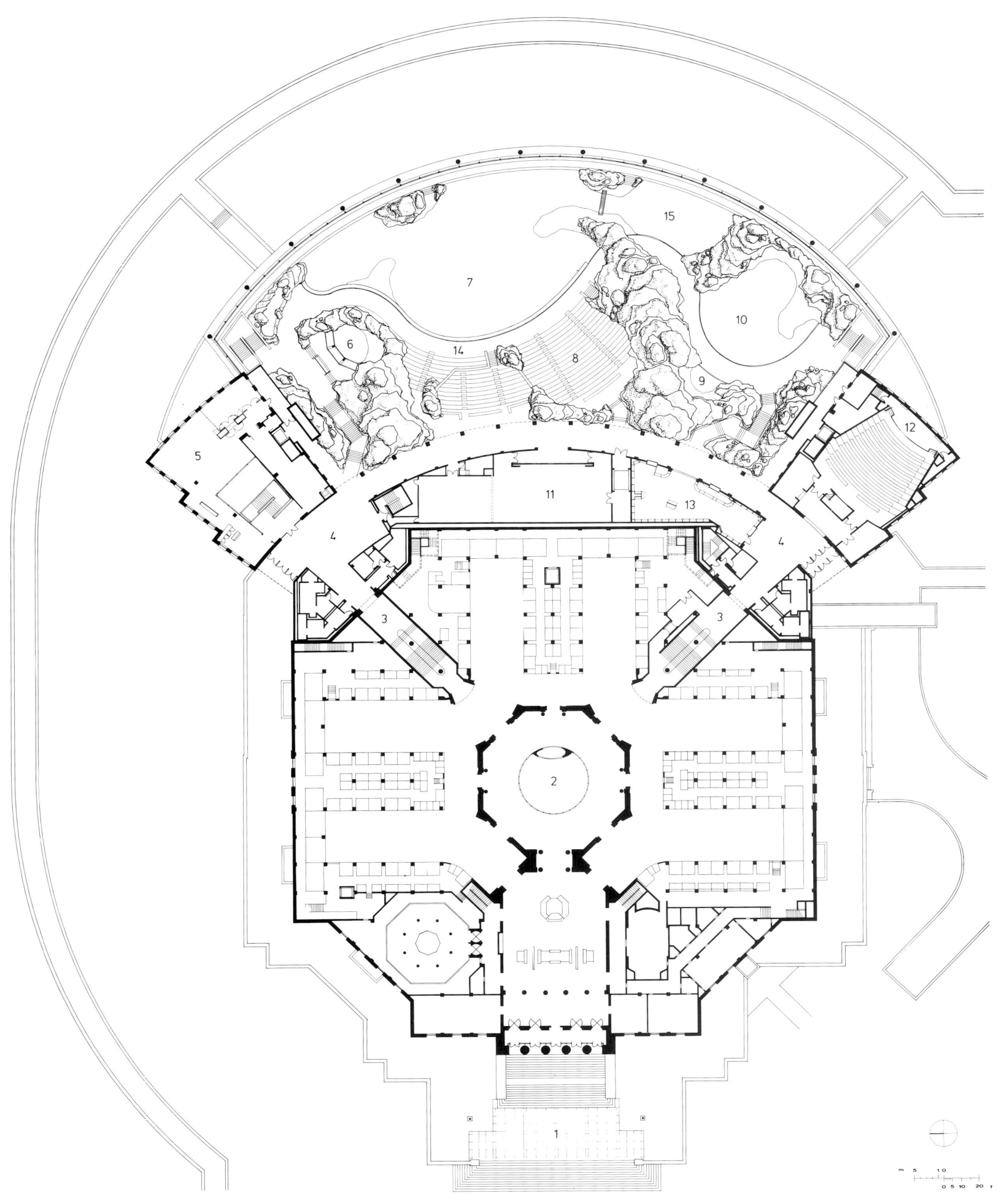

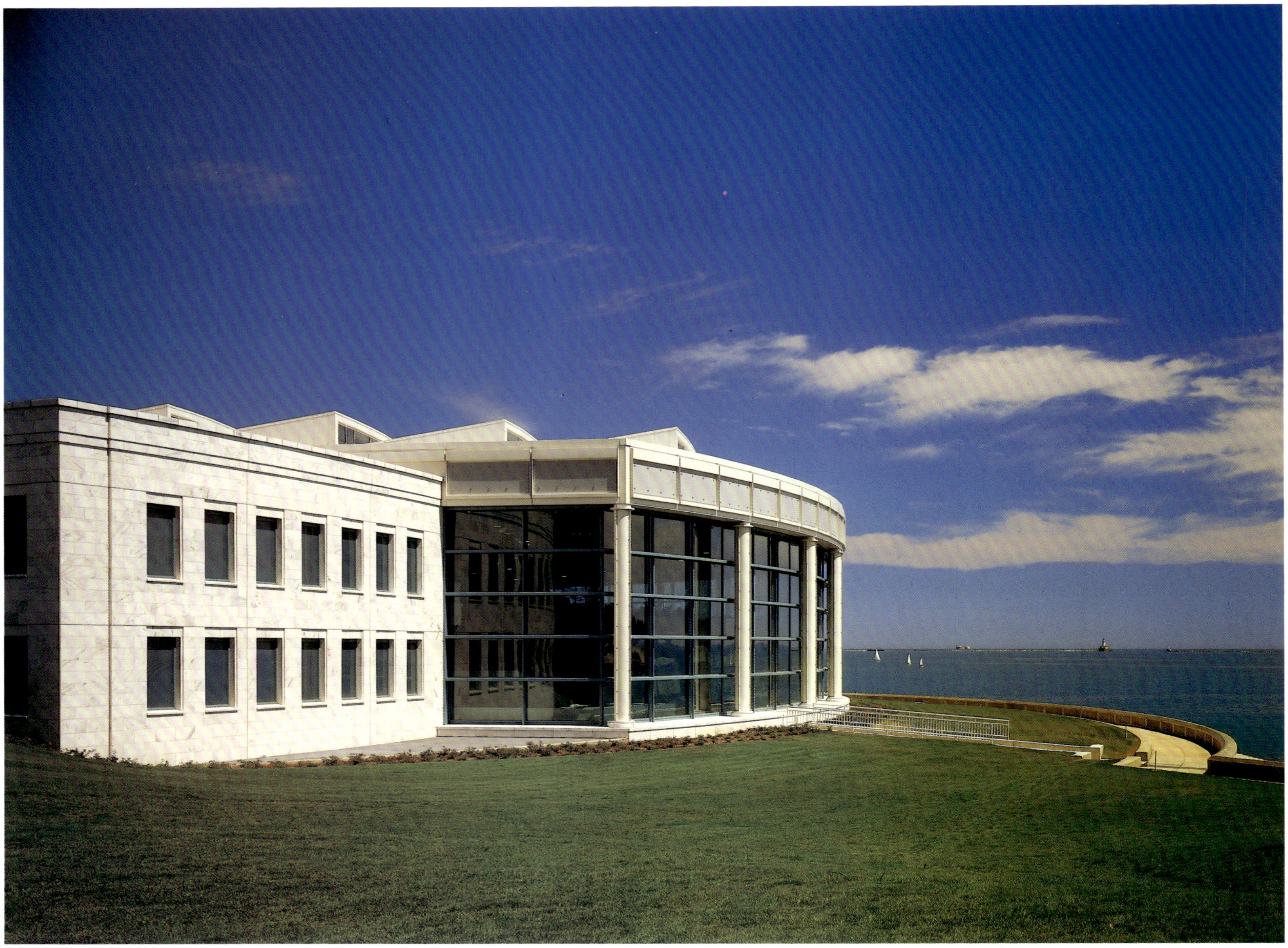

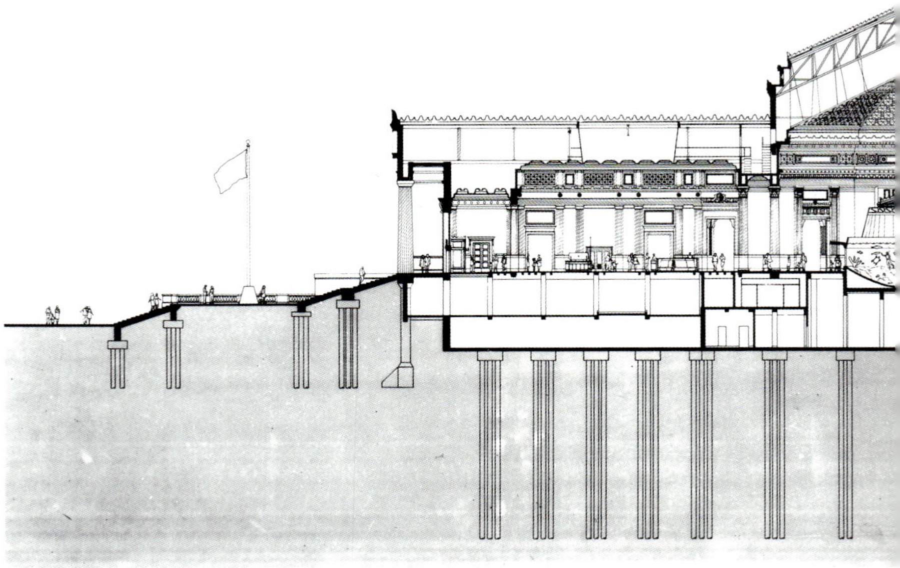

7. Marble-clad pavilions on either side of the curtain wall are transitions from the Oceanarium to the Shedd Aquarium.
8. Interior detail.
9. Section.

p. 64/65
10. View of the large whale habitat during a demonstration.

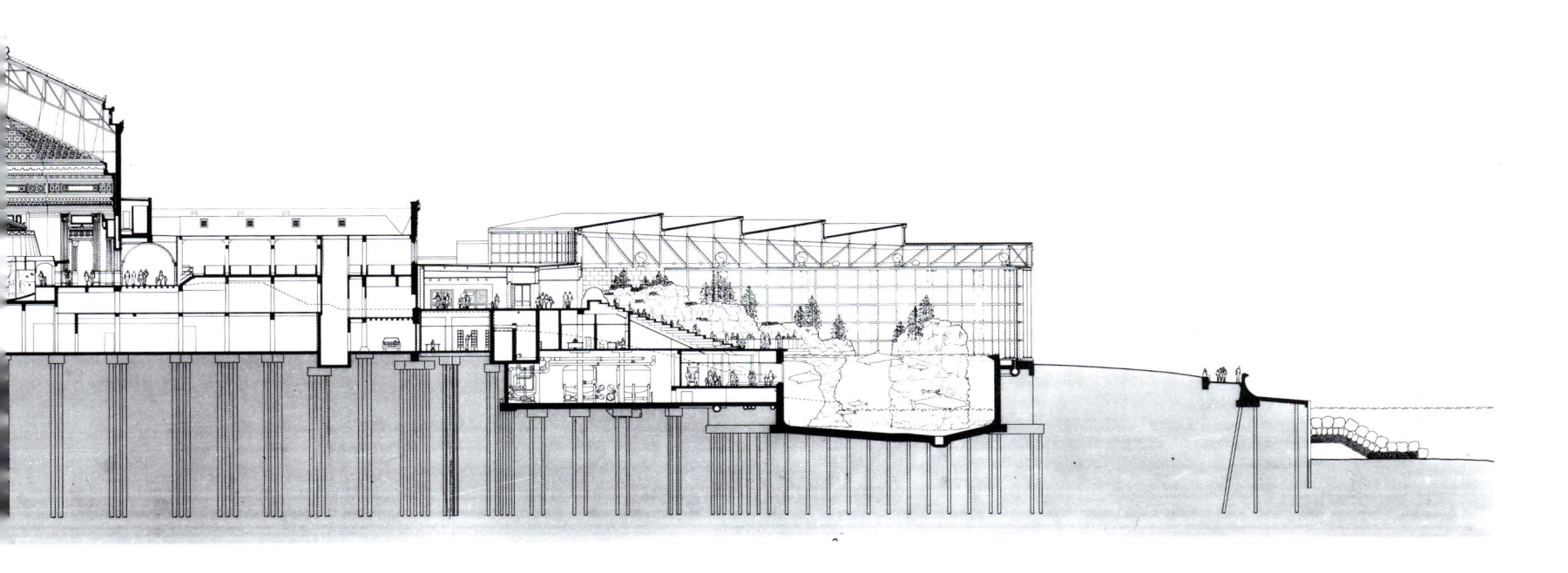

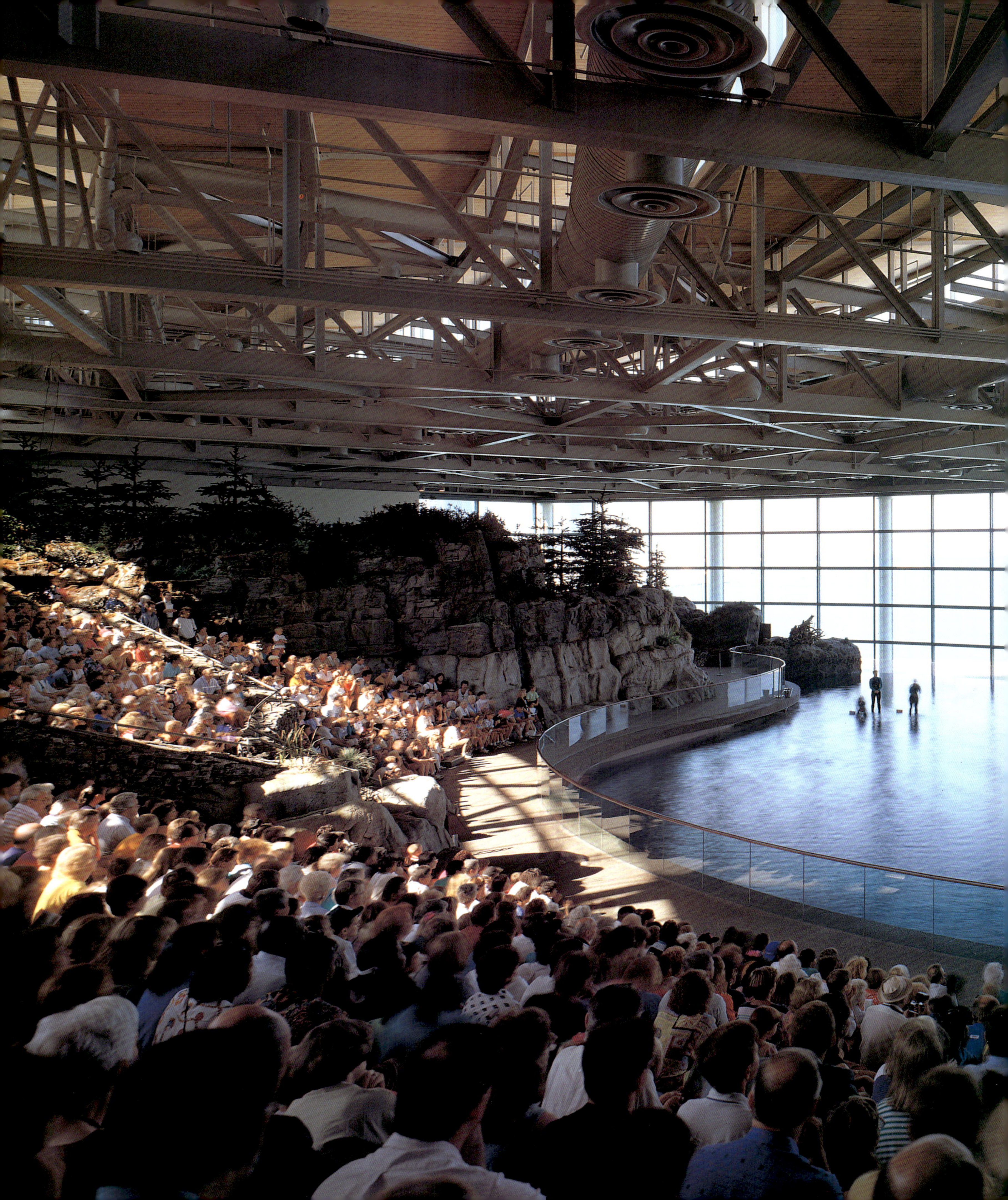

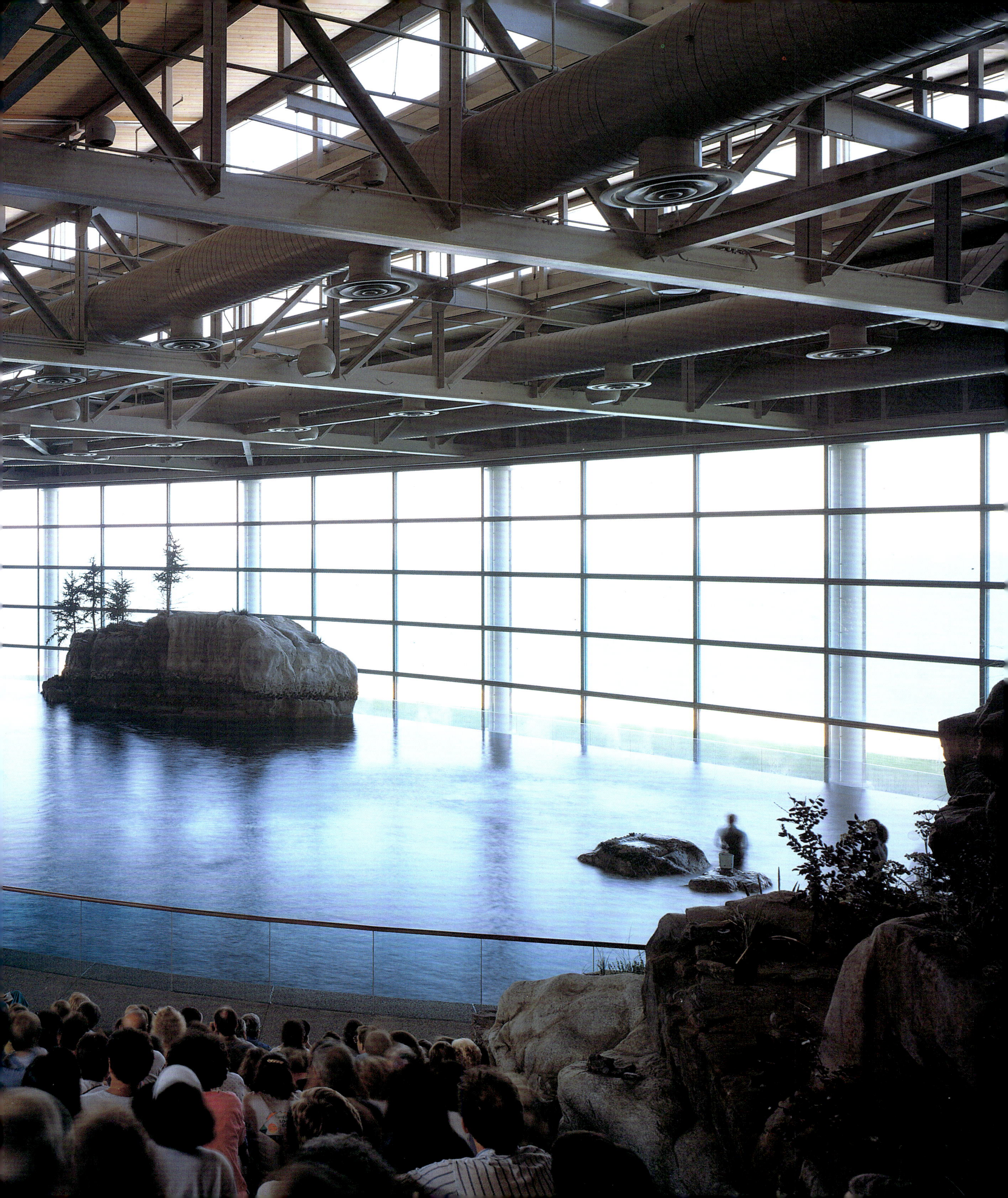

Museum Campus, Chicago, Illinois
1984–

For years, the benefits of having three of Chicago's cultural institutions as next-door lakefront neighbors have been undermined by Lake Shore Drive, a high-speed road whose north-bound lanes separate the museums from one another.

The ongoing Museum Campus plan capitalizes on the proximity of the Field Museum of Natural History, the John G. Shedd Aquarium and the Adler Planetarium to one another by proposing to remove the barrier between them. The long-term goals of the plan are to shift Lake Shore Drive's north-bound lanes to the west creating acontinuous campus among these cultural institutions. A narrow looping boulevard will be created out of the former roadway where slower, two-way traffic can circulate within the campus and among its parking lots. The plan also proposes to replace parking in front of the Field Museum with a formal plaza.

Access from the west to the museums and lakefront would be improved by two features of the plan. A bridge crossing Lake Shore Drive would make it easier for pedestrians to walk to Lake Michigan from Grant Park or the Loop. Both automobile and pedestrian access would be improved by extending Roosevelt Road across existing Illinois Central rail lines.

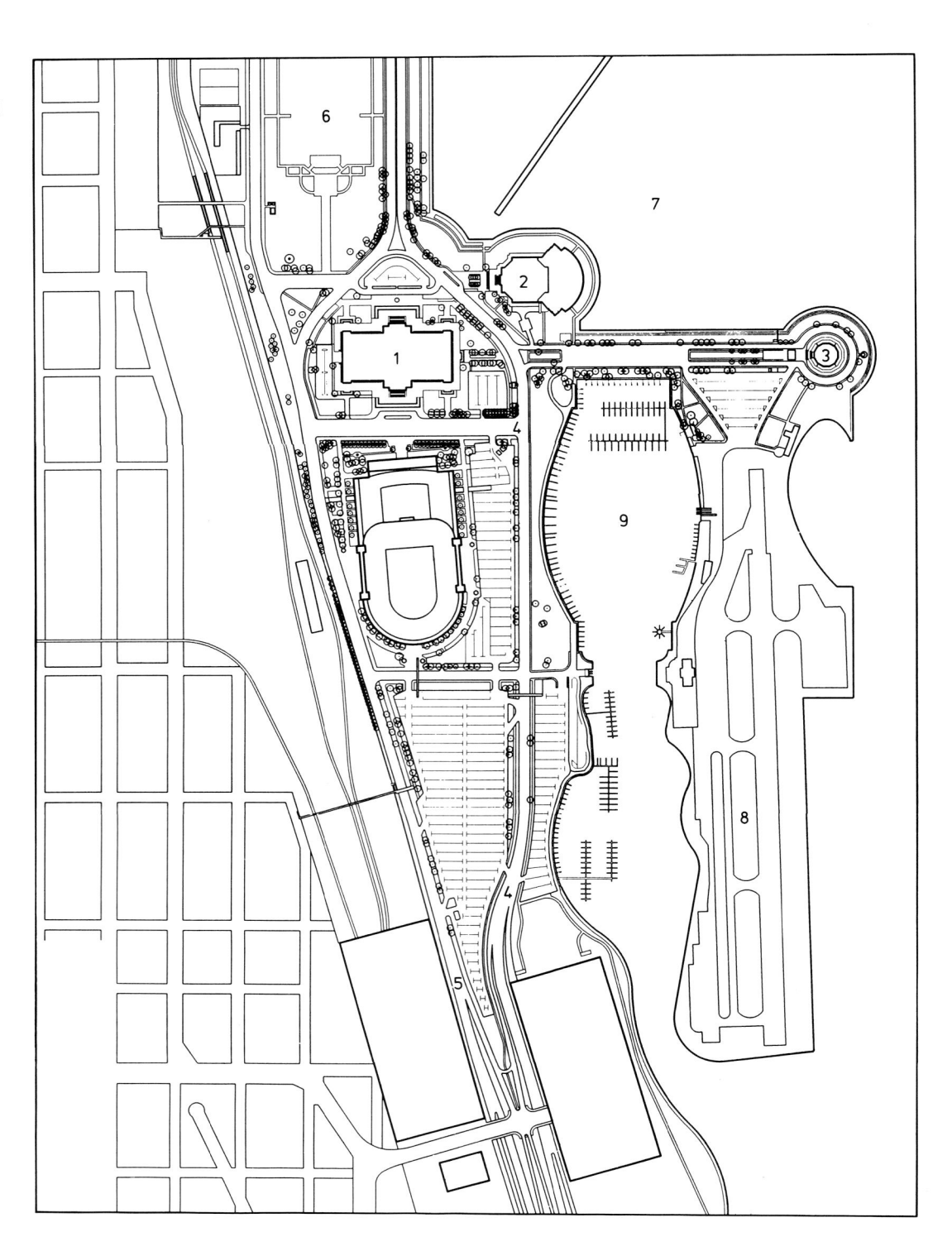

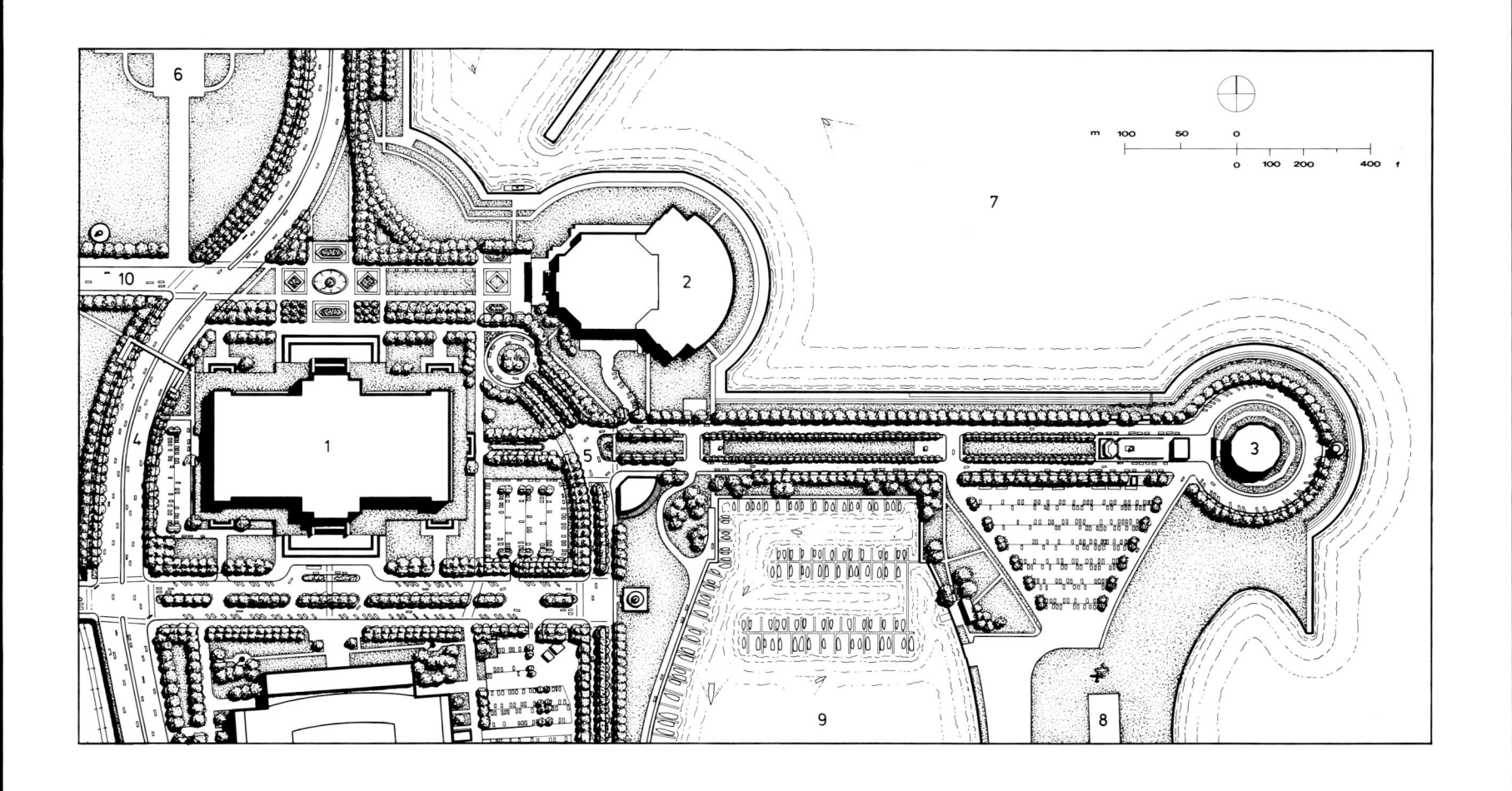

1. Site plan (existing). Key: 1 Field Museum of Natural History, 2 Shedd Aquarium, 3 Adler Planetarium, 4 Lake Shore Drive north-bound lanes, 5 Lake Shore Drive south-bound lanes, 6 Grant Park, 7 Lake Michigan, 8 small-craft airfield, 9 harbor.
2. Site plan (proposed). Key: 1 Field Museum of Natural History, 2 Shedd Aquarium, 3 Adler Planetarium, 4 Lake Shore Drive north- and south-bound lanes, 5 campus circulation road, 6 Grant Park, 7 Lake Michigan, 8 small-craft airfield, 9 harbor, 10 Roosevelt Road extension.

Cityfront Center, Chicago, Illinois
1984–

Cityfront Center lies at the confluence of the Chicago River and Lake Michigan and adjacent to the central business district. Until recently, this 52-acre site was occuppied by rail lines and warehouses, the remnants of a shipping industry. As Cityfront develops, this once-isolated area is being integrated into the city.

Before development began, however, the owner of 40 acres of this development, the Chicago Dock & Canal Trust, hired Lohan Associates to develop a conceptual plan by Cooper Eckstut into a detailed master plan and to oversee its implementation for their site.

In addition, Lohan Associates prepared the internal design standards and designed the public spaces and infrastructure for the Dock & Canal development. A modern infrastructure is now in place; streets that once stopped at Cityfront's edge continue through the site; and, hotel, office and residential structures have been erected.

The goal at Cityfront is to create an environment that is at once urban and conducive to residential living. Design standards requiring developers to incorporate retail at building bases will support street life, day and night. Generous plantings of trees will make the area inviting to pedestrians.

Among the major public spaces designed and completed by Lohan to date are the River Esplanade, Mayor Ogden Park and Centennial Fountain. As the development of Cityfront continues, more parks and public amentities are planned.

The River Esplanade runs along the edge of the Chicago River. The walkway is sheltered by a landscaped bank that slopes up to the street nine feet above. The architects designed the pedestrian-scaled railings and light fixtures after decorative fixtures from the Chicago Plan of 1909 by Daniel Burnham. Lighting has been placed along the length of the esplanade at 30-foot intervals – rather than the city standard of 100 feet – and provides a softer, more continuous illumination than is typical. Cityfront is one of the first riverfront developments in the city to treat the Chicago River as a pedestrian amenity.

Mayor Ogden Park serves as the entry to the Dock & Canal development and is bordered by office and hotel developments. The formal and richly landscaped park is on two stepped levels carved from a steep slope. The park masks a 400-car garage. Partial walls on all sides shelter the park from traffic and create a sense of repose in a busy area of the city. A strong geometry, expressed as a grid by the pergola and a grove of pear trees, is softened by varied and dense plantings. In the center of the park is a sculpture by Vito Acconci, a monumental working clock that lies on the granite pavement.

Centennial Fountain commemorates the reversal of the Chicago River in 1889. Shifting the direction of the polluted river flow away from Lake Michigan, the city's source for drinking water, quickly improved sanitary conditions in Chicago at the turn of the century. The fountain stands on the bank of the Chicago River and is the terminus of McClurg Court Boulevard. Water from an elevated basin cascades down a series of semi-circular steps into a pool. Every hour an 80-foot arc of water is shot to the opposite bank of the river 220 feet away forming a gateway to the city. A sculptural sun dial will top the fountain.

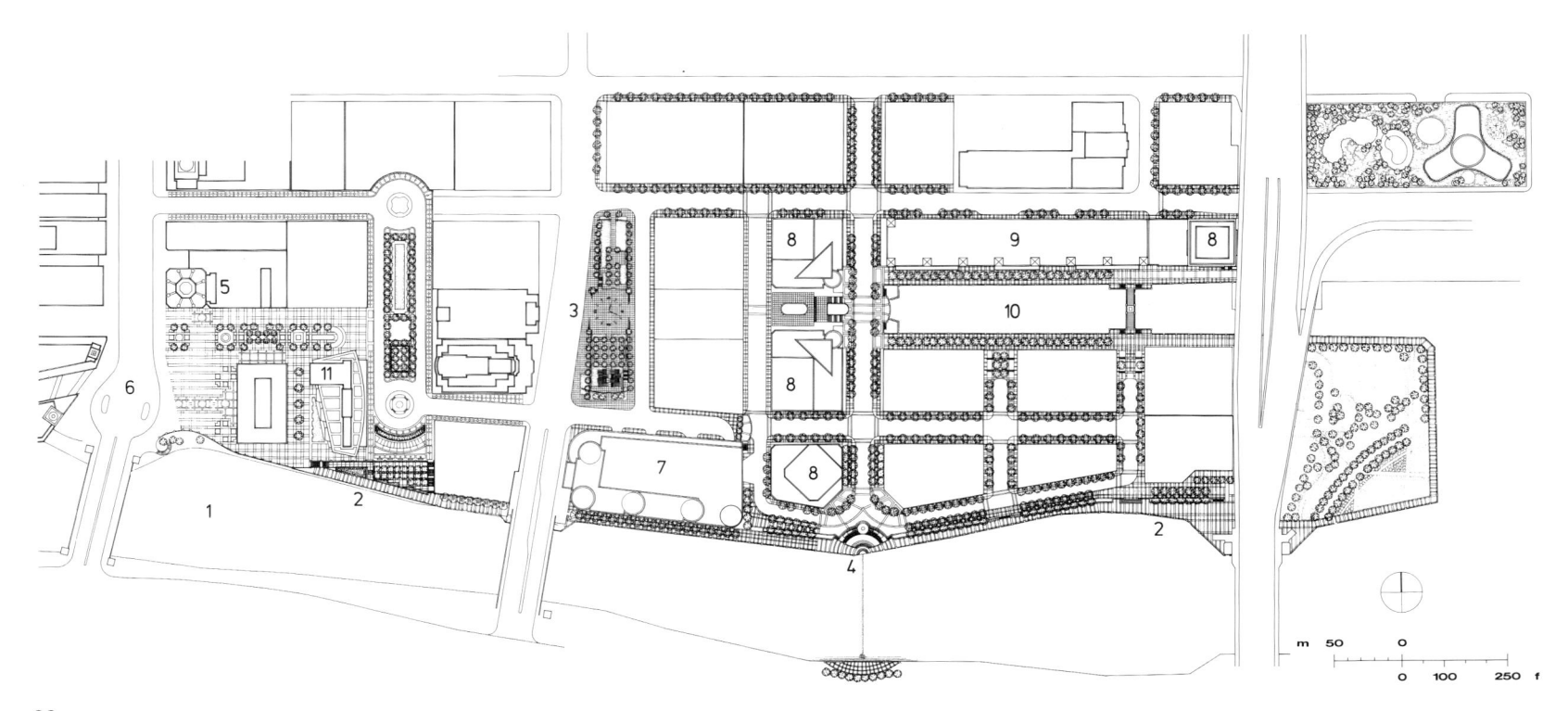

1. Site plan. Key: 1 Chicago River, 2 River Esplanade, 3 Mayor Ogden Park, 4 Centennial Fountain, 5 Tribune Tower, 6 Michigan Avenue, 7 hotel, 8 residential, 9 retail and office, 10 Ogden Slip, 11 University of Chicago Graduate School of Business.
2. General view of the development from the east. Model.
3. Rendering of Ogden Slip.

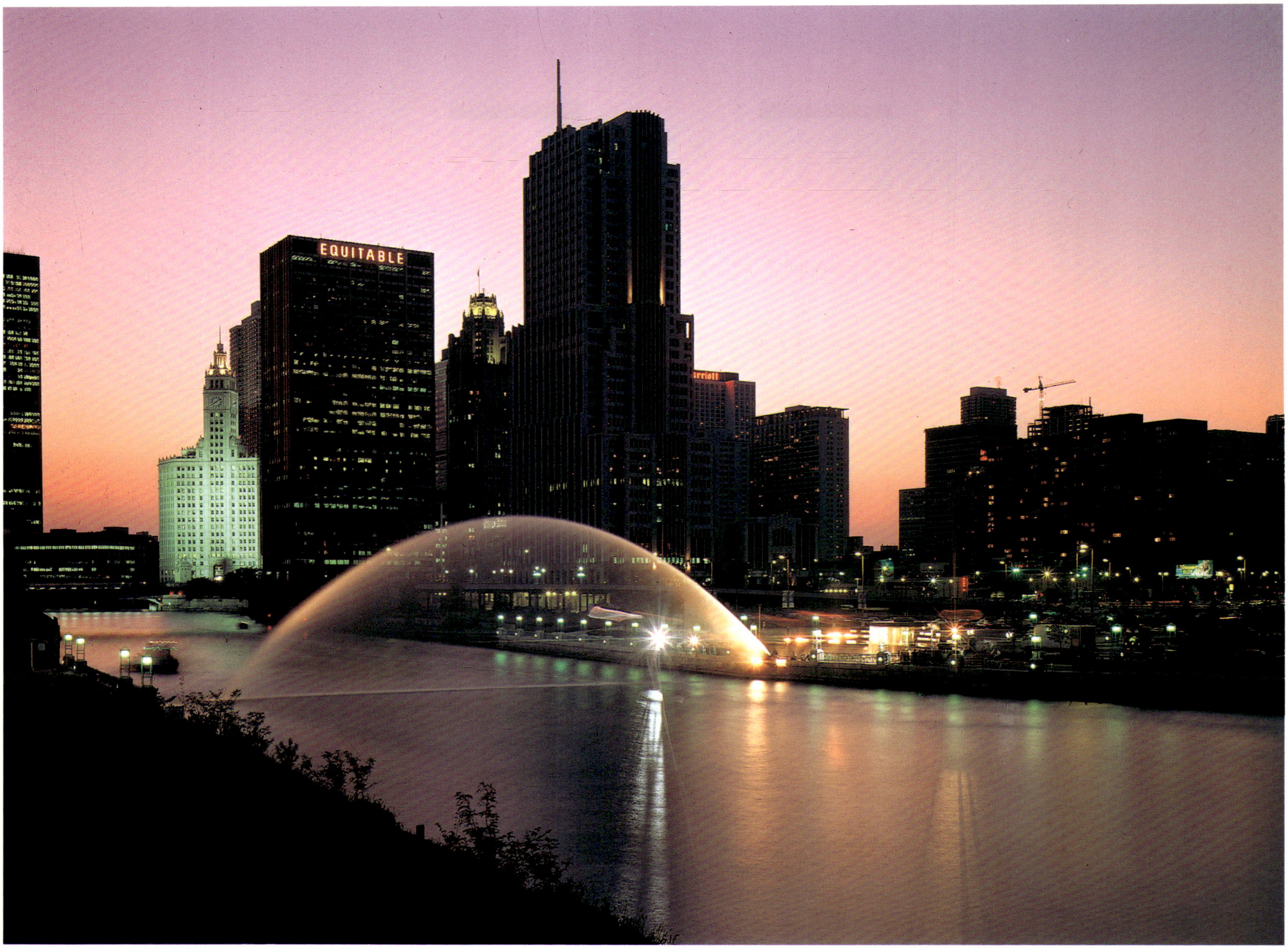
EQUITABLE

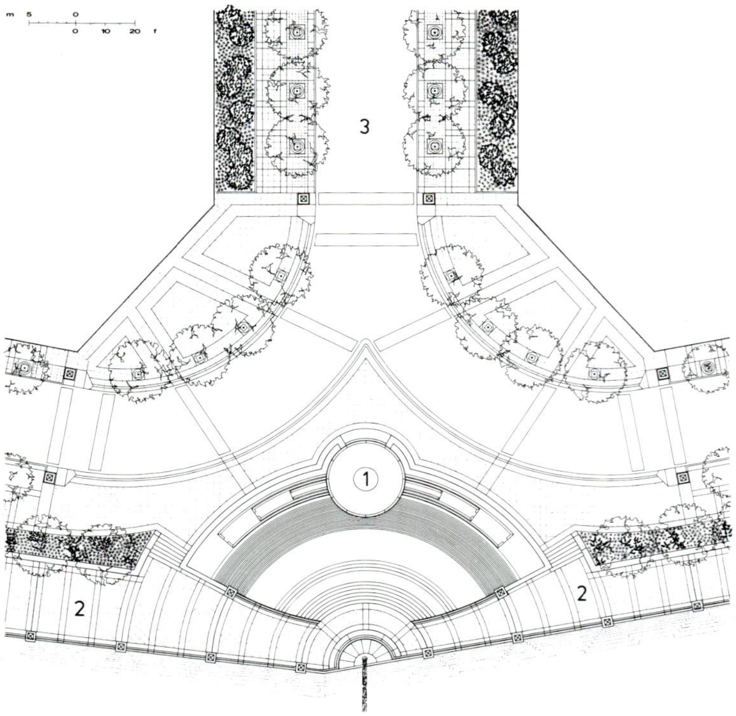
3
1
2
2

4. An arc of water is shot on the hour from Centennial Fountain.
5. Plan. Key: 1 Centennial Fountain, 2 River Esplanade, 3 McClurg Court.
6. A sundial sculpture will top Centennial Fountain. Model.
7. View from the east across Centennial Fountain to the River Esplanade.

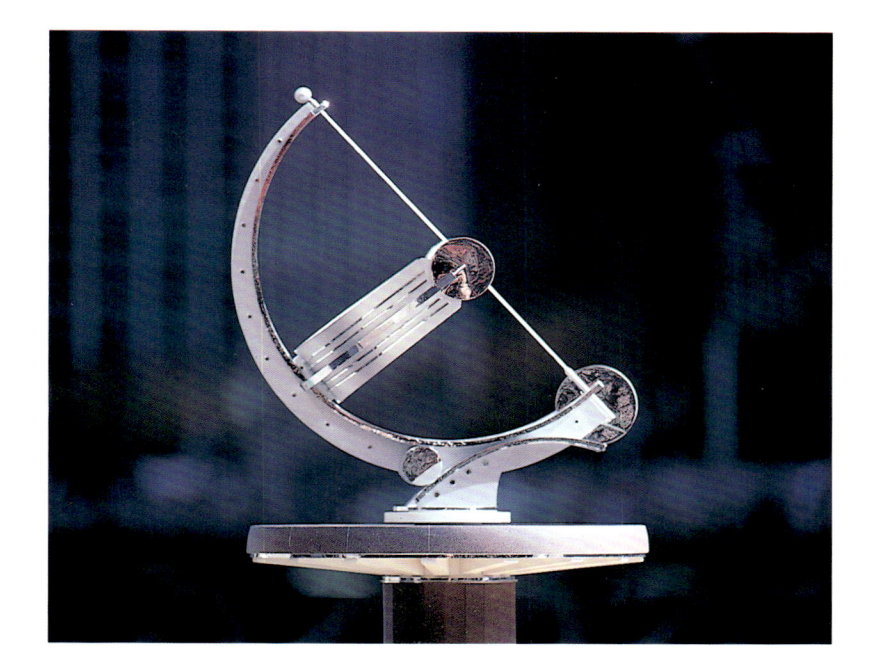

72

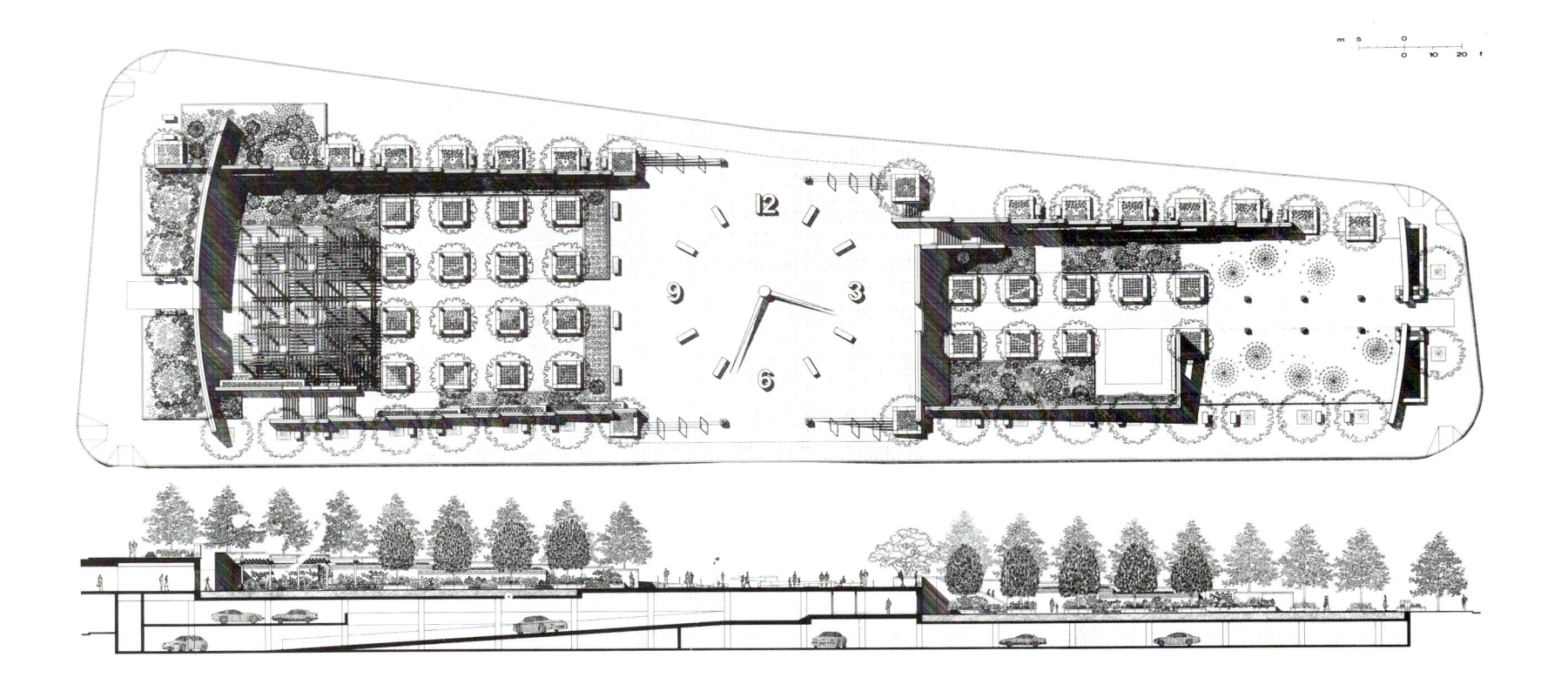

8. Plan and section of Mayor Ogden Park.
9. Aerial view of Mayor Ogden Park.
10. The pergola frames a view of the park.

Market Tower, Indianapolis, Indiana
1984–1988

Market Tower stands near Monument Circle, the most important public space in Indianapolis. The Circle contains an imposing stone and bronze war memorial and is on axis with the State Capitol two blocks away. The monument was once entirely ringed by stone-clad buildings, a number of which survive.

Market Tower is designed to relate to the original fabric around the Circle. The 32-story speculative office building is clad in a pink granite with certain window sprandels accented by a polished red granite. Its pronounced cornice line matches the height of a next-door building. As it ascends, it steps back echoing the massing of skyscrapers in the area. Its angled copper roof recalls a nearby mansard. The four-story broken-arch entryway echoes several arched entries around the Circle.

But the borrowed features are interpreted in a modern way. An aluminum frame supports the cladding. Where the upper setbacks occur the façade is pulled back to expose structural supports beneath. Fifteen-foot-deep cantilevers on the east and west sides are expressed by a transformation from stone to a taut glass curtain-wall cladding.

The first three stories of the building are devoted to services and retail. Shops and restaurants are accessible by escalators. A conference center that is available to all the building's tenants is located on the fourth floor. In all, the building has 568,000 square feet with floors averaging 18,400 square feet. On most floors the cantilevers have created a cruciform plan with eight corner offices.

1. Plans (ground floor and typical floor). Key: 1 escalators to the retail mezzanine, 2 fountain, 3 loading dock, 4 bank.
2. Entry detail.

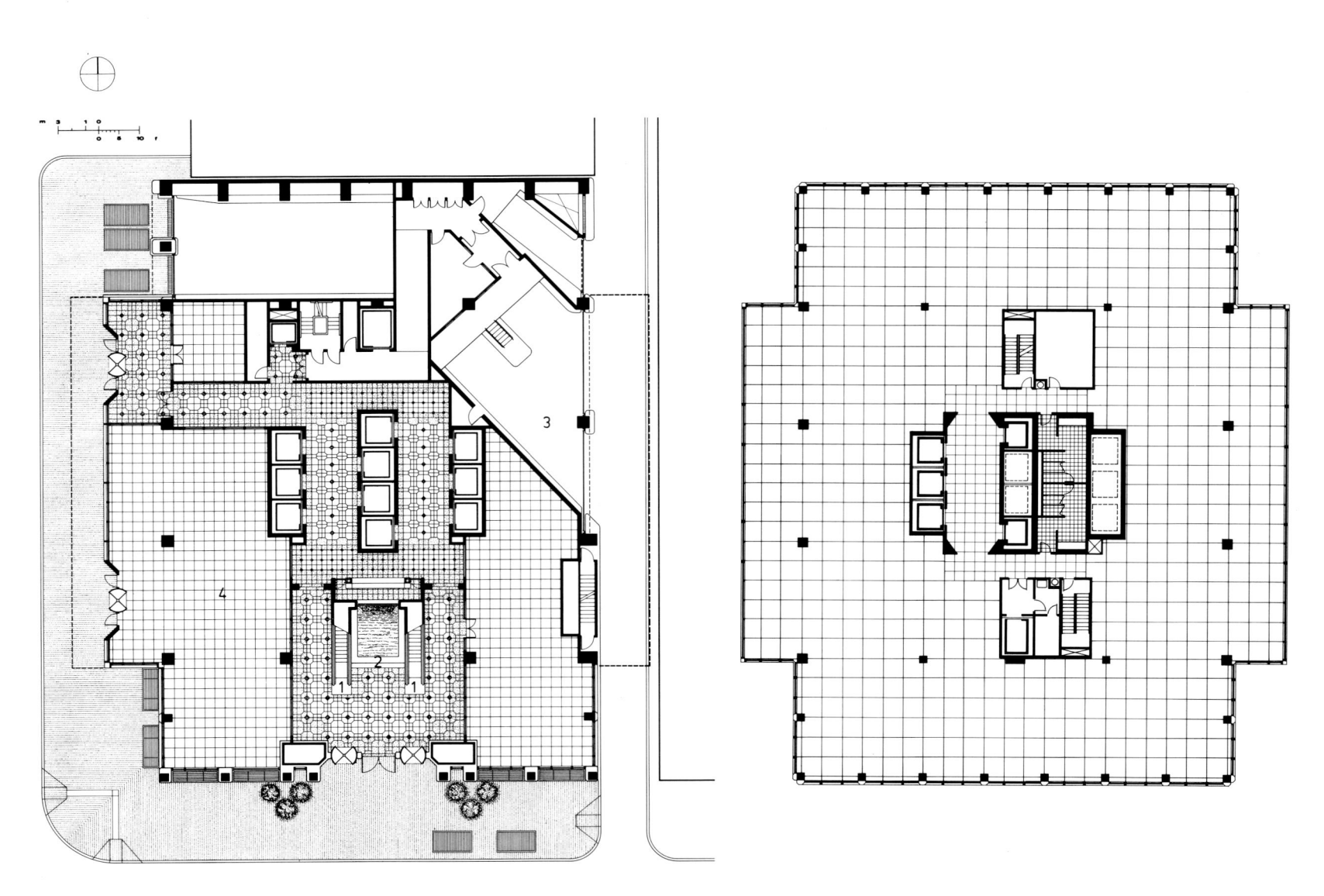

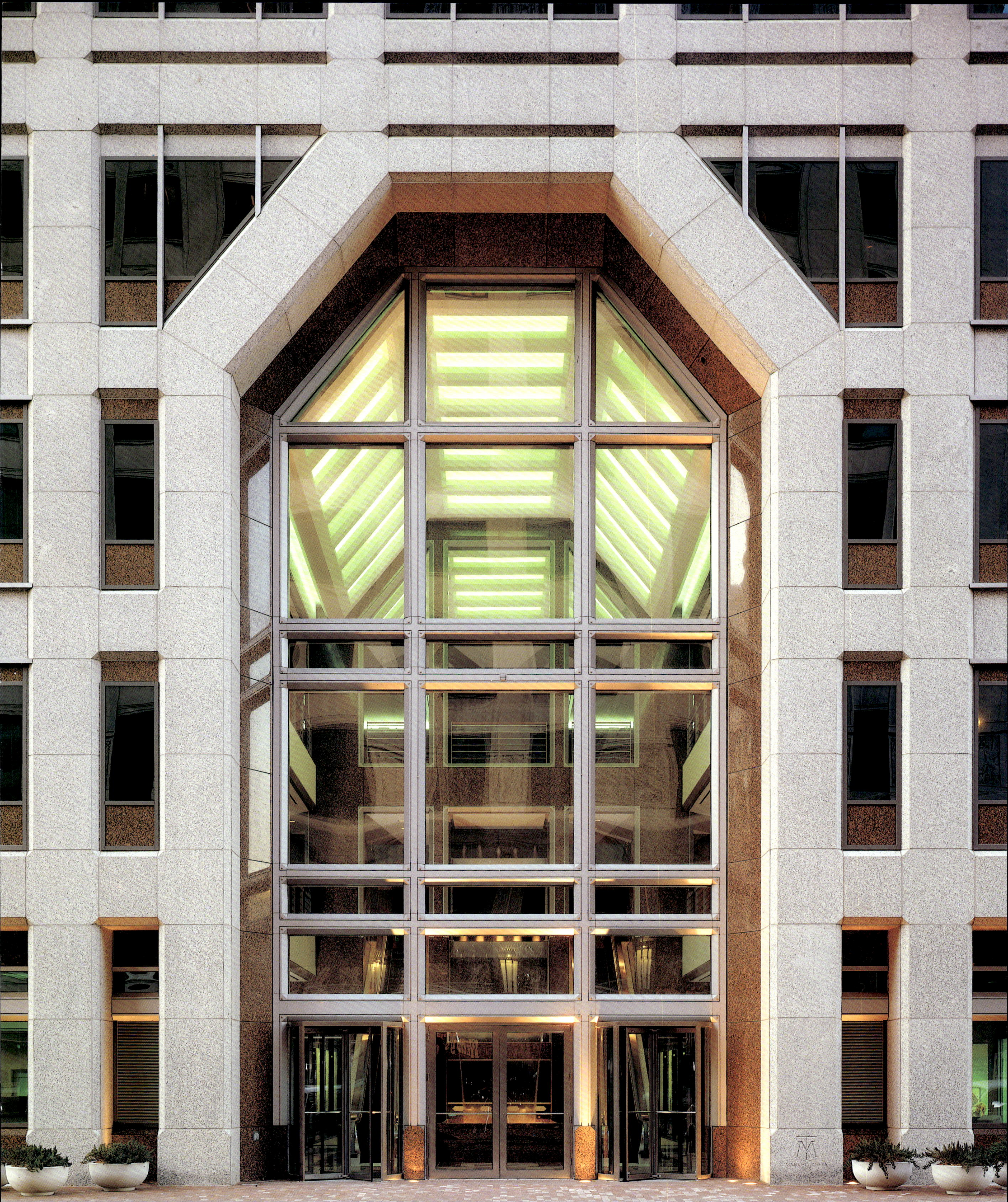

3. The upper setbacks and mansard roof recall details in older neighboring buildings.
4. The tower stands near Monument Circle.

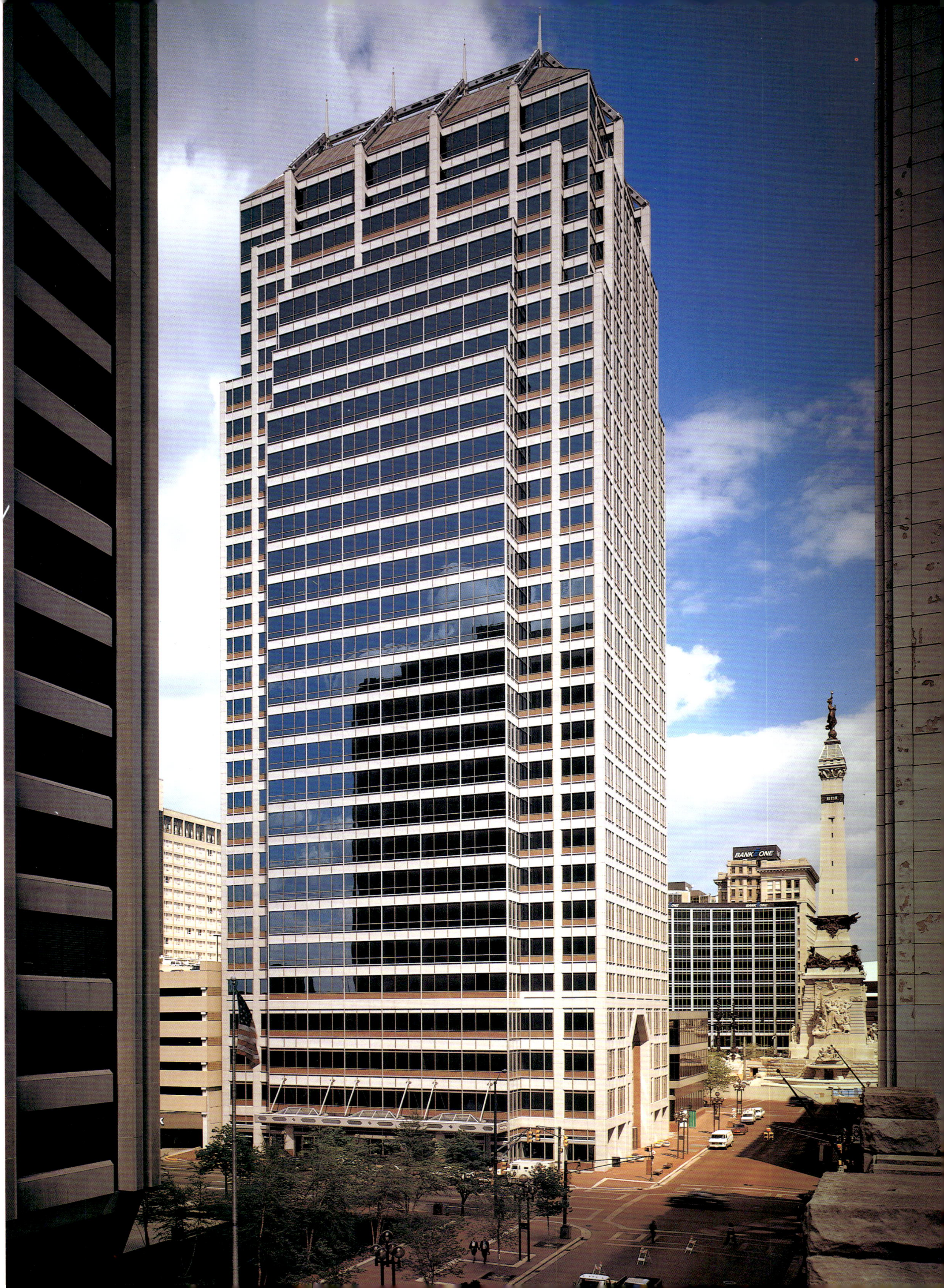
BANK ONE

Dean Witter Financial Services Headquarters, Riverwoods, Illinois
1986–1988

Approaching the Dean Witter campus along a formal tree-lined road, two wings of the building appear to reach out on either side of the entry in an embracing gesture. This first impression is telling. Warmth and human scale were the animating principles behind the design. In addition to the building design, Lohan Associates designed the common areas, rotunda, gallerias, dining facilities, and executive offices.

The 600,000-square-foot building is composed of four wings that resemble, in plan, two interlocking L-shapes. The backward wings are four stories high, the forward wings are three stories and reduce the building's mass at the entry. It is clad with polished and rough-finished imported granite. Polished stainless steel window frames are a gleaming addition. The dome, which marks the center of the building, is topped with a copper roof.

The form of the building permits penetration of natural light into worker areas. Each wing is 100 feet wide with windows on either side. Together, the four wings contain offices and work stations for approximately 1,800 people. In the hallways there are skylit, double staircases with ornamental railings. Granite and limestone flooring is used. The walls are painted a faux granite pattern that mimics the exterior walls.

The wings radiate from a soaring four-story rotunda with circling lobbies at the upper floors, a clerestory, and a ribbed domed ceiling painted a shade of blue suggesting the color of the sky. A pattern in the granite and limestone floor picks up the curve of the rotunda above and the custom circular lobby rug, measuring 45 feet in diameter, reiterates the theme. The same green granite that is used on the exterior is used in the rotunda for walls and floors, unifying the building design in a fundamental way. In a ground-level common area at the back of the building there is a semi-circular dining area with upper and lower levels overlooking an outdoor terrace and landscaped pond.

At the request of the client, traditional materials and finishes have been used in the second-floor executive area where there are nine offices, three conference rooms, a dining room, pantry, reception and administrative spaces.

The landscaping is formal close to the building and naturalistic further away from it.

1. Plan (ground floor). Key: 1 lobby rotunda, 2 standard office wing, 3 tiered dining area, 4 reception, 5 terrace.
2. Entry detail.

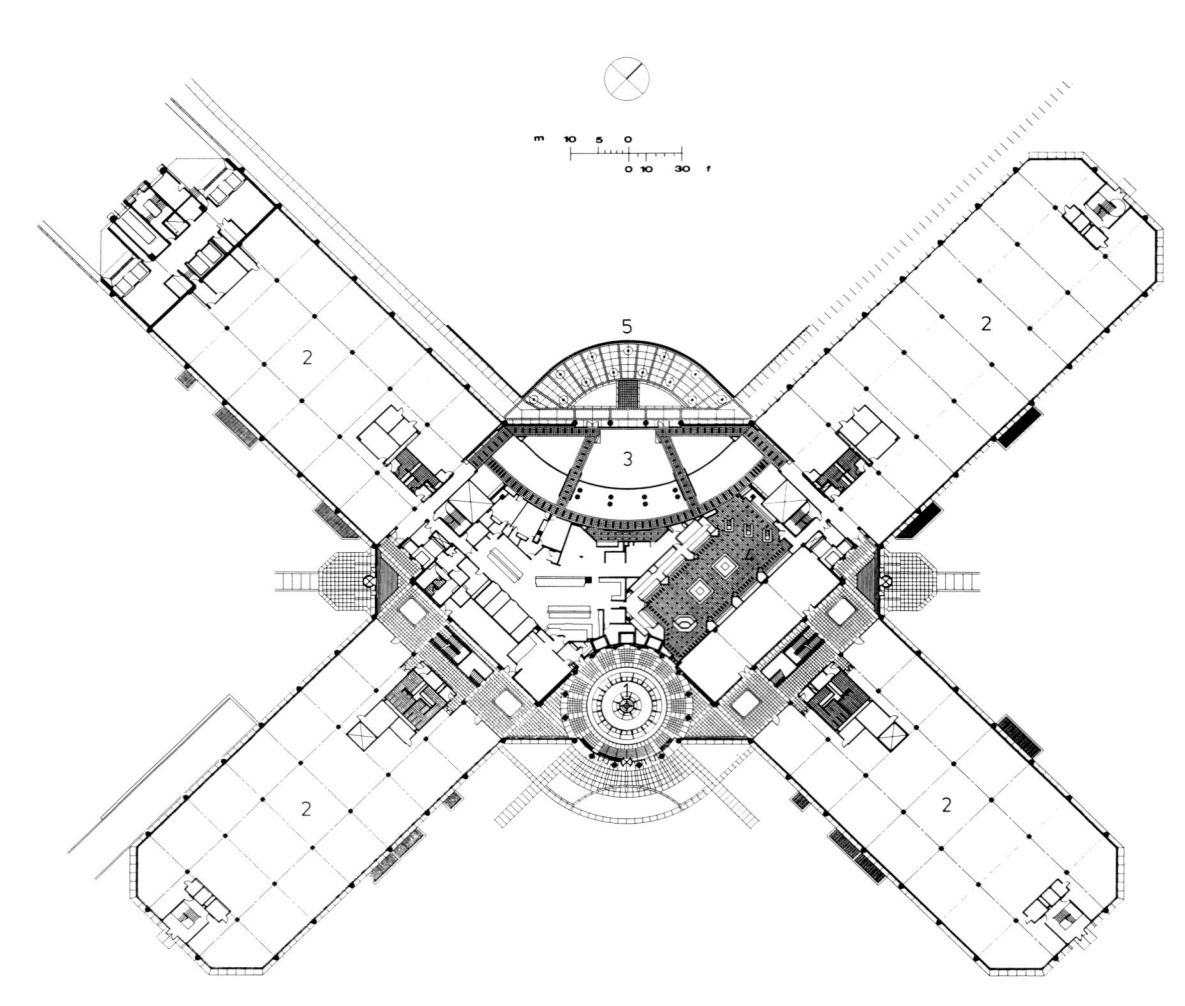

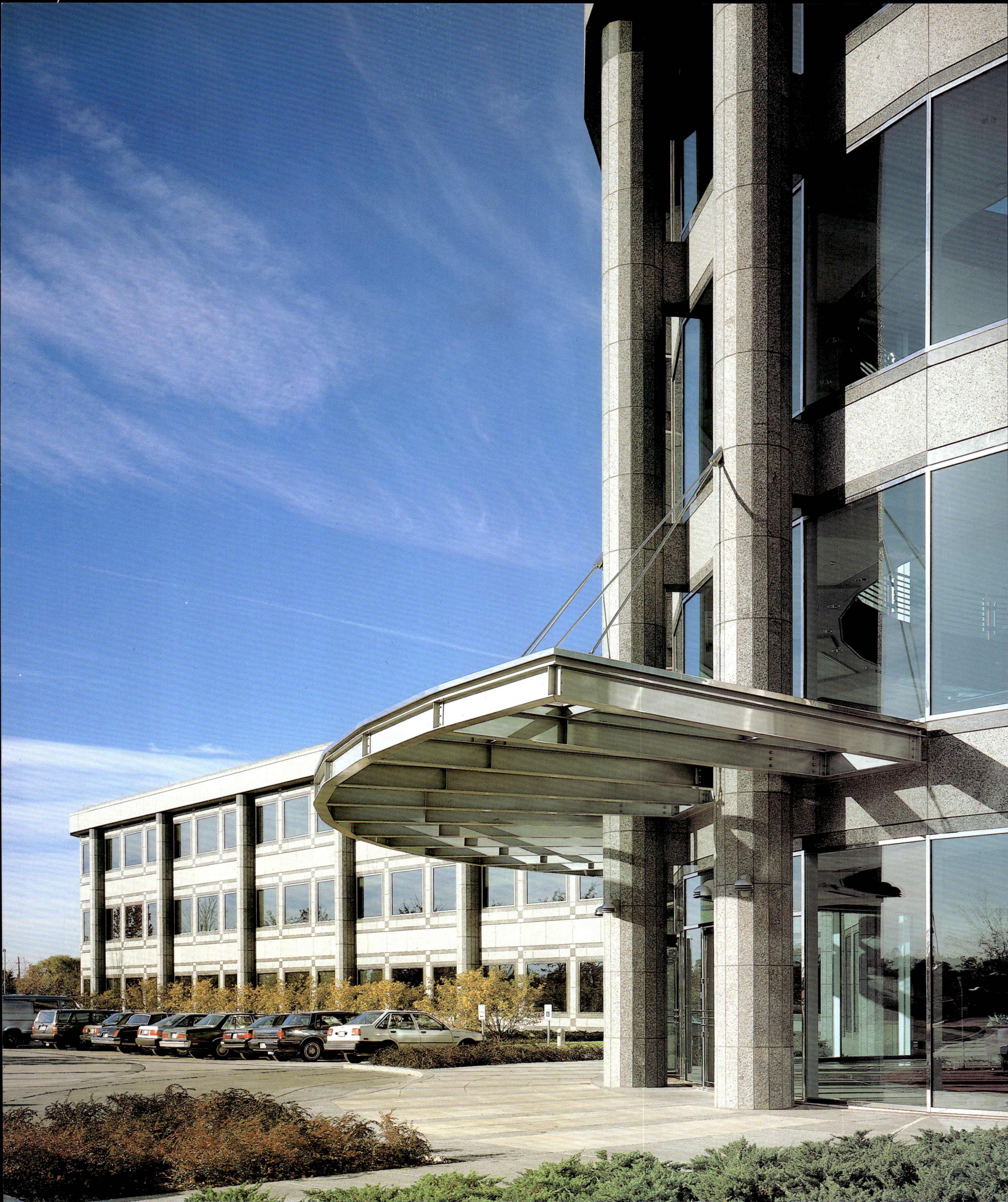

3. The rotunda crowns the lobby.
4. The same materials are used on the exterior and interior of the building.
5. Skylit hallways have double staircases with ornamental railings.

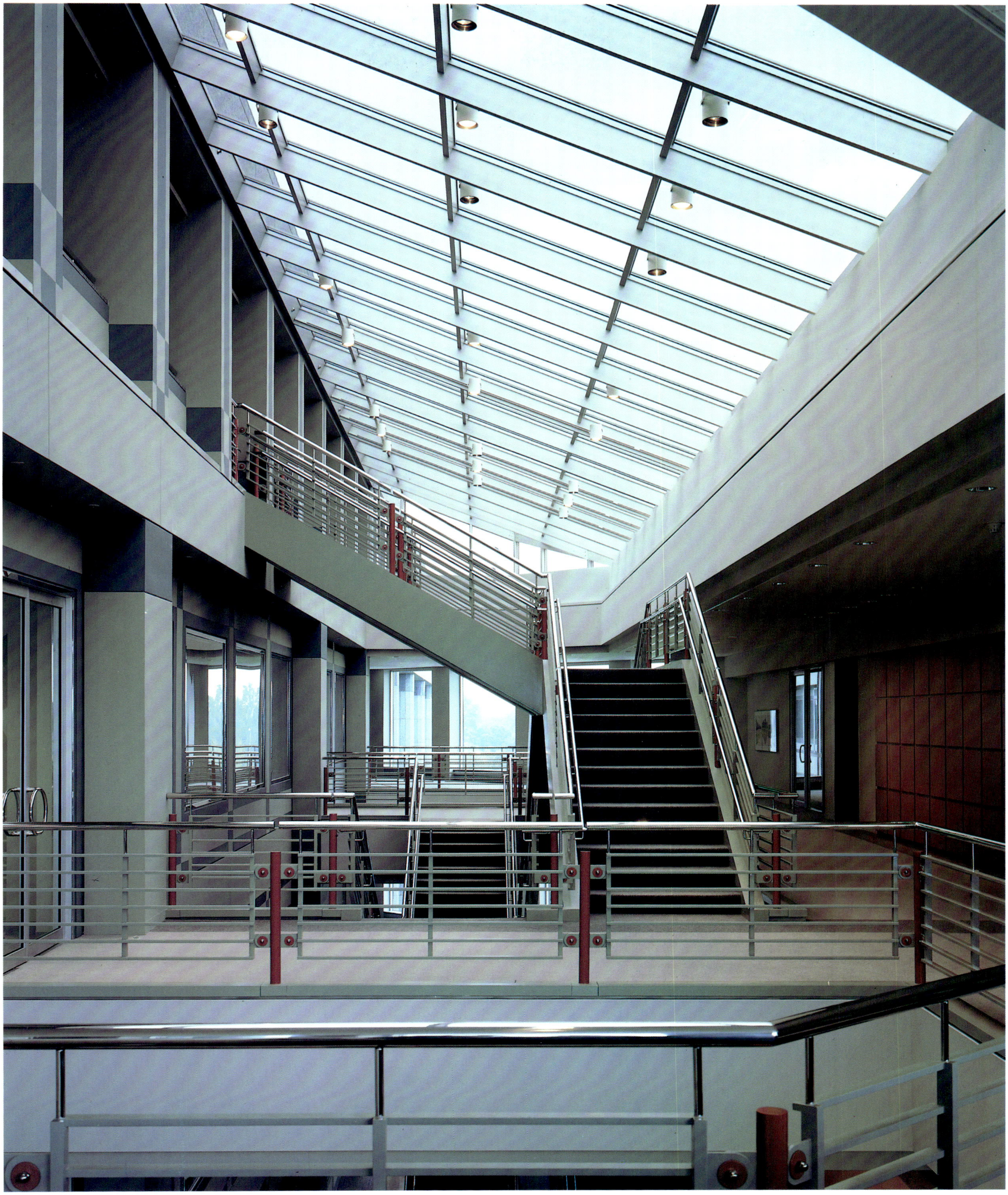

Rockwell International Graphic Systems Headquarters, Westmont, Illinois
1986–1988

The challenge of the project lay in reconciling a stringent budget with the desire for a distinctive building. Added to the mix was a height restriction on the site.
The problem suggested a low massive box. Lohan's solution is more complex. It is a low-rise building with four components, each resembling a separate building. But the four structures are joined by 15-foot-wide light wells that admit natural light into the center of each unit. The four building components are of varying heights – the tallest rising three stories above grade – and follow a slope, stepping down the site to a retention pond.
The two-story entry is distinguished by a steel-and-glass canopy and flanking walls of amber-colored marble. The building is clad in deeply articulated precast concrete panels that help to screen windows from direct sunlight and give the building a richly textured appearance. An octagonal motif is introduced in a pattern of medallions on the façade. The shape is reiterated throughout the interior, extending to the layout of the executive office and ornamental elements.
Three of the structures together contain roughly 262,000 square feet in office and support space for 800 workers. The fourth structure houses a research and development hall of 23,000 square feet laid out on a single floor with a three-story ceiling height. This area is used principally to test and demonstrate prototype printing press equipment.
Other office facilities include research laboratories, a technical library, a cafeteria, dining rooms, and a conference and sales area.

1. Plan (site and ground floor). Key: 1 lobby, 2 galleria, 3 research and design.
2. Natural light is admitted through the gallerias into the center of each building unit.
3. View of the entry.

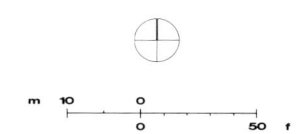

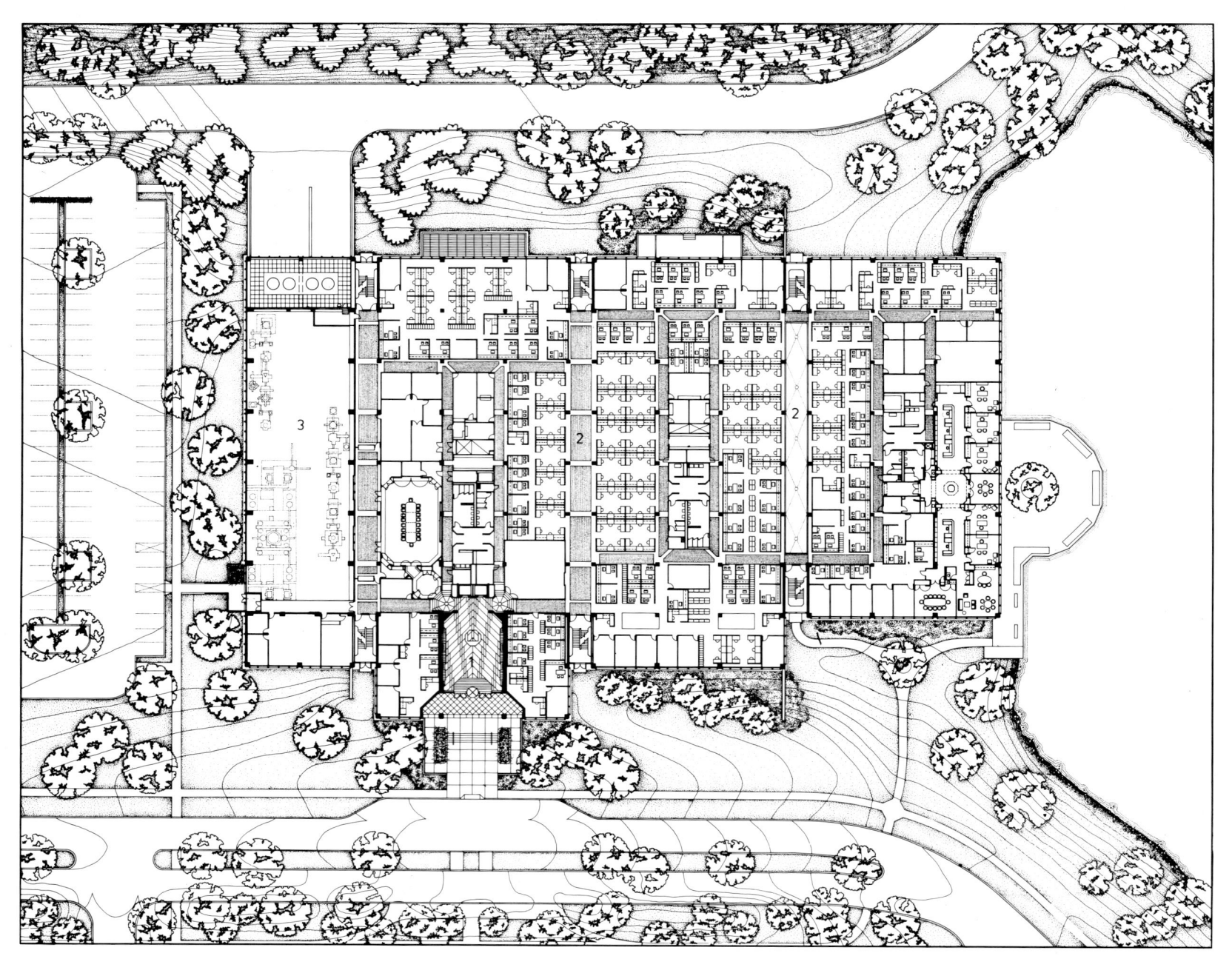

83

Lakefront Lagoon, Chicago, Illinois
1987. Project

In 1987 when Lake Michigan rose to its highest recorded level, severe winter storms caused flooding along Lake Shore Drive and damage to lakefront buildings. That spring Lohan Associates offered a plan to the City of Chicago to stabilize the lakefront water level.

The plan proposes to join existing breakwaters to create an enormous lagoon enclosing Meigs Field to the south and Navy Pier to the north. The locks, which serve river traffic and are currently at the mouth of the Chicago River, would be moved to the outer breakwater. The resulting lagoon would be a stable body of water at the same level as the river and would provide a good place for recreational sports like wind surfing and sailing for boats too small for Lake Michigan. The development would spark recreational activity along the Chicago River by making it easy for boats to travel from the river to the lagoon. Bicycle paths, landscaped walks and beaches would be located along the new breakwater. A marina for larger, lake-going craft would be located on the outer edge of the breakwater.

The project was planned for completion in two phases: existing breakwaters would be extended in stage one and the locks would be erected in stage two.

1. View of the lakefront lagoon looking south.

One-Fifty North Dearborn Office Tower, Chicago, Illinois
1987. Project

For a speculative 40-story office building Lohan Associates invented a distinctive design that recalls Chicago's traditions and refines them for the present day.

The tower is rectangular with cantilevered faceted corners that soften its form and reflect light in interesting ways. The cladding is stainless steel, painted aluminum and green glass. Simple bands of windows wrap the corners of the building. Elsewhere, glass tinted a darker green is recessed within the frame of the curtain wall to emphasize the play of light and shadow over the surface of the building. The pattern of recessed and flush-to-surface glass resembles the turn-of-the-century Chicago window and invites recollection of the city's oldest and most distinguished architectural traditions. The building is topped with a sloped glass roof and ornamental spires that are lighted at night.

The 850,000-square-foot tower is an important element in the redevelopment of an area called the North Loop. To stimulate its daytime use and draw more people to the North Loop, a series of retail galleries link One-fifty North Dearborn with other buildings in the vicinity. Retail occupies the entire first floor. Two landmark theaters next door are being restored and are expected to draw nighttime crowds. In deference to the theaters, Lohan Associates has matched its ground-floor cornice line to their height. Entries to the tower are located at the corners. Elevators to the offices are on the mezzanine level and can be reached by way of a lobby escalator.

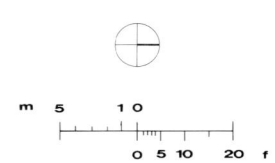

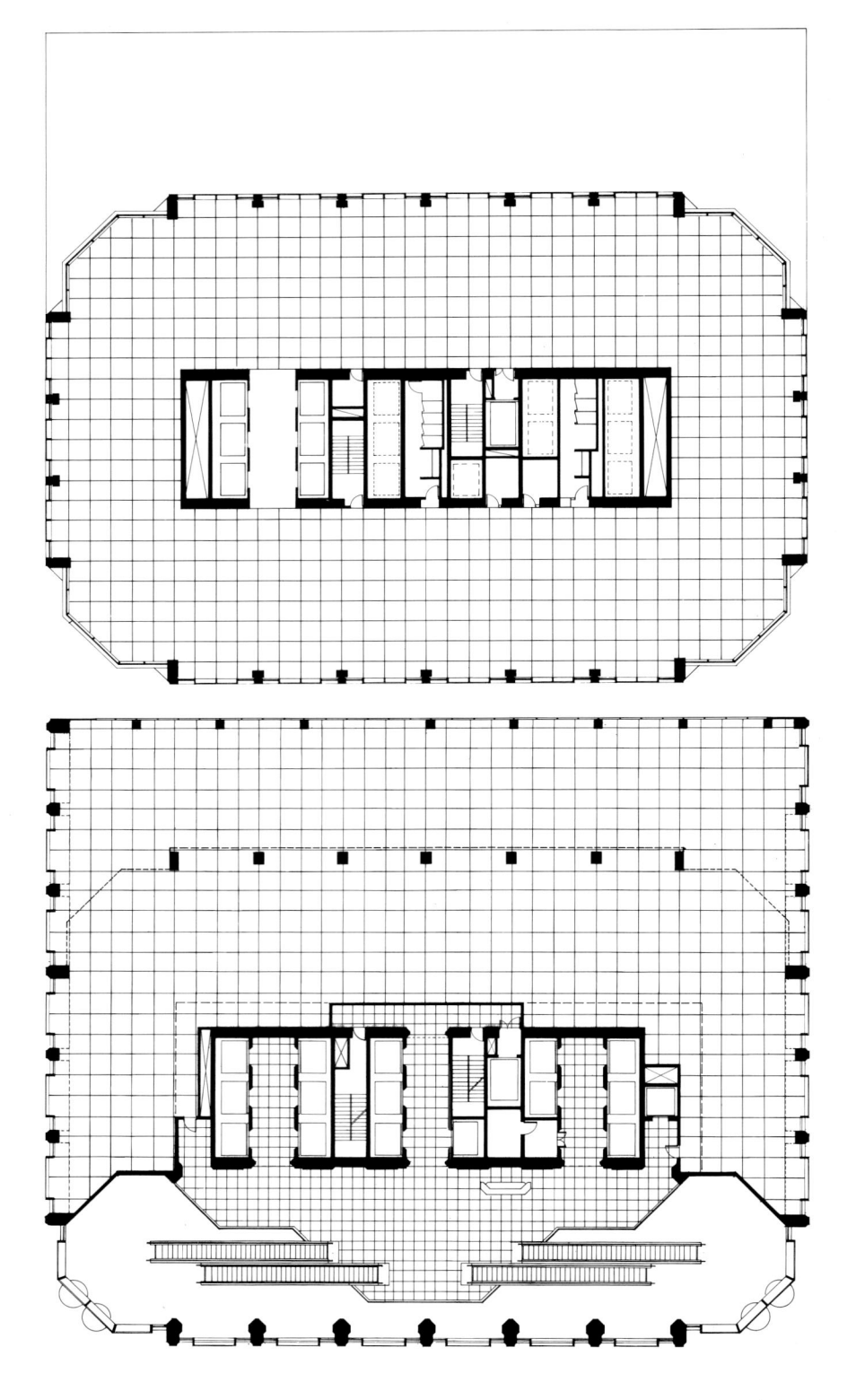

1. Plans (mezzanine, typical floor).
2. Rendering.

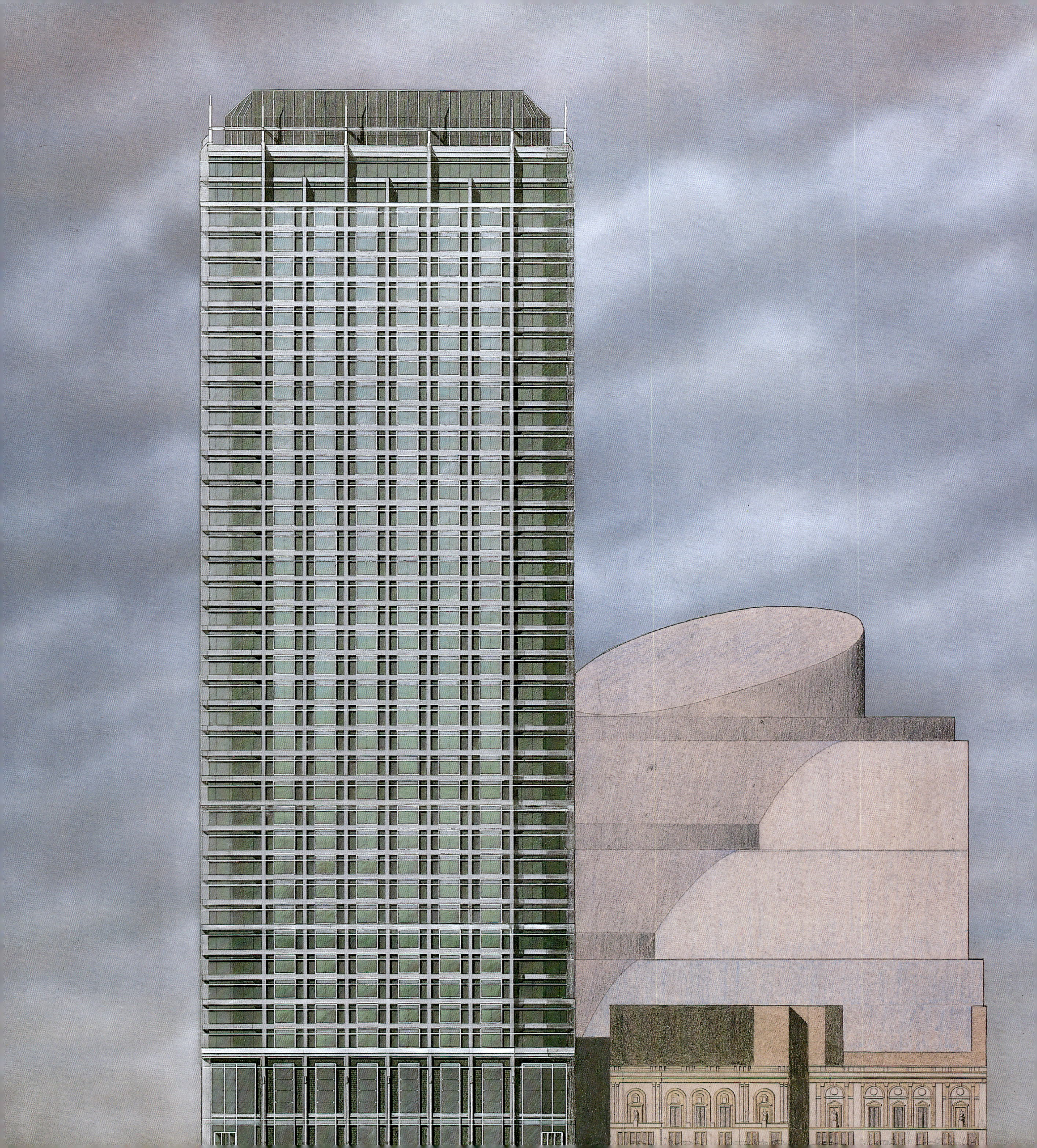

Ameritech Center, Hoffman Estates, Illinois
1987–1991

Formal planning principles were used to organize the site and the four-story, 1.3 million-square-foot building the Ameritech Corporation required for its regional office in suburban Chicago.
From either side of the building's central hub a series of symmetrically adjoined L-shaped wings emerge. There are eight such wings, each measuring 30,000 square feet and defining a contained work area. The wings' internal boundaries are defined by gallerias and suspended walkways that are the principal circulation avenues within the building. Two enclosed atria occur where the gallerias converge. These soaring spaces, which are animated by fountains and landscaping, are circulation hubs and informal meeting places. The logical repetition of the formal plan makes the building immediately comprehensible.
In a reversal of the typical office hierarchy, work stations are placed along the window wall and private offices are on the interior. The work stations have low wall dividers and the private offices have glass fronts so that sunlight can penetrate into the interiors. Sun screens are mounted on the exterior of the building in a way that prevents direct light from hitting the windows while permitting reflected light to bounce off the ceiling.
The exterior of the building has a highly detailed surface with expressed bays that reflect the interior layout. A pattern of red granites set in precast panels forms the cladding.
The plan for the 240-acre site is as formal as the building plan and works to make the site easily understandable. A horseshoe-shaped drive passes an existing lake, ponds and wetlands and leads to the building's entry on the second level.
At the center of the building is a conference center with 71 meeting rooms that can accommodate as many as 3,000 people. Under a central skylight on the fourth floor is the cafeteria.
Parking lies on either side of the main building in two-story landscaped structures masked from view by high berms. Employees approaching from the parking area enter the building on the third level and take the suspended interior walkways to their work places.
The Ameritech plan anticipates expansion. Eventually, the site will accommodate as much as 3.3 million square feet in office and support space.

1. Cladding detail.

p. 90/91
2. General view of the complex.

89

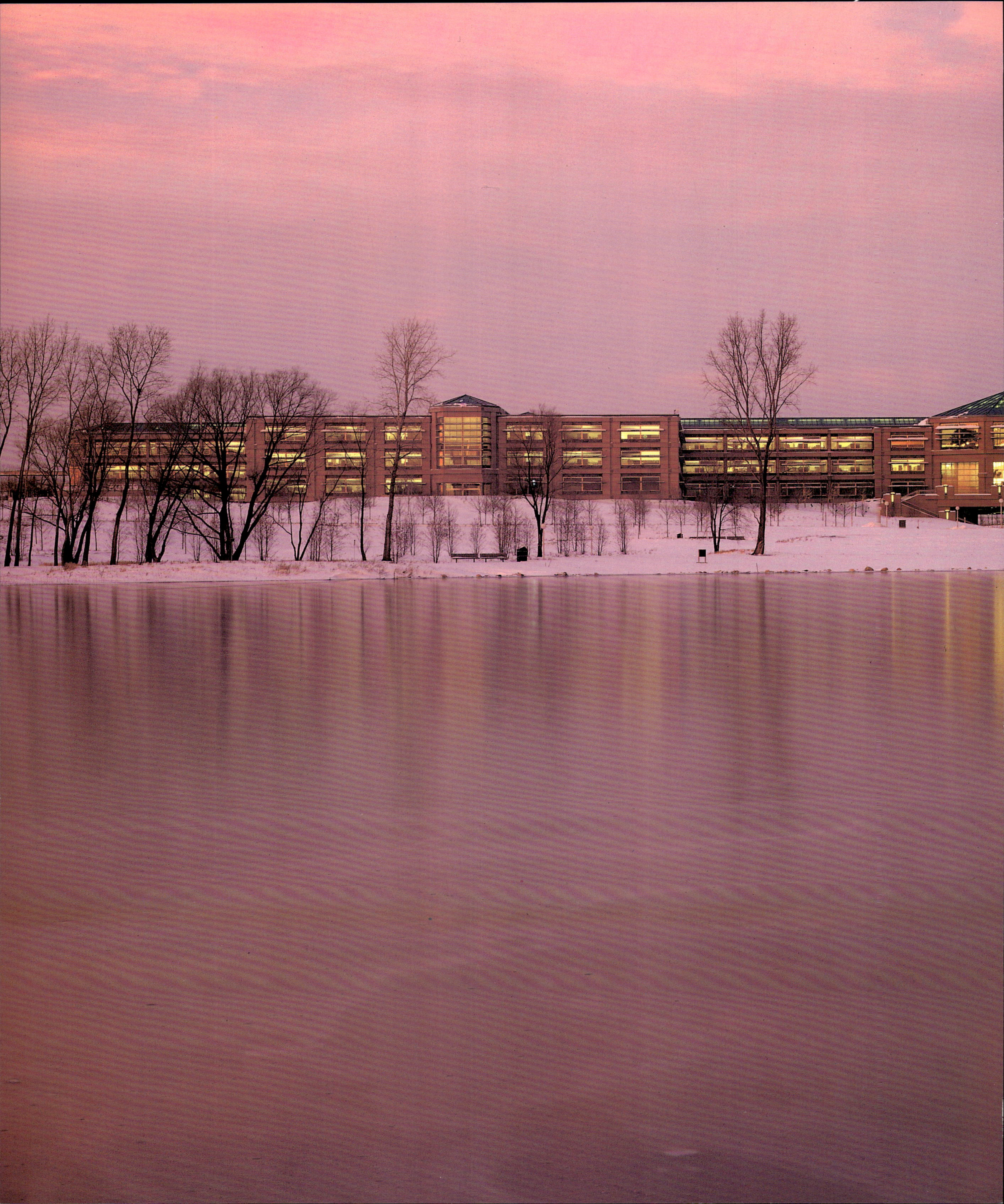

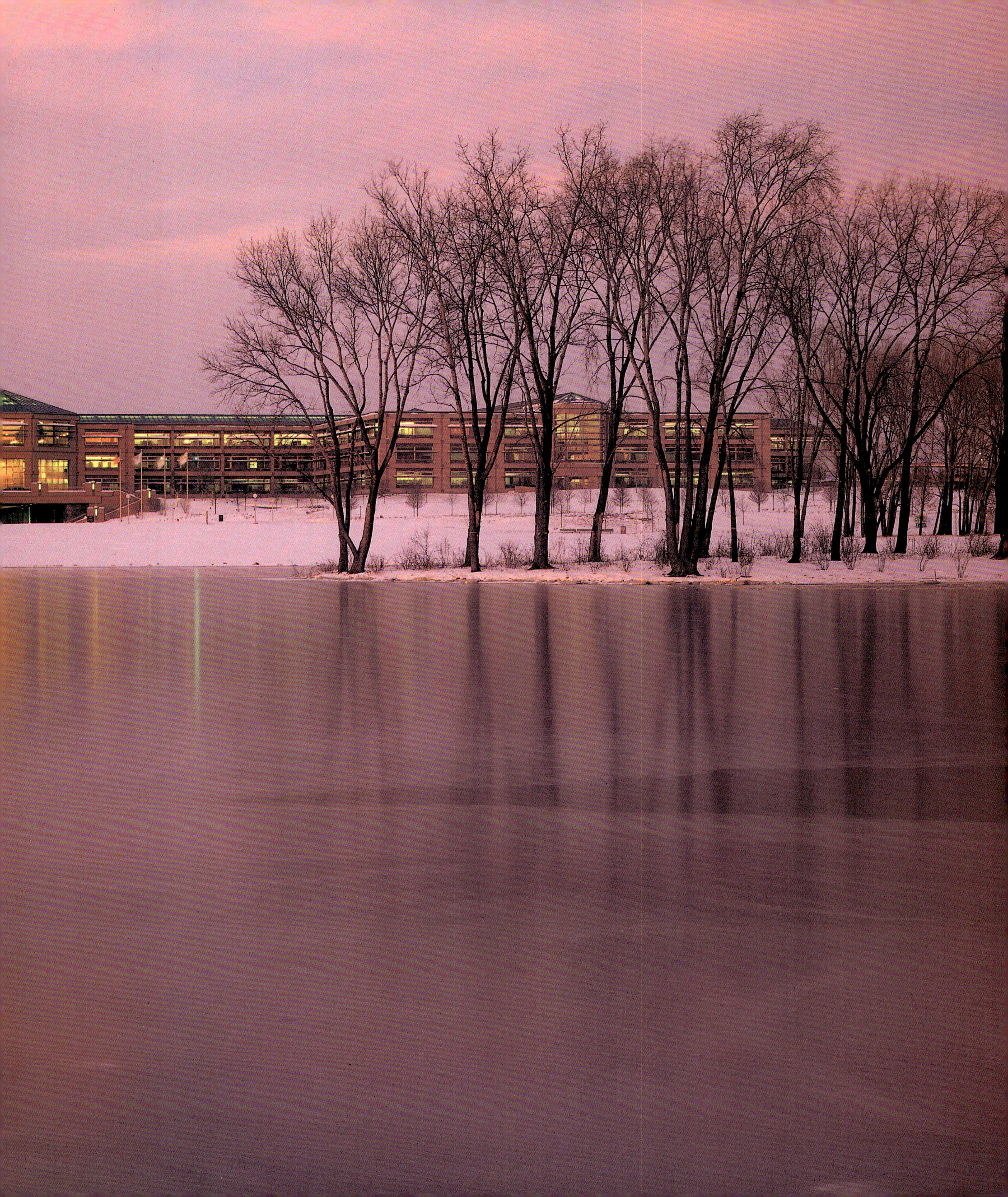

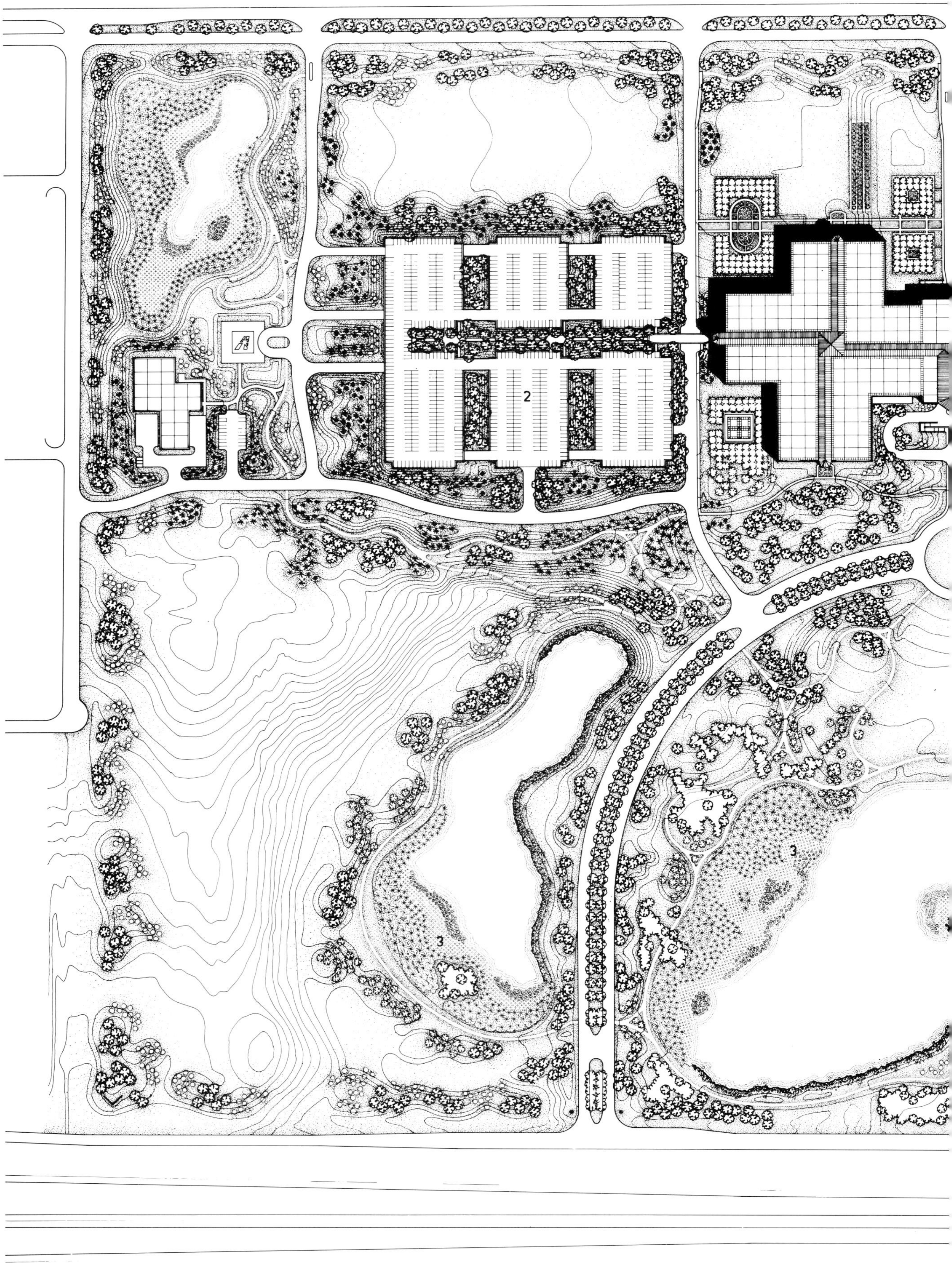
2
3
3

93

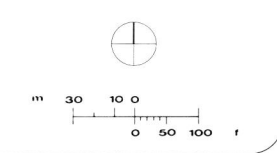

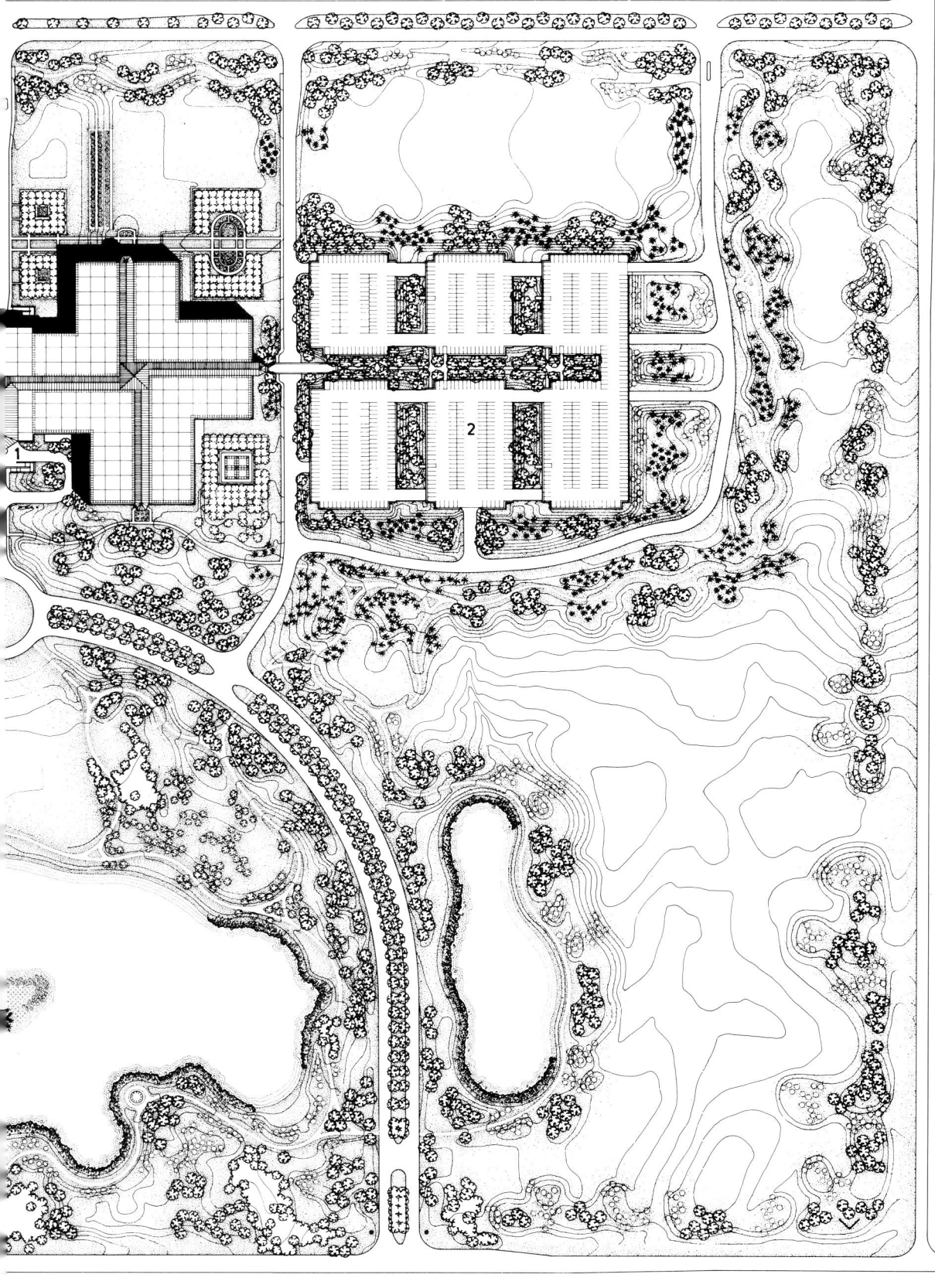

94

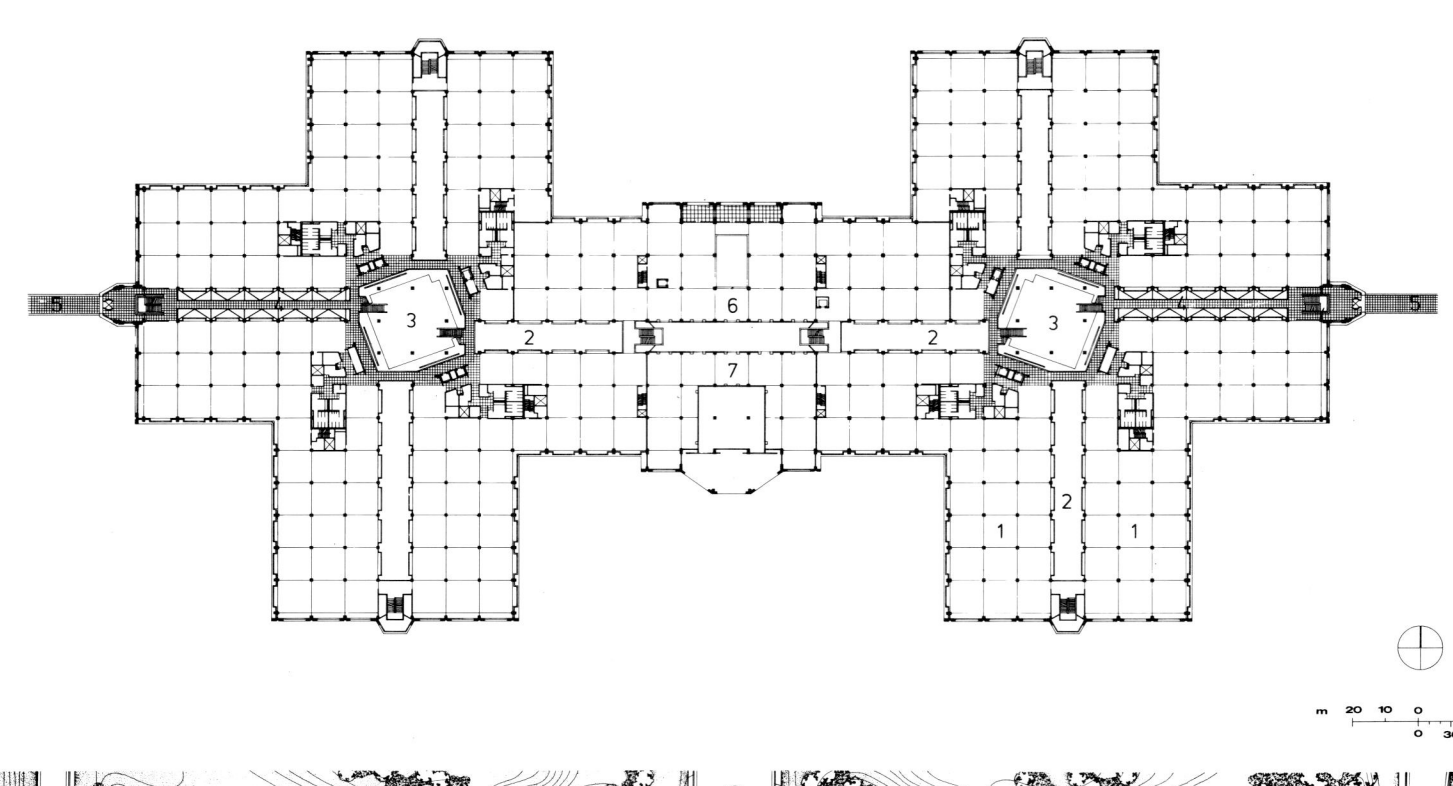

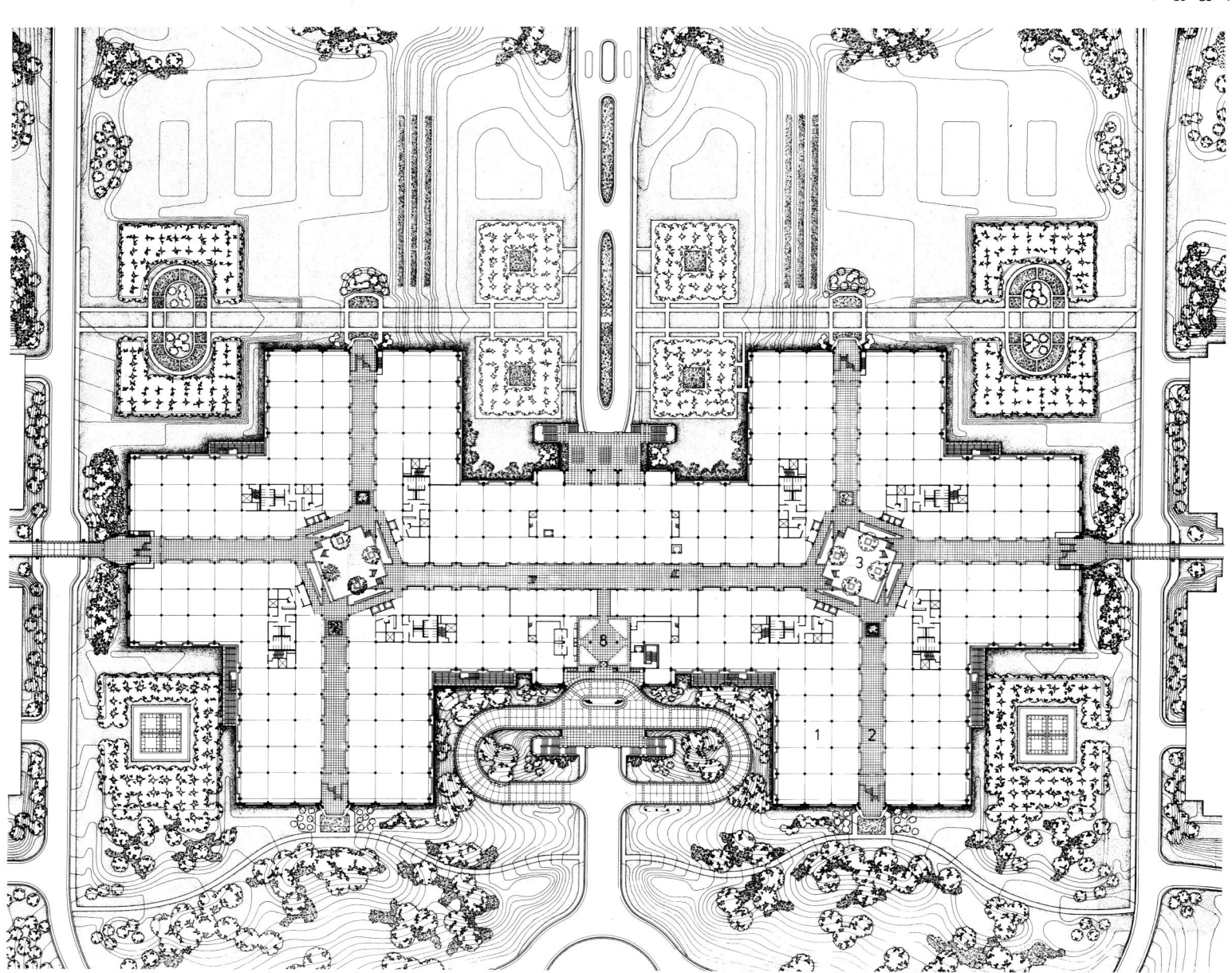

p. 92/93
3. Site plan. Key: 1 main entry, 2 parking, 3 wetlands.

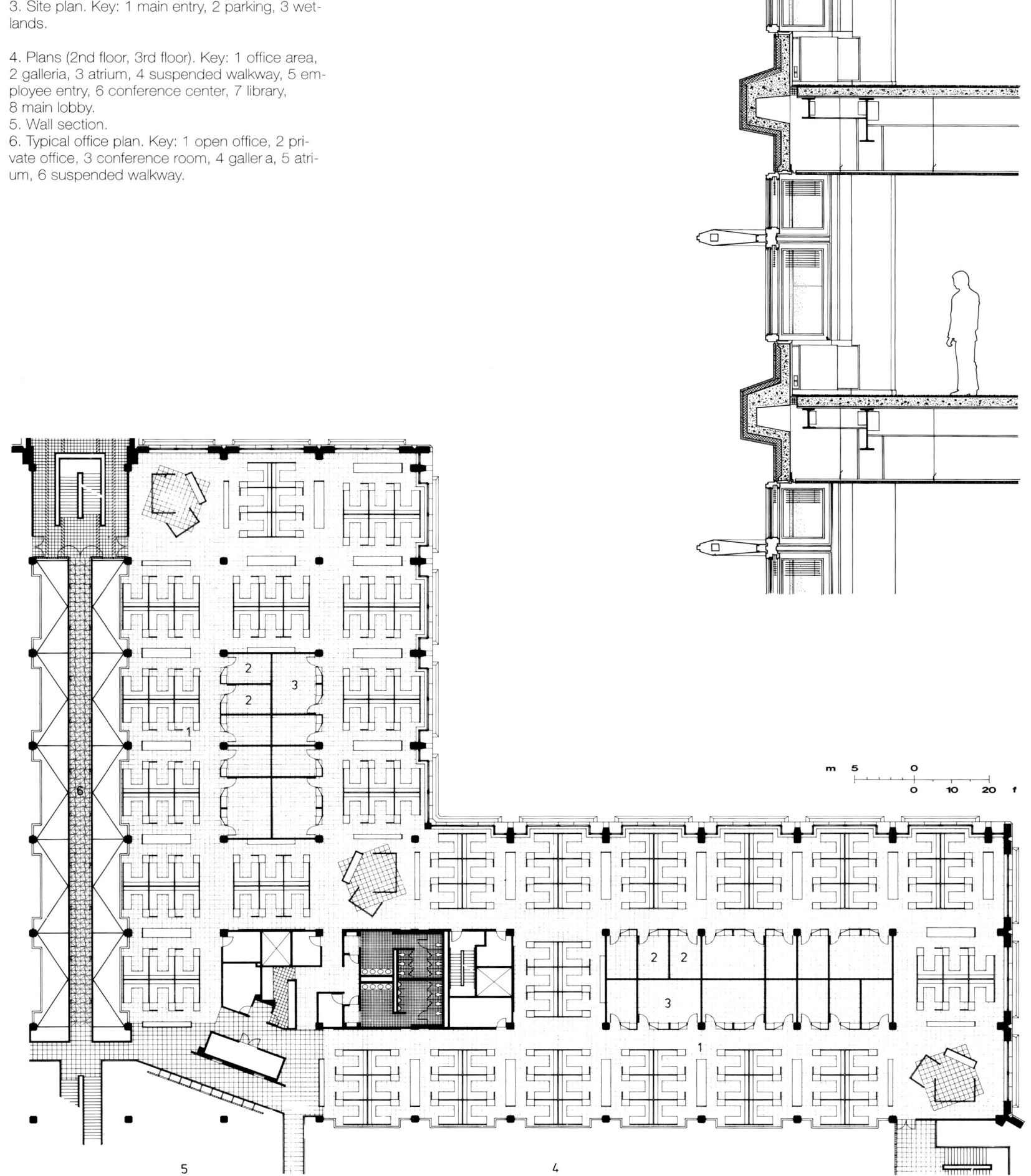

4. Plans (2nd floor, 3rd floor). Key: 1 office area, 2 galleria, 3 atrium, 4 suspended walkway, 5 employee entry, 6 conference center, 7 library, 8 main lobby.
5. Wall section.
6. Typical office plan. Key: 1 open office, 2 private office, 3 conference room, 4 galleria, 5 atrium, 6 suspended walkway.

7. The main entry is on the second level.
8. The road passes beneath the building.

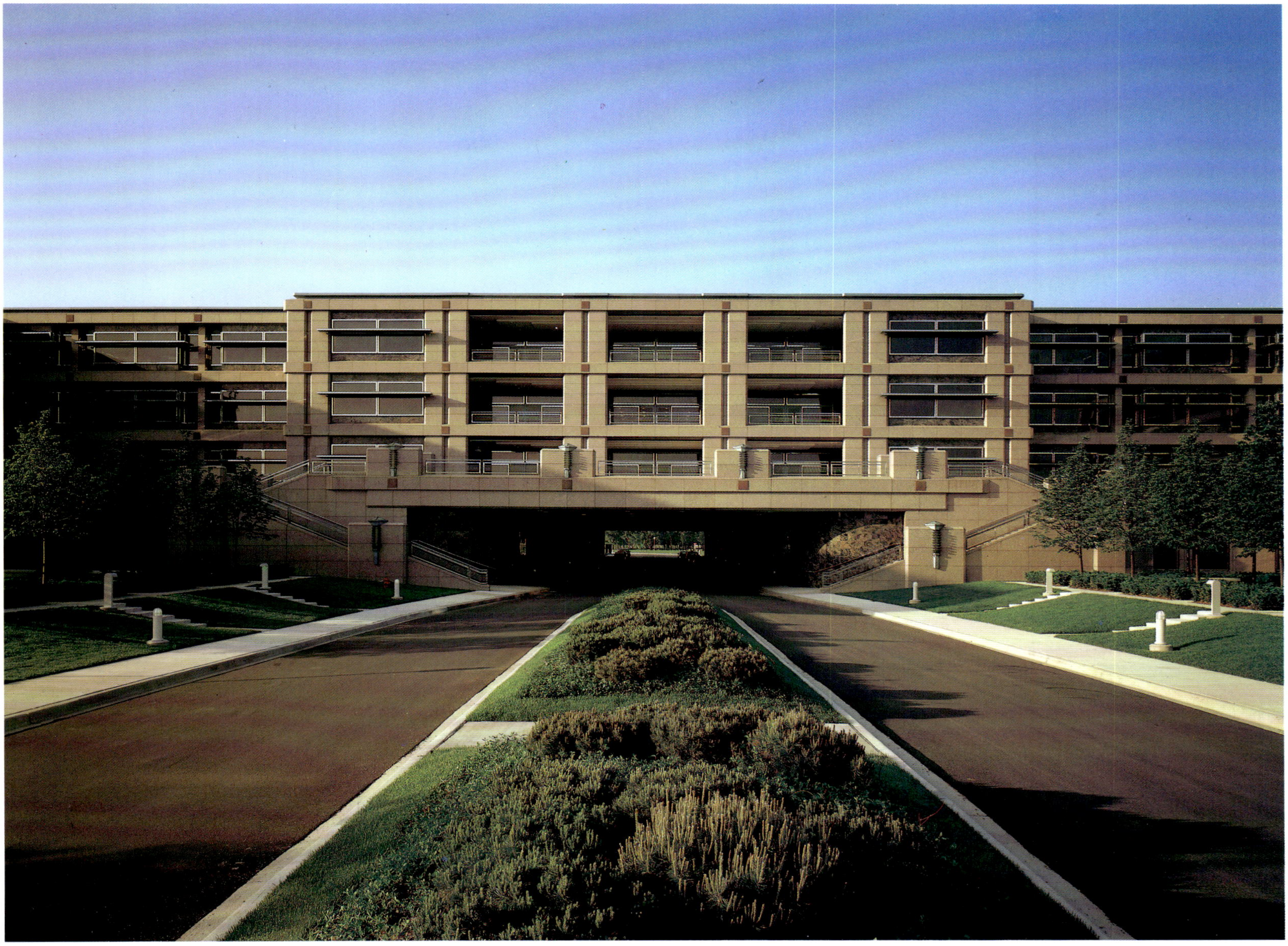

9. Suspended walkways are the principal means of circulation.
10. View of work stations from the suspended walkways.
11. Atriums are located where circulation paths converge.

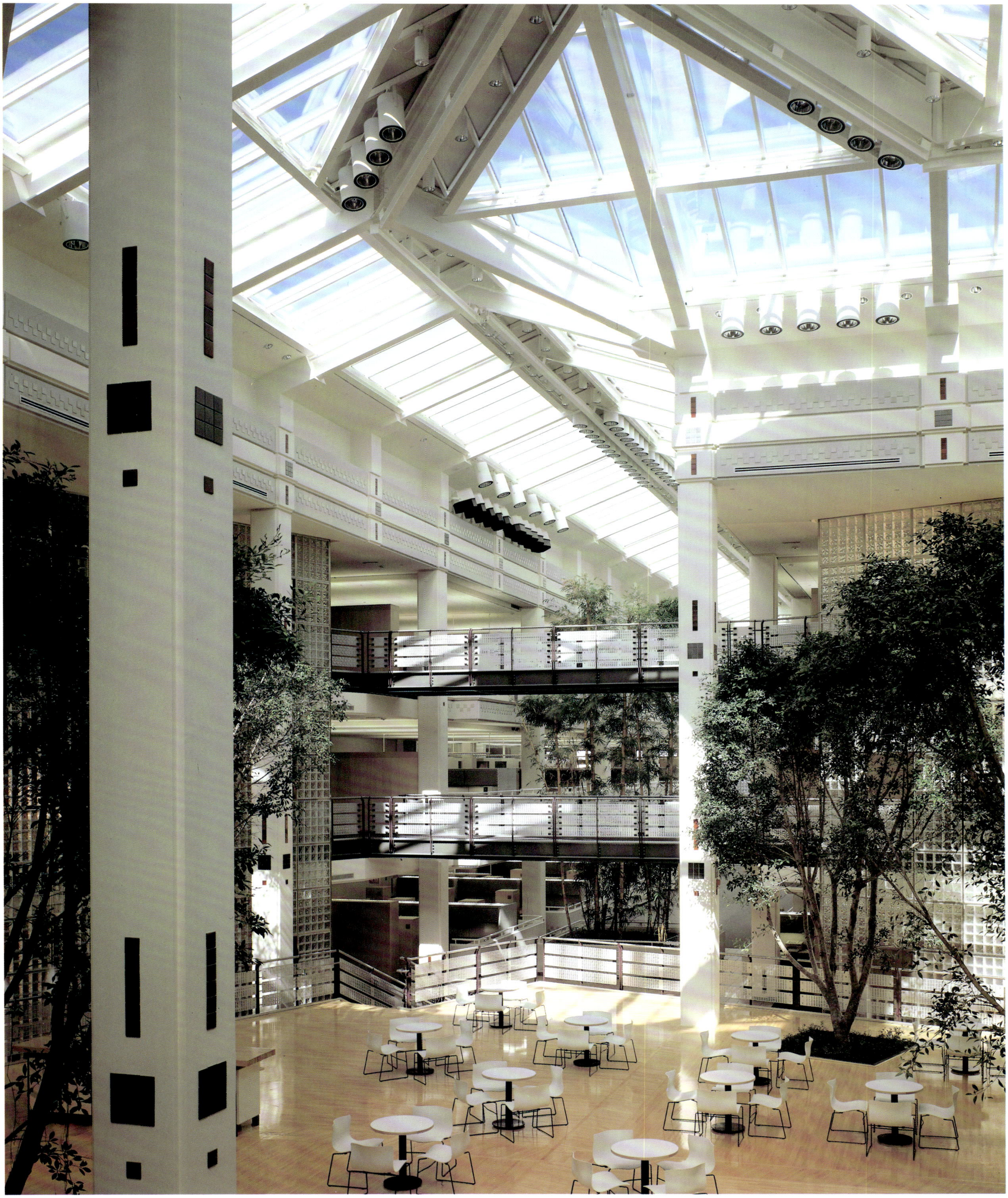

Illinois State Toll Highway Authority Headquarters, Downers Grove, Illinois
1987–1992

The Illinois State Toll Highway Authority Headquarters has a dynamic form with an angled façade of green glass and cast-concrete detailing. The three-story building is nearly 400 feet long and just over 100 feet deep. Inside are offices and the boardroom for the Toll Authority, a day-care facility and an Illinois State Police station. On the two floors below grade are truck docks and a secure zone where money collected daily at highway toll booths is counted and stored in a vault.

The 185,000-square-foot structure is divided longitudinally by a three-story atrium that brings natural light into offices on either side. Stairs made of cast terrazzo carry people up the atrium. Suspended bridges bear glass-enclosed conference rooms at the second- and third-story levels.

Office areas are free of columns. The structural supports for the 46-foot free spans are dramatically articulated in the atrium.

The formal visitors' entry is marked by a circular, clear-glass vestibule. Soaring towers of granite lend a suitable dignity to side entries that will be used daily by employees approaching the building from nearby parking lots.

1. Site plan.
2. Entry detail.

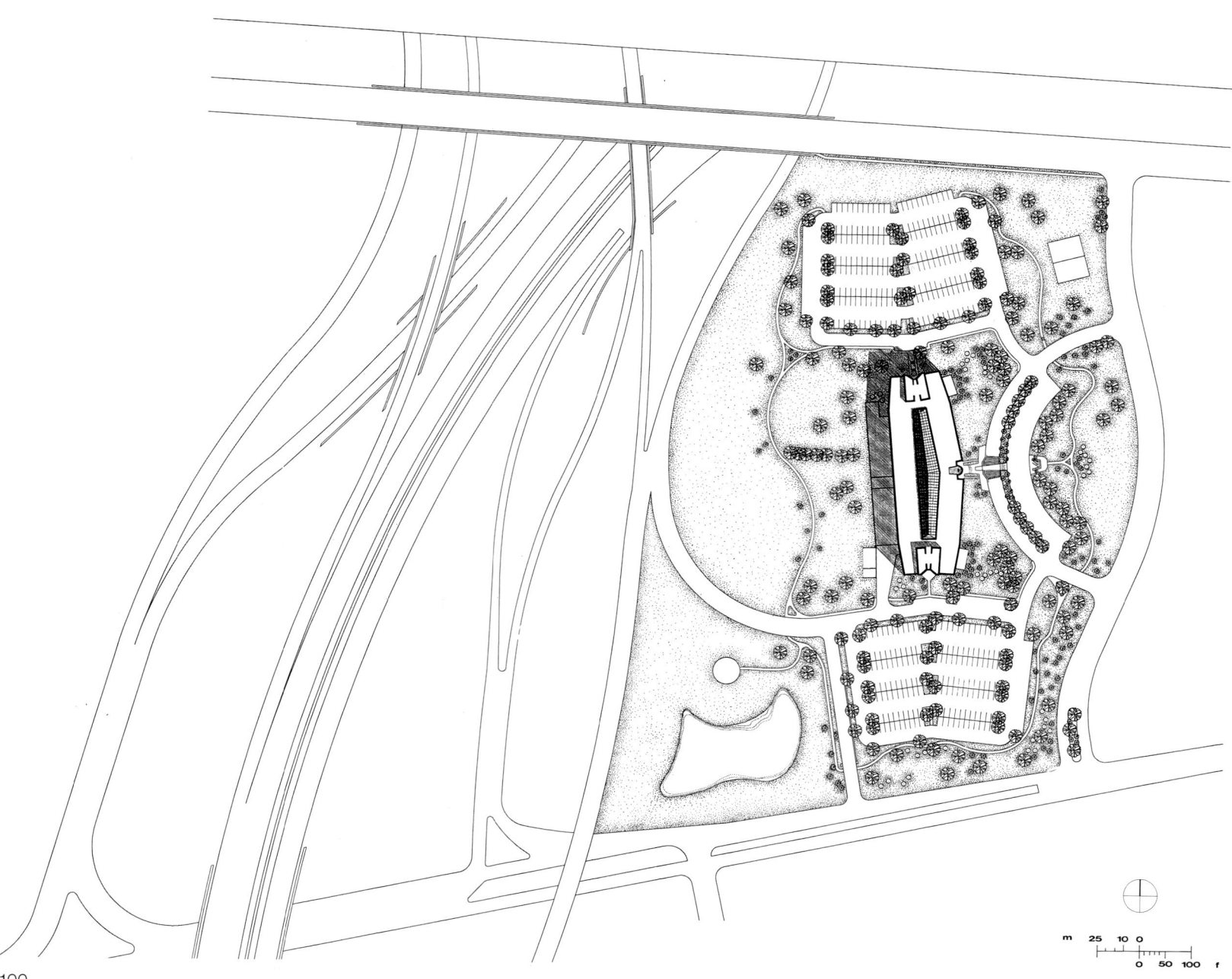

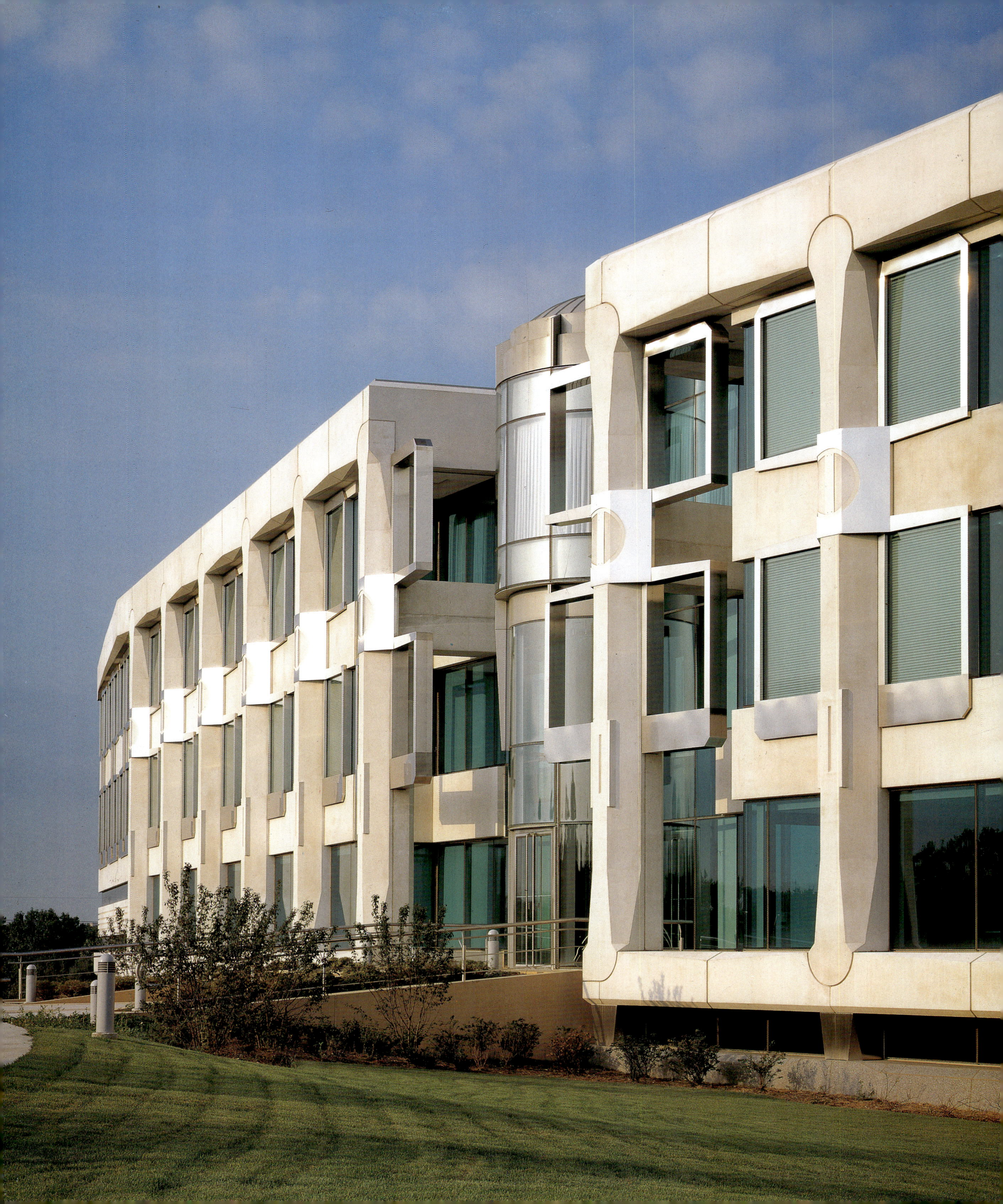

3. Plan (2nd floor). Key: 1 lobby, 2 atrium, 3 conference rooms, 4 bridges, 5 employee entry.
4. Section.

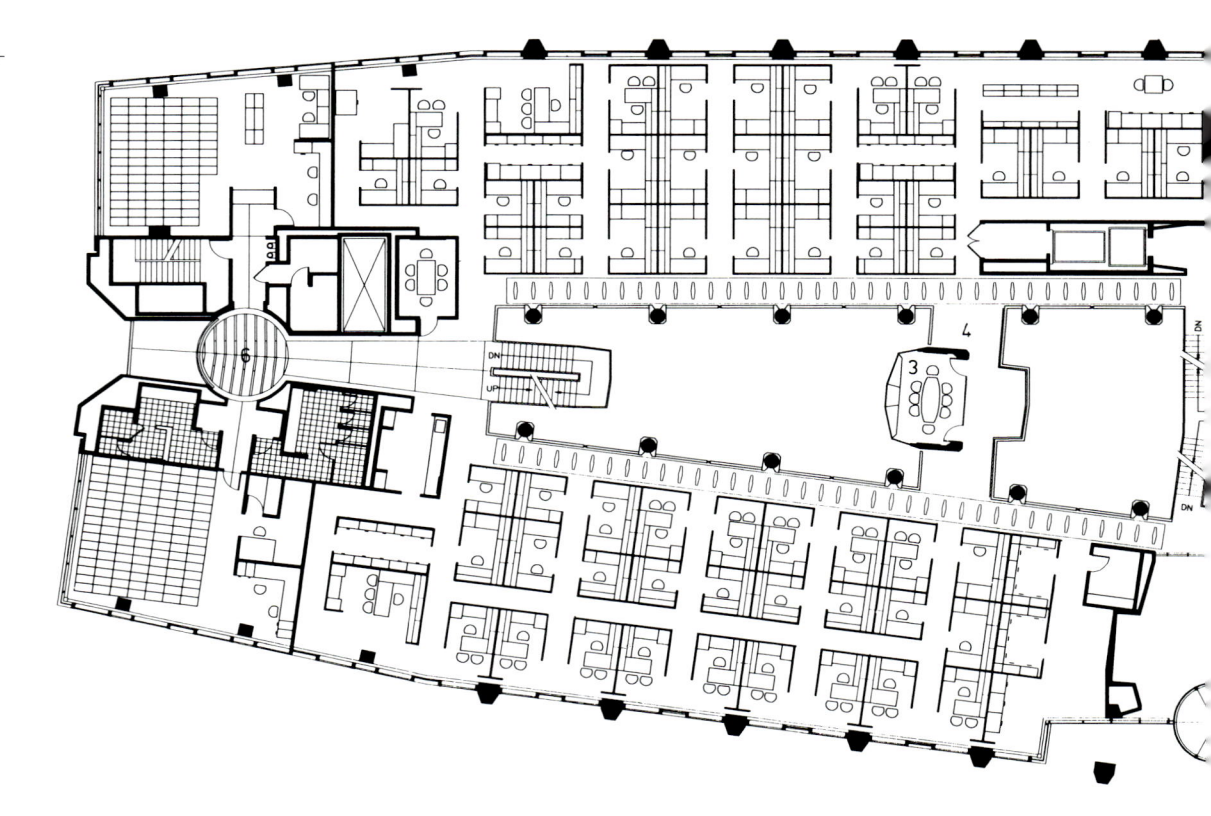

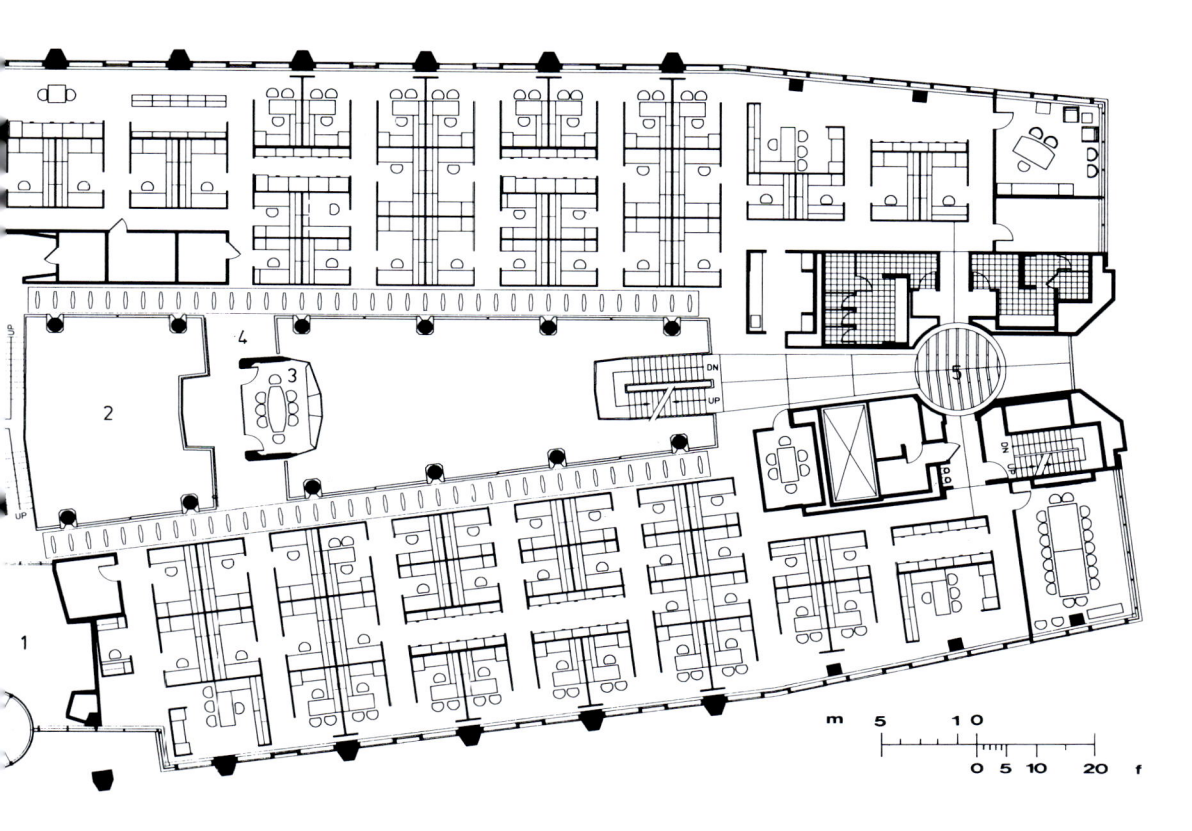

p. 104/105
5. Conference rooms are suspended on bridges that cross the atrium.
6. Atrium stair detail.

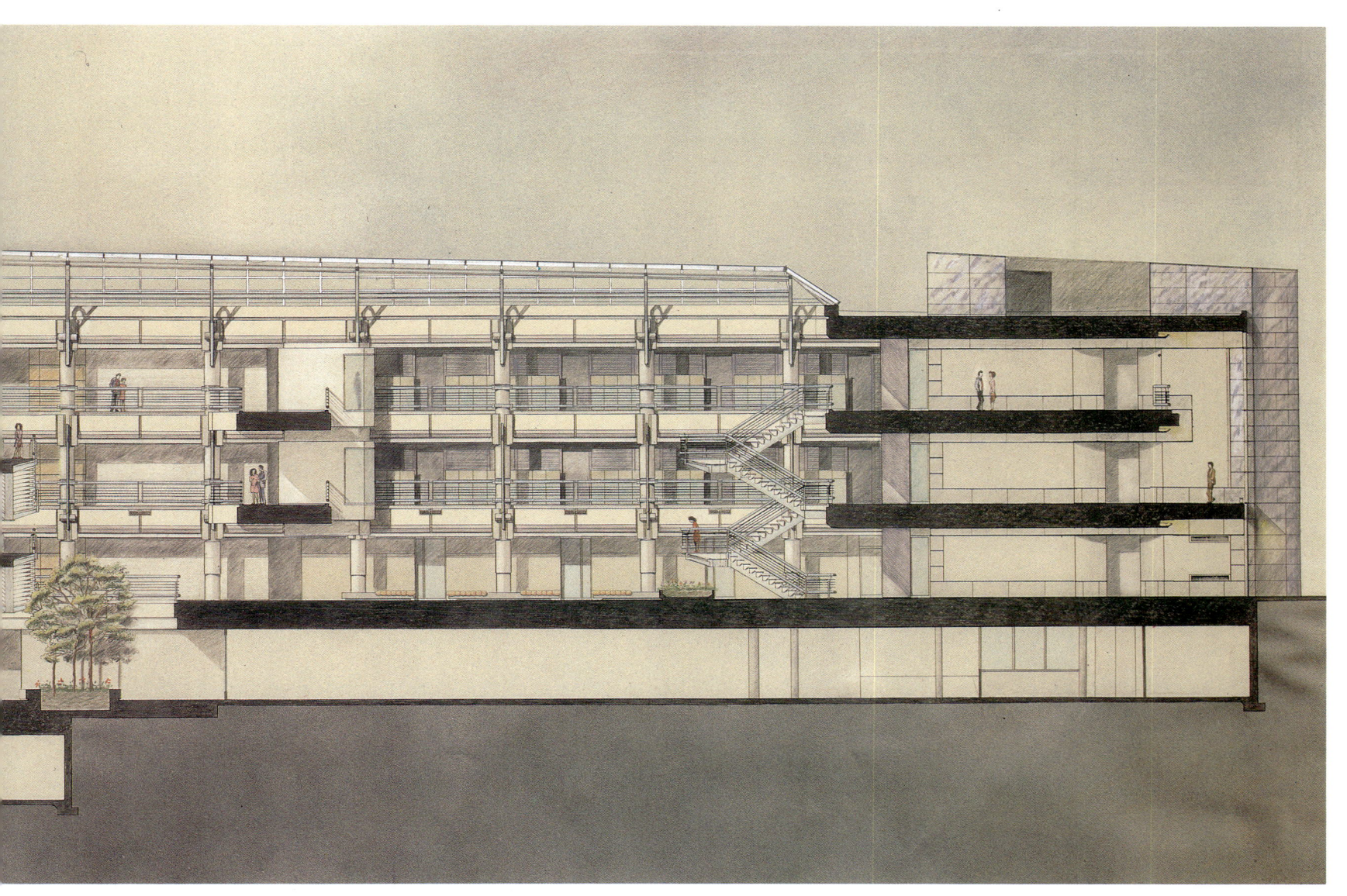

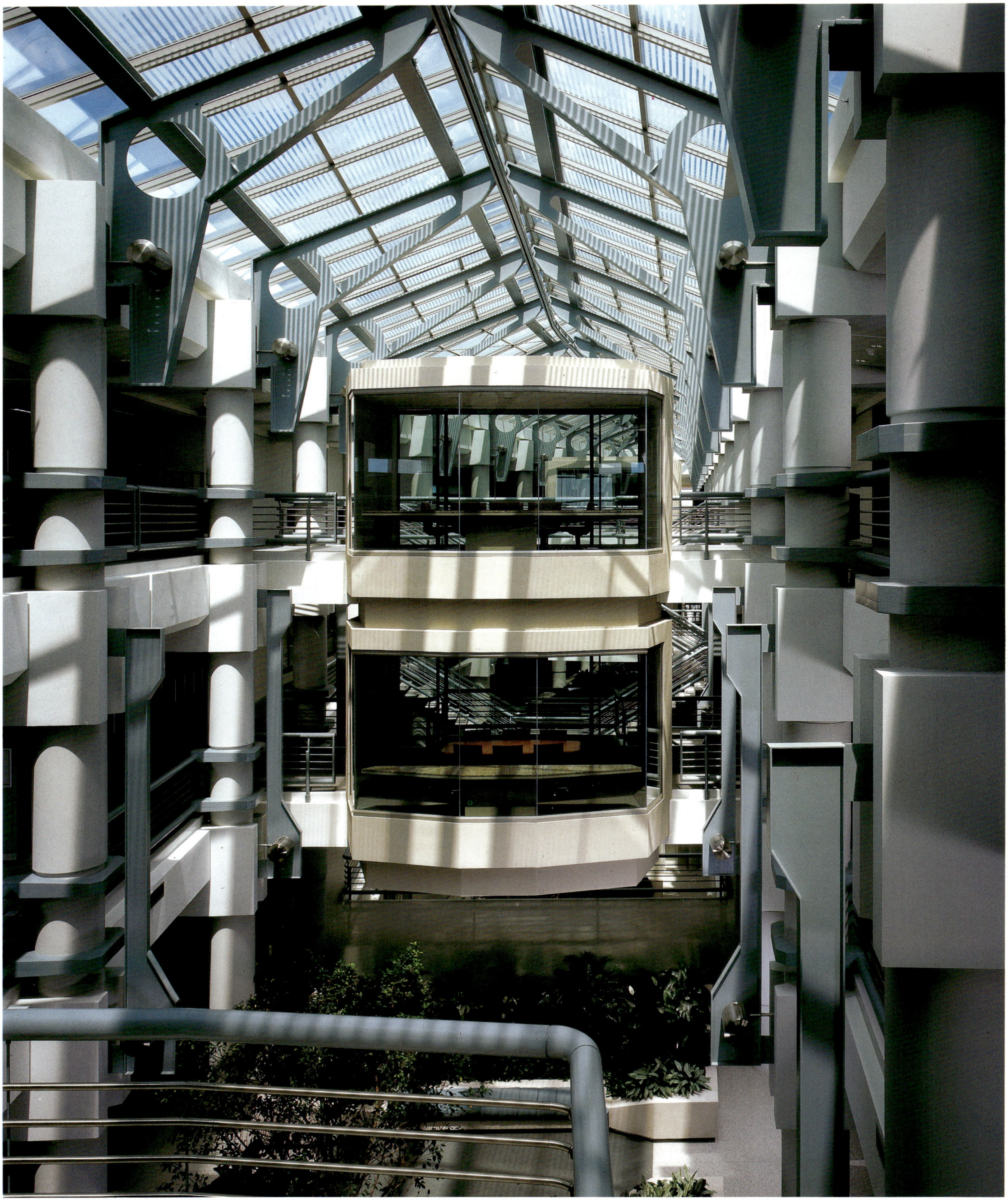

105

Devon House, Ada, Michigan
1987–1992

The Devon House's white frame and strict geometry stand in deliberate contrast to its rural Michigan setting. The house is on a slight hill overlooking an emerging hardwood forest to the south, and a mature evergreen forest to the north.

The house is a perfect 42-foot cube with an inventive plan that emphasizes the volumetric possibilities. The structure is three stories tall, but guest bedrooms are set at half-story levels for privacy and economy of space, creating staggered interior spaces. There are other level changes as well. The living room, which is two-stories high, is set three steps below the dining room and kitchen.

The house revolves around the stair which, as it turns at each landing, offers changing impressions of the interiors and of the outdoors, seen variously through clear glass windows and rippled glass block.

The house's complex plan is faithfully expressed in elevation, creating rich Mondrianlike patterns and rhythms articulated in the exposed frame, clapboard siding, glass block and custom windows.

Teak decks wrap the corners at some levels and are contained within the building grid by the wood frame. The top of the house is given over to a sun deck in the same material.

Maple floors are used throughout the house with the exception of the entry where green slate is employed for flooring and for a bench. Verde Antique marble has been used for counter tops.

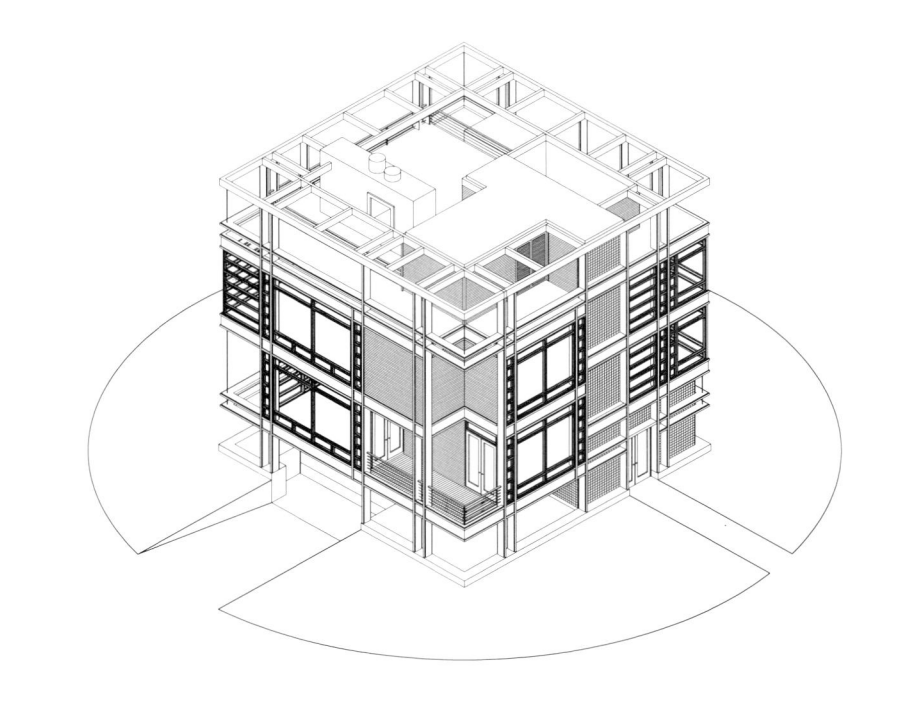

1. Isometric view of the building.
2. Plans (ground floor, 2nd floor, 3rd floor, roof).
3. View of the house from the southeast.

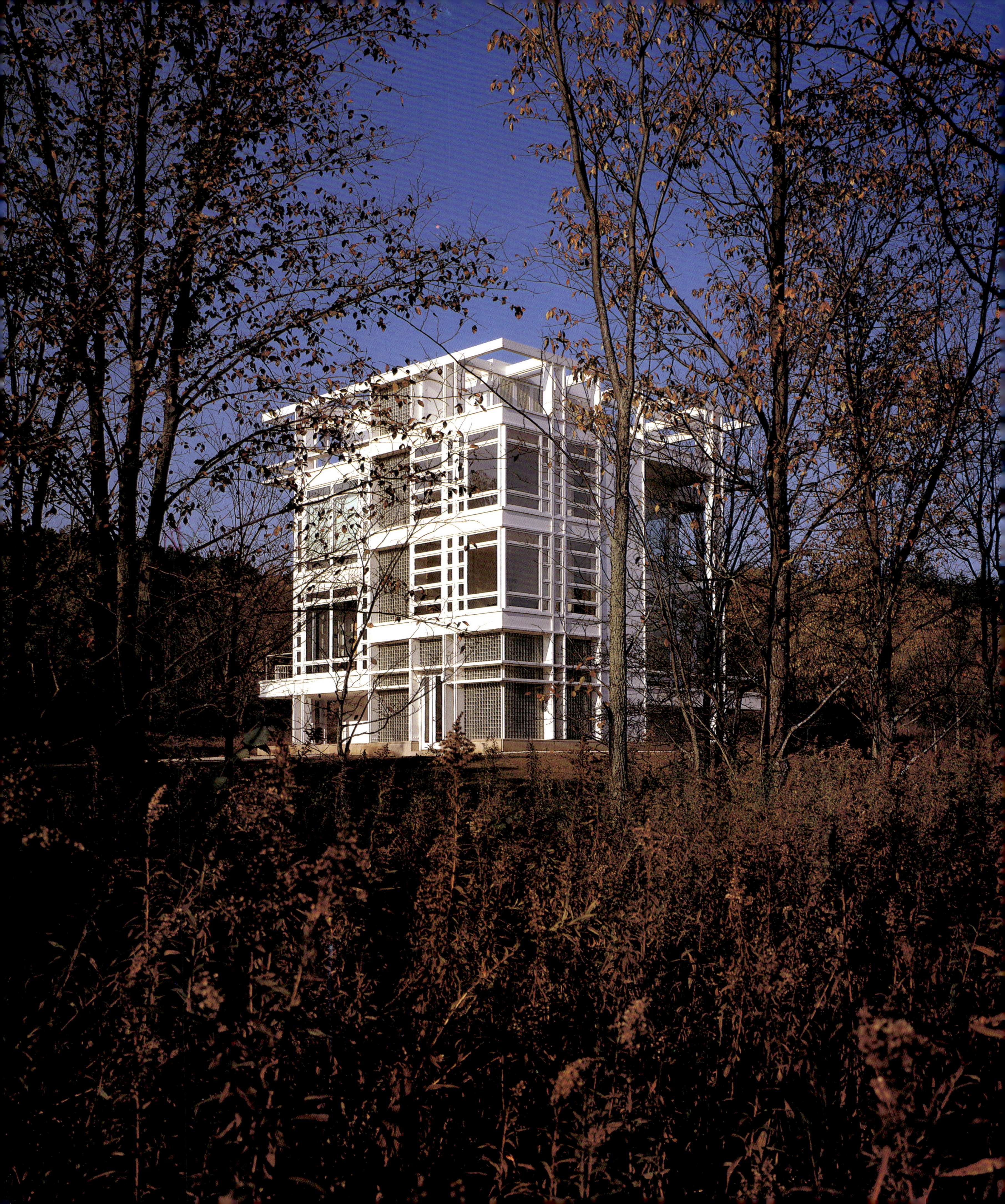

4. Corner detail of the roof trellis.
5. Stair detail.

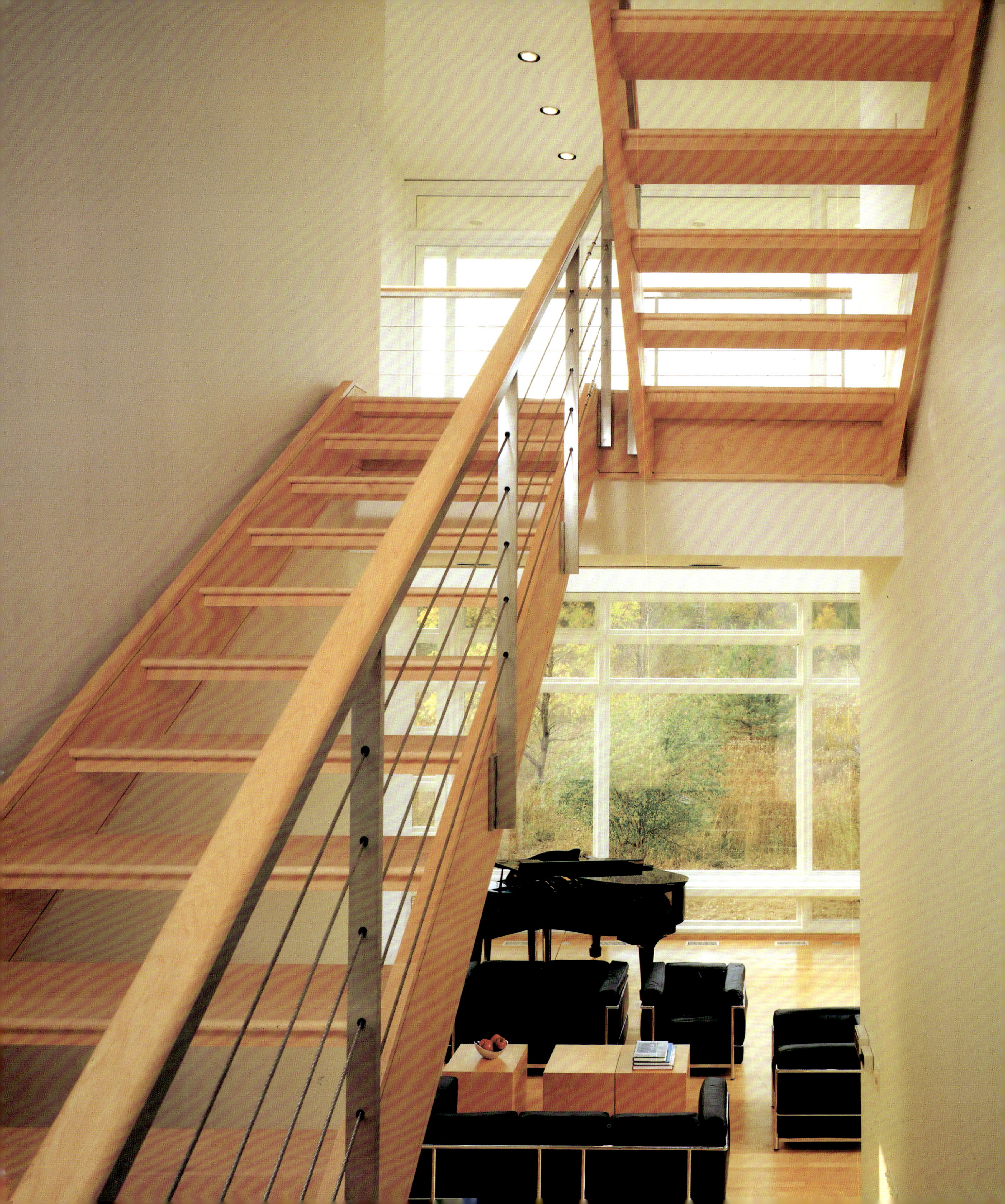

Harold Washington Library Center, Chicago, Illinois
1988. Competition entry

The scheme for the Harold Washington Library Center is both a functional plan for Chicago's new central library and one that celebrates the civic ideals suggested by this prominent public institution.
The design proposes a 10-story, 740,000-square-foot building with a concrete frame clad in limestone, aluminum and glass. A dramatic four-story glass façade with 30-foot lanterns marks the principal entrance. Its transparency symbolizes the library's openness and accessibility. Inside is a naturally lit hall with monumental staircases rising on either side. This public space is comparable in gesture and intention to the Roman piazza and, being enclosed, is appropriate to Chicago's climate.
On the first floor of the library is a public auditorium, a restaurant and shops, facilities compatible with State Street, the retail street the library faces. Each of the upper floors includes stacks and public reading spaces. Information desks are placed at the center of each floor where they are immediately visible to library users arriving by escalators or elevators. The upper floors were left open and flexible to accommodate alteration as future information technology dictates.
The site for the library is at the edge of Chicago's downtown office and retail district. It was the expressed hope of Chicago's city officials that placing the library there would help to stimulate growth in the area. The two principal bisecting streets are Congress and State which are, respectively, a heavily travelled road leading to an expressway, and a retail street. The architects chose to turn the library to State Street because of its pedestrian scale. The old department stores along State became models for the height and massing of the Harold Washington Library Center. The plan calls for creating underground subway connections and a new elevated train station to be developed inside the building.

1. Section. Key: 1 hall, 2 auditorium, 3 subway.
2. General view from the southeast.
3. View of the hall.

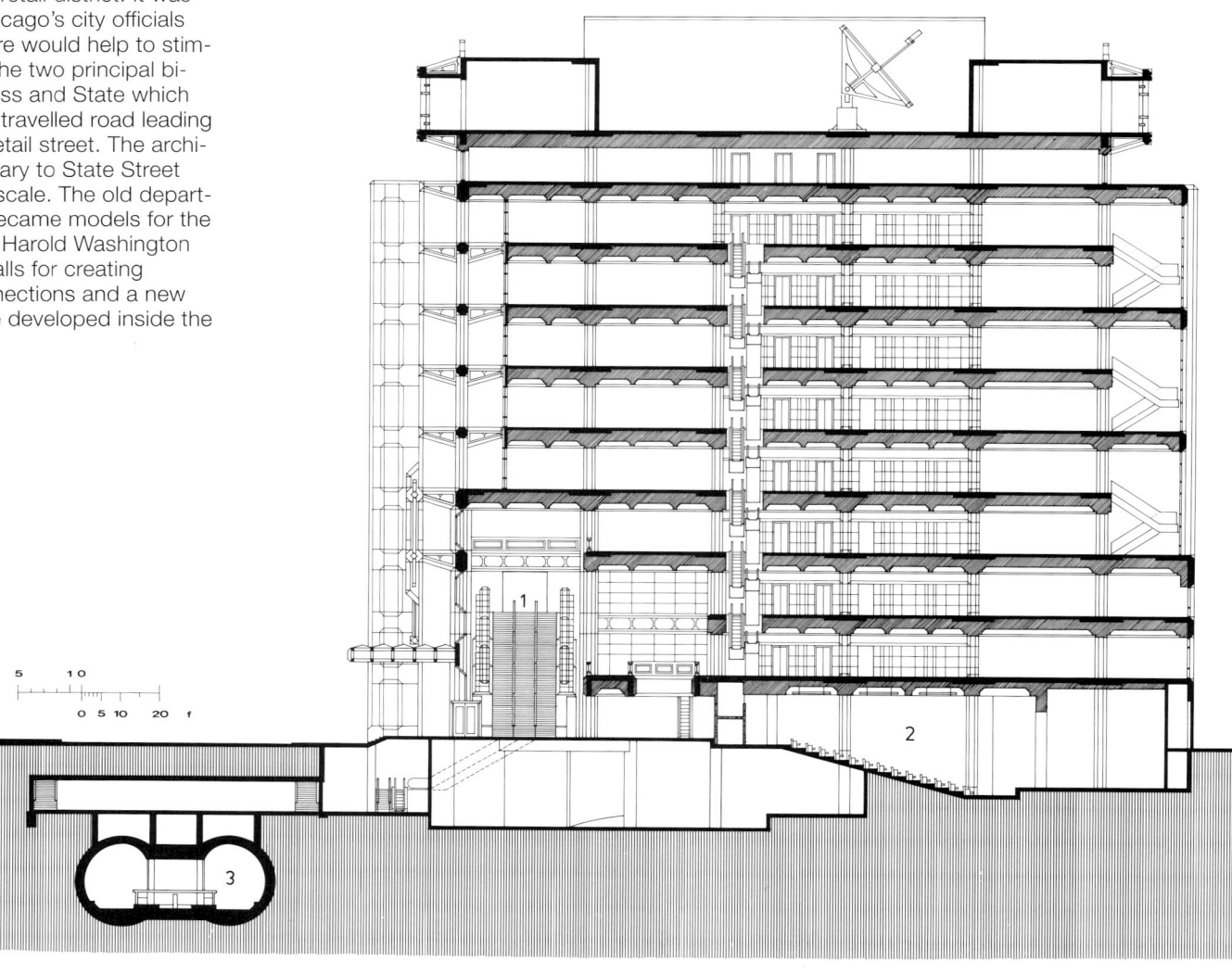

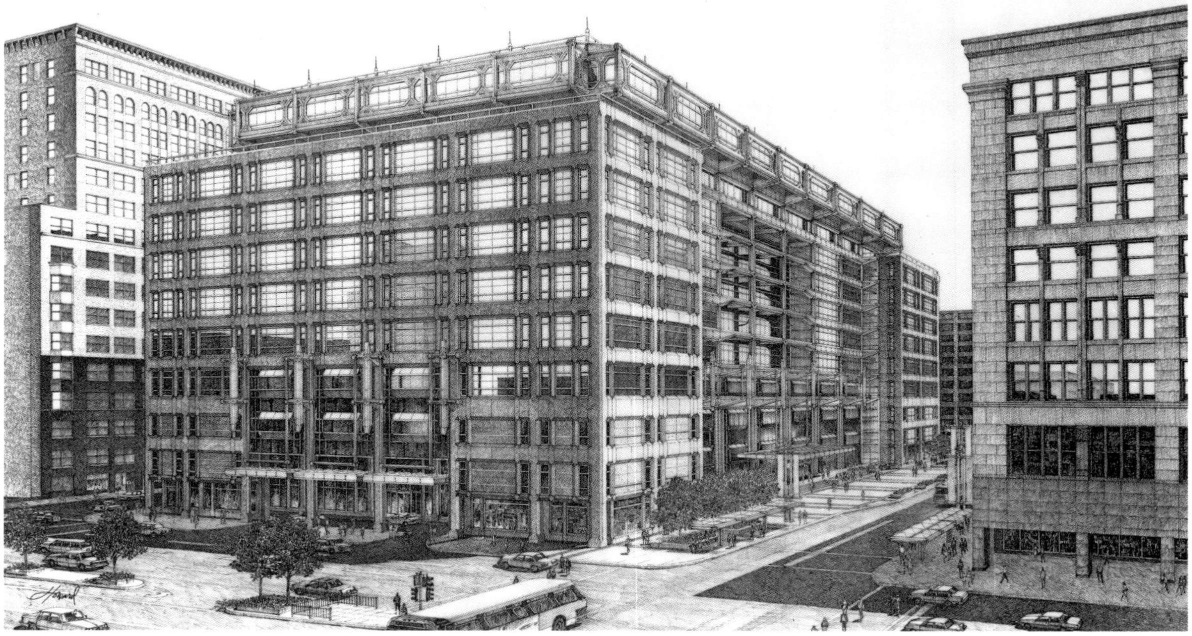

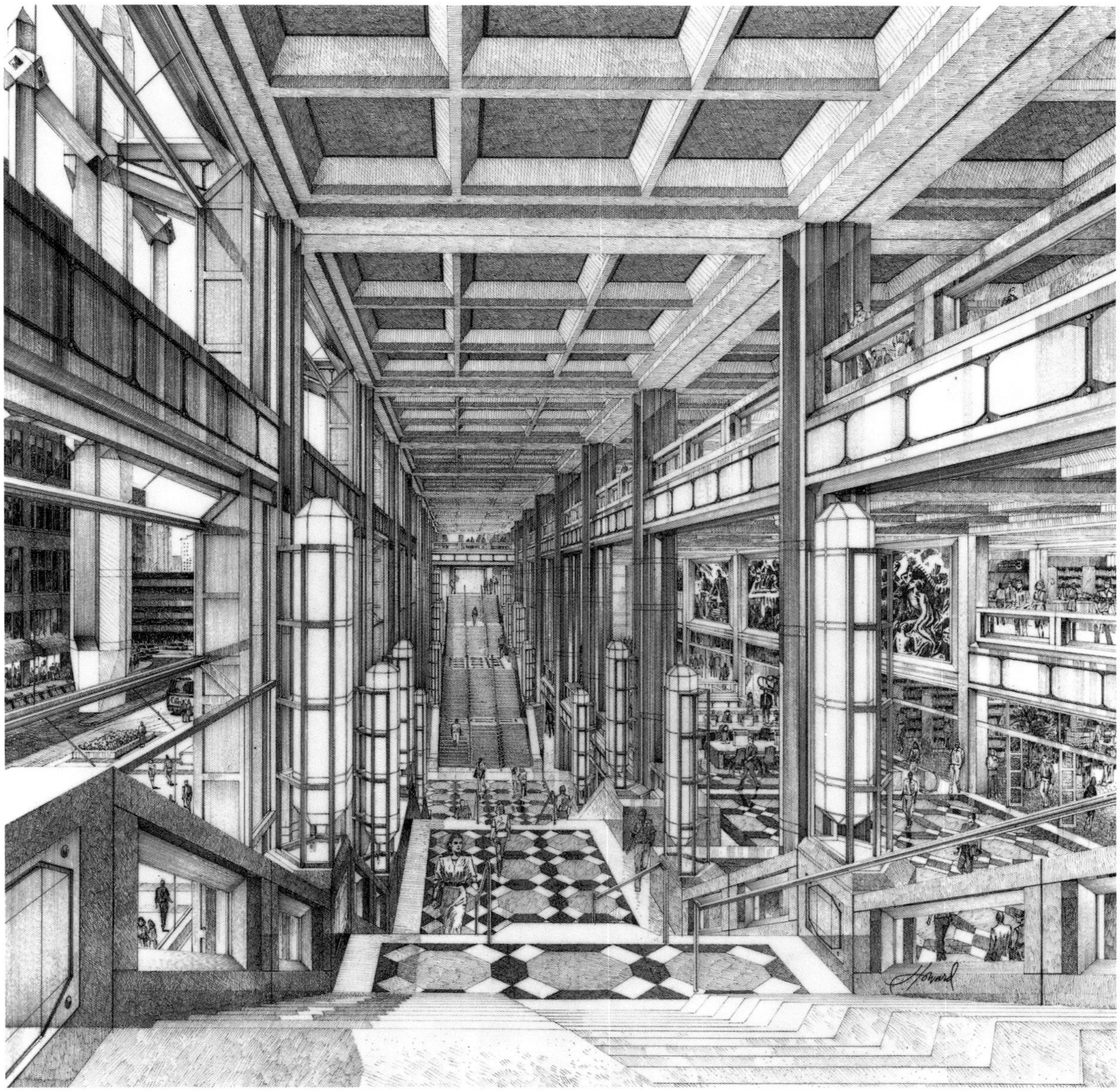

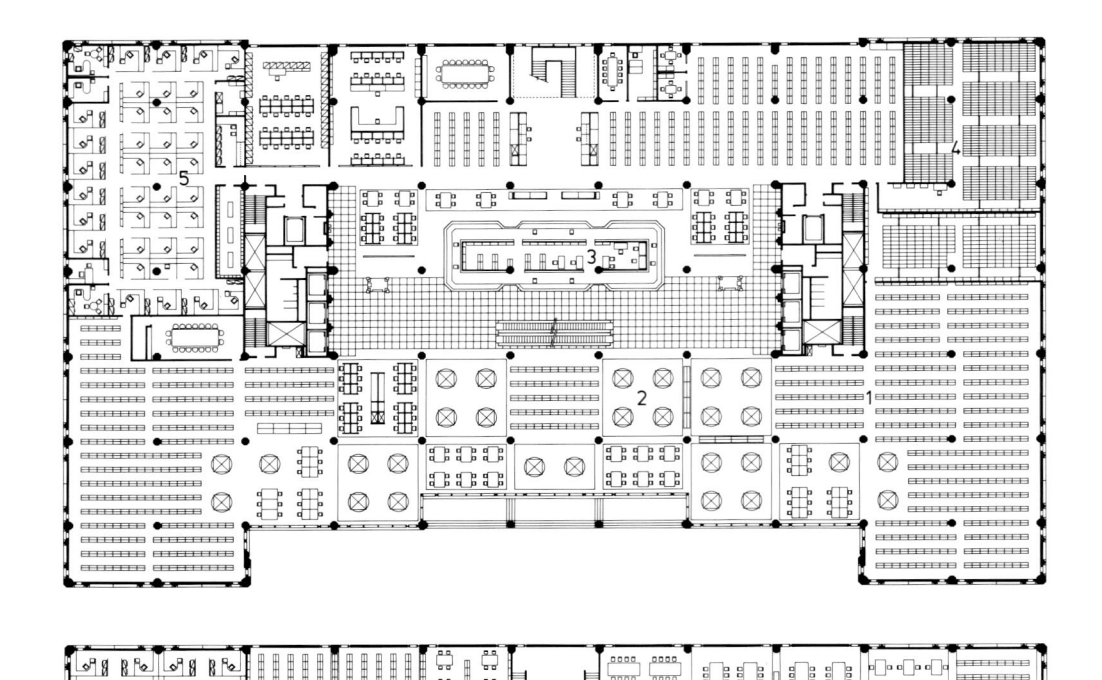

4. Plans (ground floor, 2nd floor, typical floor). Key: 1 stacks, 2 reading areas, 3 information, 4 compact shelving, 5 staff offices, 6 book circulation, 7 hall, 8 auditorium, 9 café, 10 shops, 11 book drop-off.
5. Lantern detail.

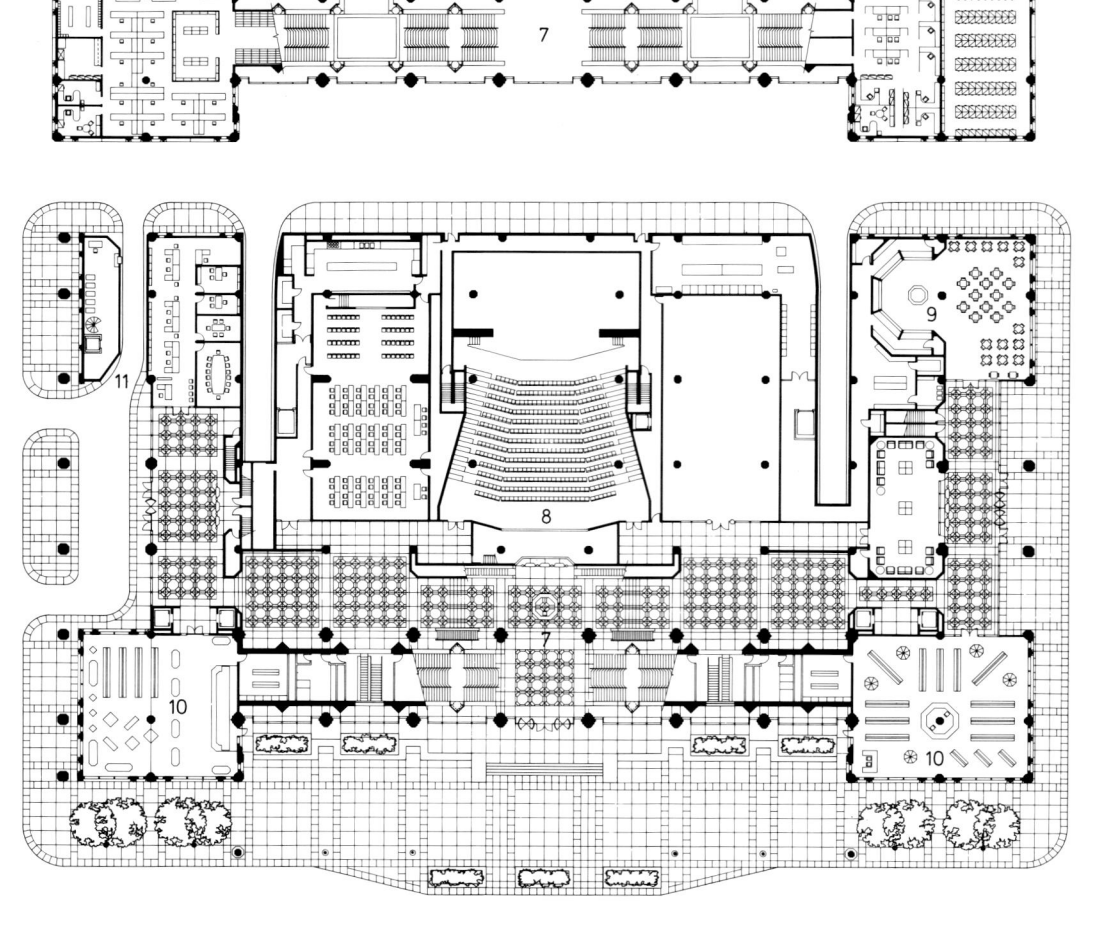

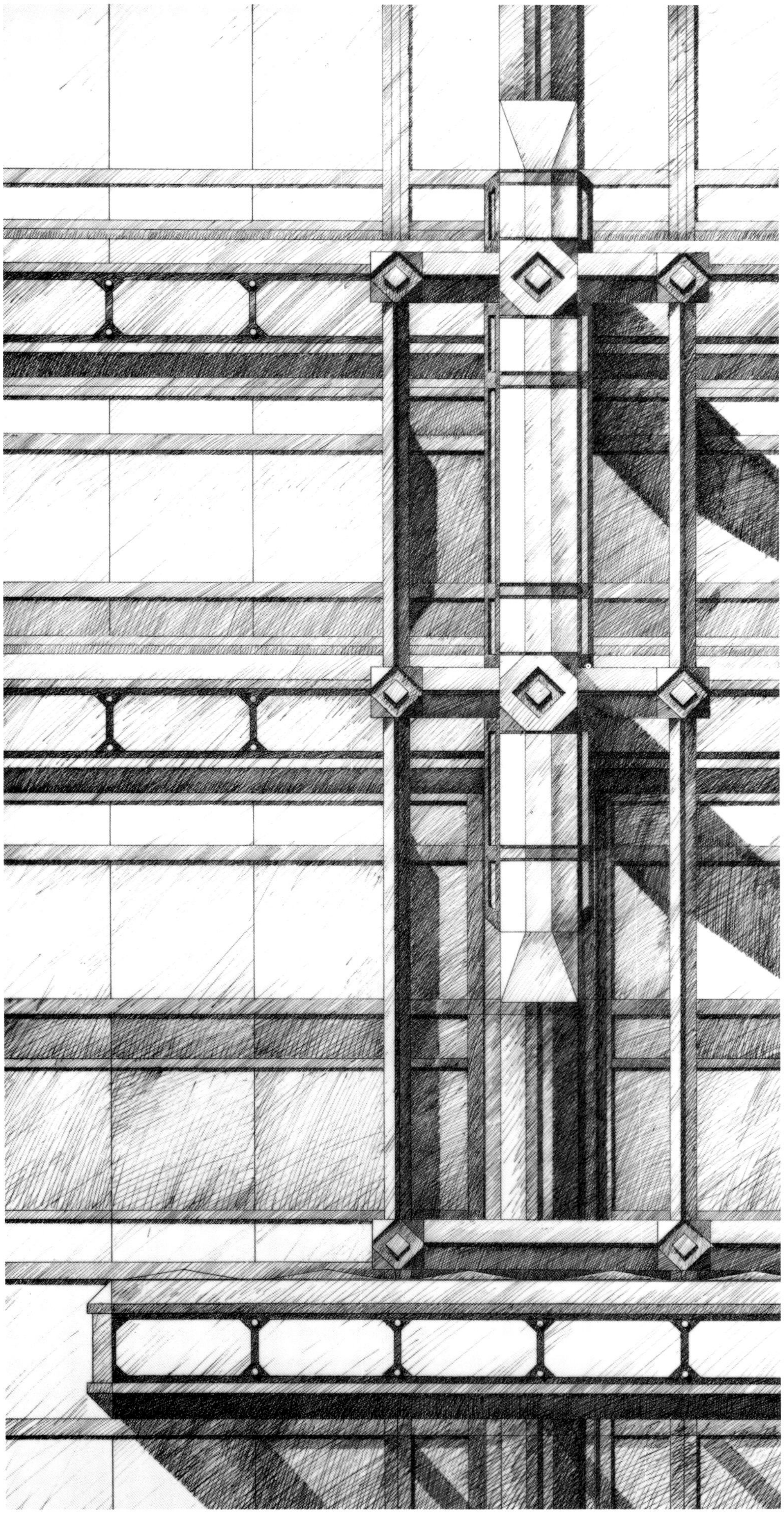

Amerika-Gedenkbibliothek, Berlin, Germany
1988. Competition entry

Lohan's entry for the competition to design a 90,000-square-foot addition to the Amerika-Gedenkbibliothek in Berlin is at once architecturally challenging and urbanistically healing. The addition is modern with a gleaming highly articulated steel and aluminum skin. The design for the addition includes stacks, reading areas, an exhibition space, a hall, a café and the new entry to the library. A pool with fountains separates the addition and the older building; emerging from the water is a drum-shaped circulation tower that joins the two structures.

The original library is a curving concrete building with an expressed frame. Berliners' have a fondness for it because it was the first library to be constructed after World War II. It was erected during the Berlin Airlift and was funded by the United States. Respectful of those sentiments, the architects took their cues from the earlier building by adopting, as a theme, a grid derived from the concrete framing of the original structure.

The motif is introduced immediately. The addition appears to be suspended within a cage. A curving gridded screen mimicking the front of the original building appears to float before the addition. Occasionally the logic of the grid is broken where the building protrudes outside the cage as it does in the two triangular glass-encased stair towers on either side of the main entry.

The architects worked to correct planning mistakes made when the library was first constructed. Rather than being knitted into the urban fabric, the library was isolated in a park easily accessible only by car. A parking lot ultimately became the doorstep to the building. The Lohan scheme proposes a public plaza as a more suitable entry, giving the building a dignity it had not enjoyed formerly. The plaza also ties the library building to the strong urban axis of the Mehringplatz and the Friedrichstraße.

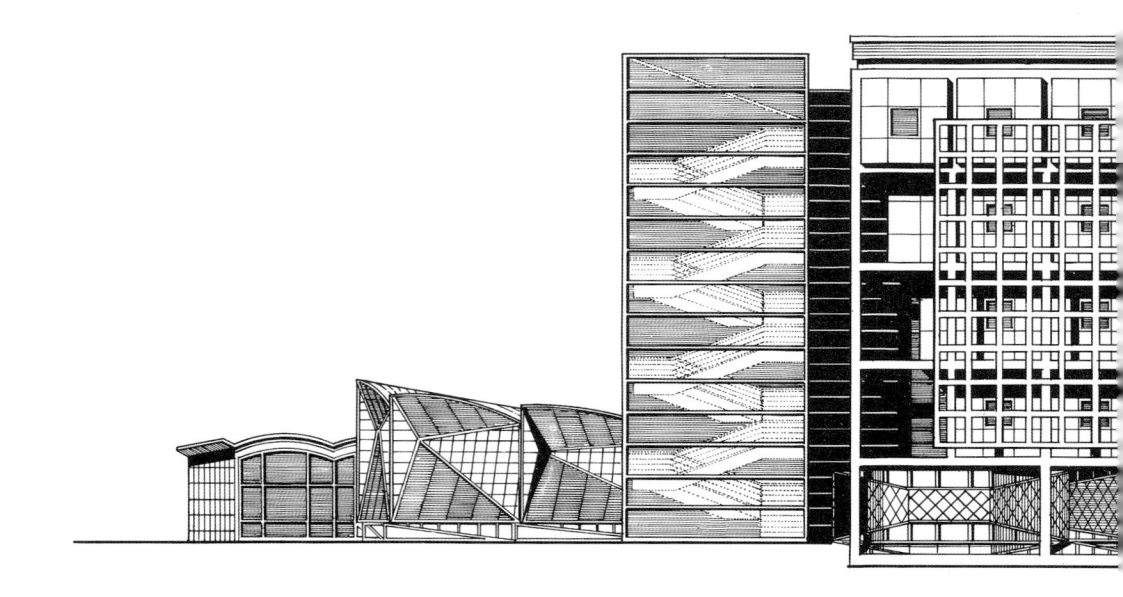

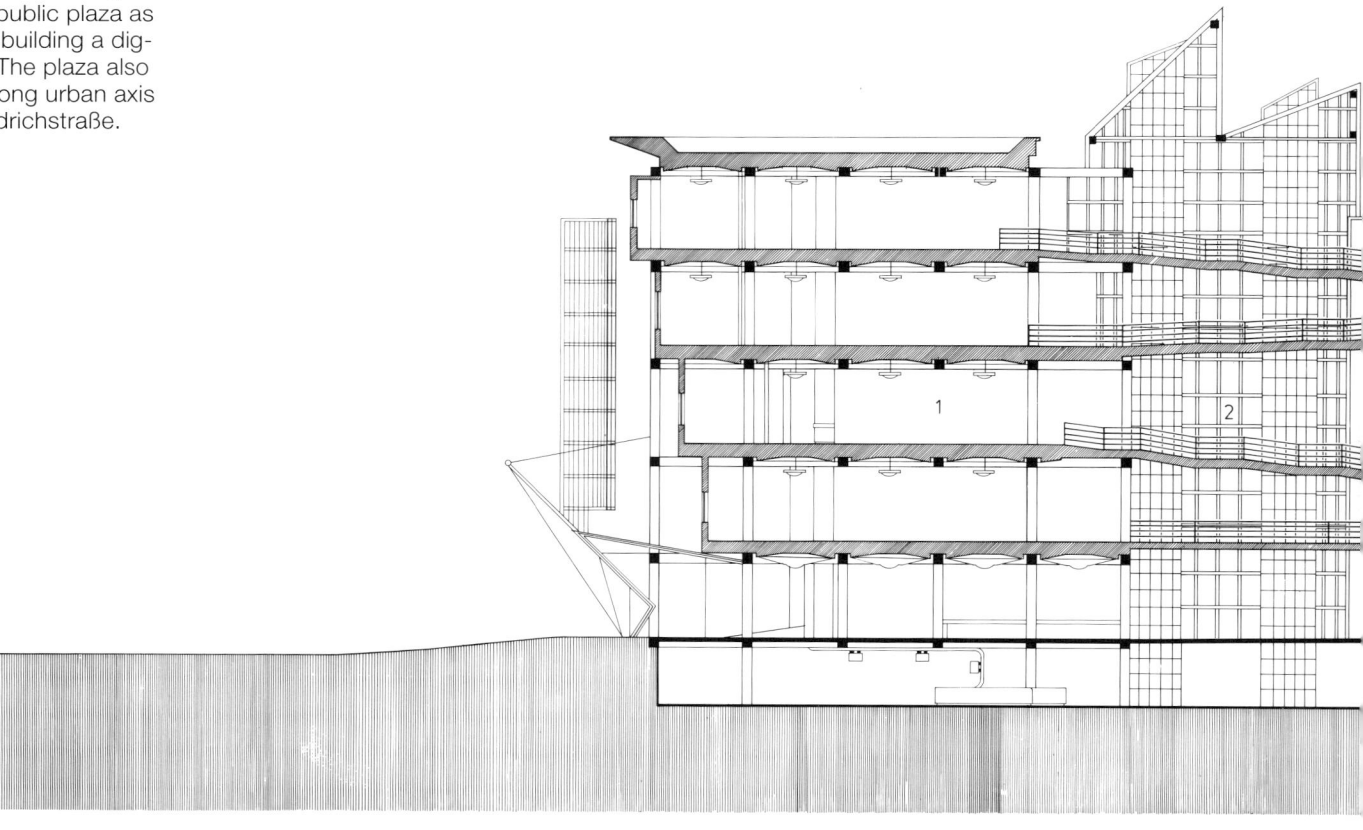

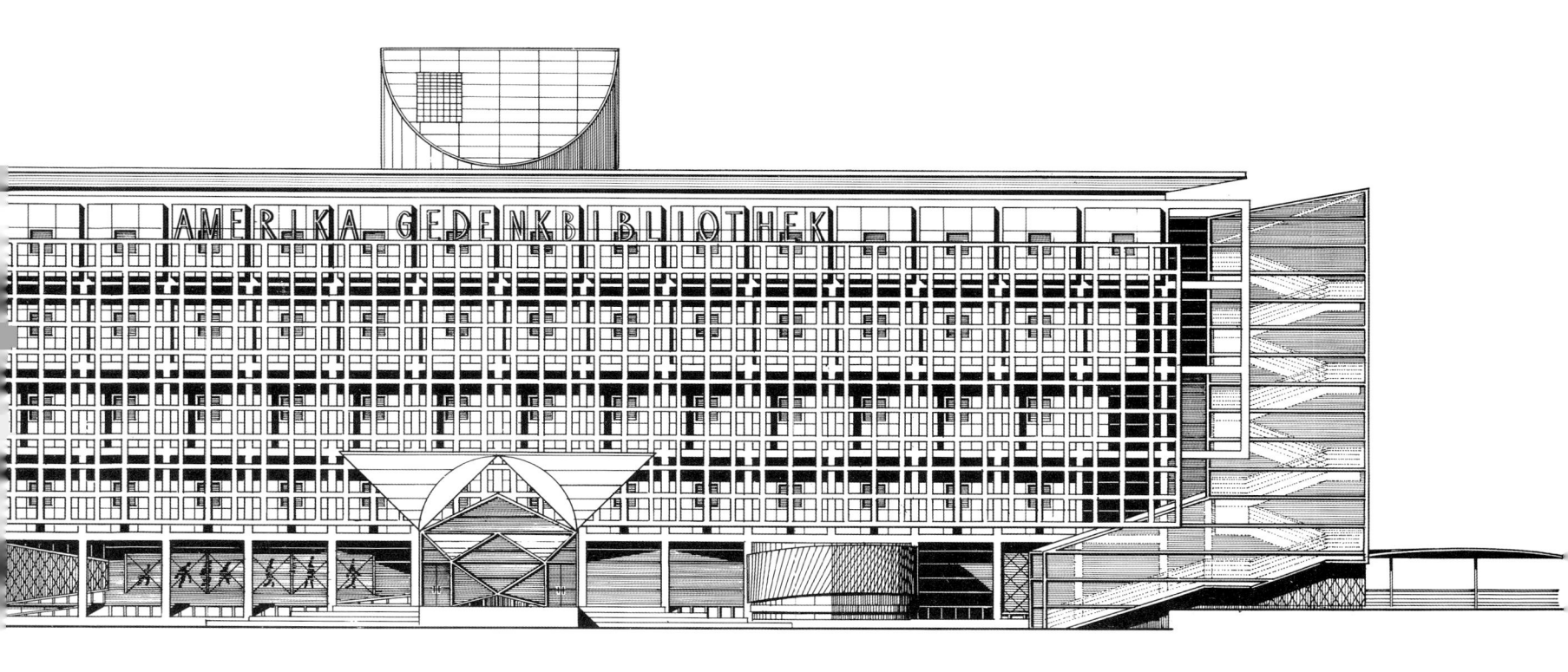

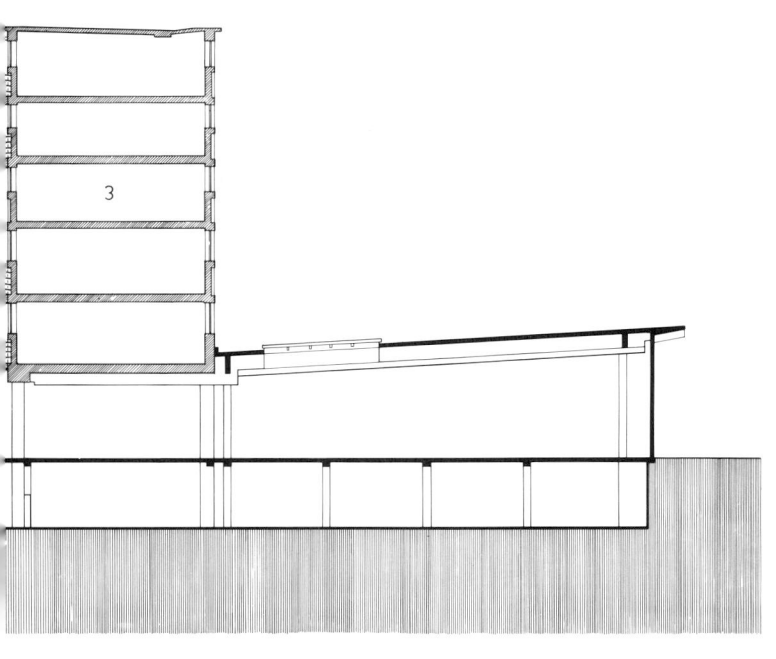

1. Elevation.
2. Section. Key: 1 new building, 2 circulation tower, 3 original structure.

116

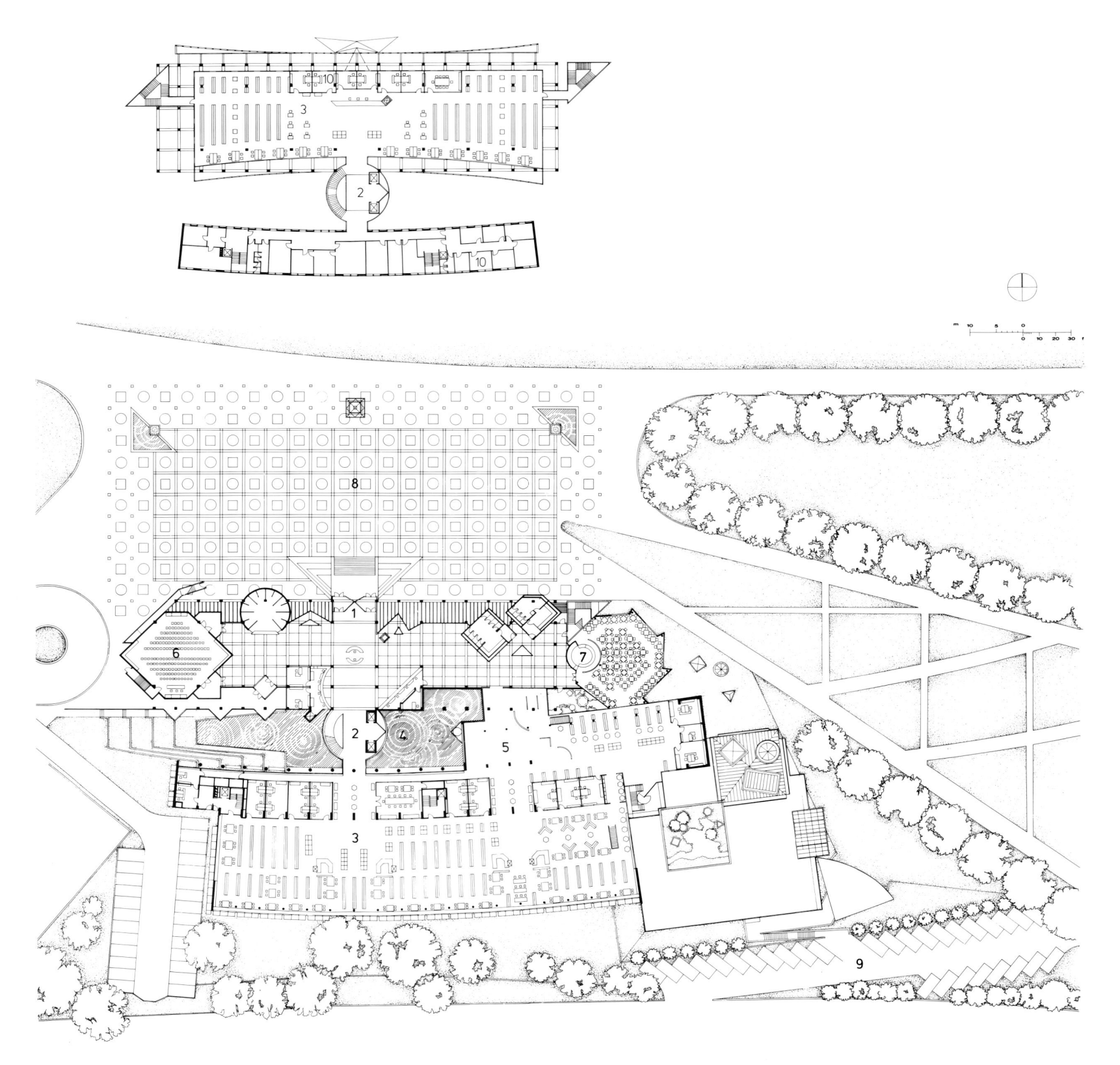

3. Plans (ground floor, site and typical floor).
Key: 1 lobby, 2 circulation tower, 3 reading room,
4 pools, 5 exhibitions, 6 auditorium, 7 café,
8 plaza, 9 parking, 10 offices.
4. General view. Model.

117

Steelcase/Stow & Davis Showroom, Chicago, Illinois
1988/1989

The program for showrooms is contradictory. The object is to create an interior that will attract attention while playing a neutral role as backdrop to the product on display. Architectonic and material devices were used to accomplish that in a showroom for Steelcase/Stow & Davis at the Merchandise Mart in Chicago.

The 28,000-square-foot showroom was reworked to take advantage of the client's unusual stacked floors. The entry was shifted to the west end where three bays were opened to expose the space's full double height.

Punctuating the entry is a high-tech stair. It springs from two small footings at its base up to the second level without intermediate supports. Tension and compression rods form an ellipse containing the stair in one geometrically logical gesture. Treads and risers are made of a continuous steel plate that, seen in profile, reinforces the essential dynamism of the stair.

The stair is the focal point of the interior. Behind it is a delicately colored and textured environment meant to support without distracting. The travertine wall that forms a backdrop to the stairs is beige. The stone panels have been rotated to alternate the grain of the stone, creating a subtle checkerboard effect. Translucent ribbed glass was rotated to similar effect where it was used to encase a conference room on the second level where the Steelcase sales staff has its offices.

The showroom is flexible with few fixed walls to impede alteration. Here, nothing is to compete with the furniture being exhibited. Panels on a fixed grid have been dropped from the ceiling with lights projecting between that are adjustable to highlight changing product displays.

Along the corridor, the architects abandoned the butt-glazing that is typical in the Merchandise Mart and introduced mock piers to mimic department store windows where products can be individually displayed. This device allows viewers to focus on the individual product display presentations.

1. View of the reception area.

p. 120, 121
2, 3. Stair details.

Stow & Davis

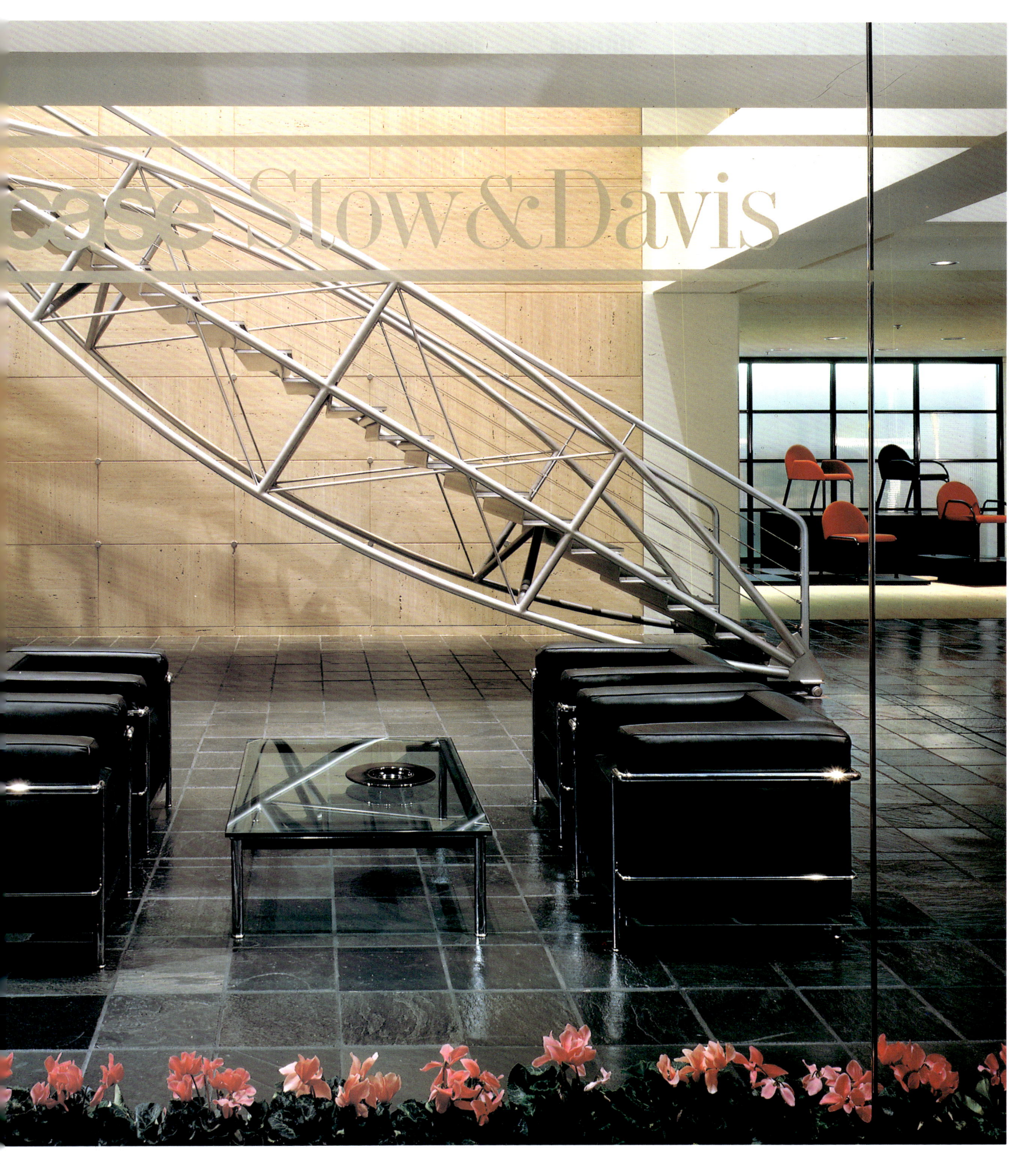

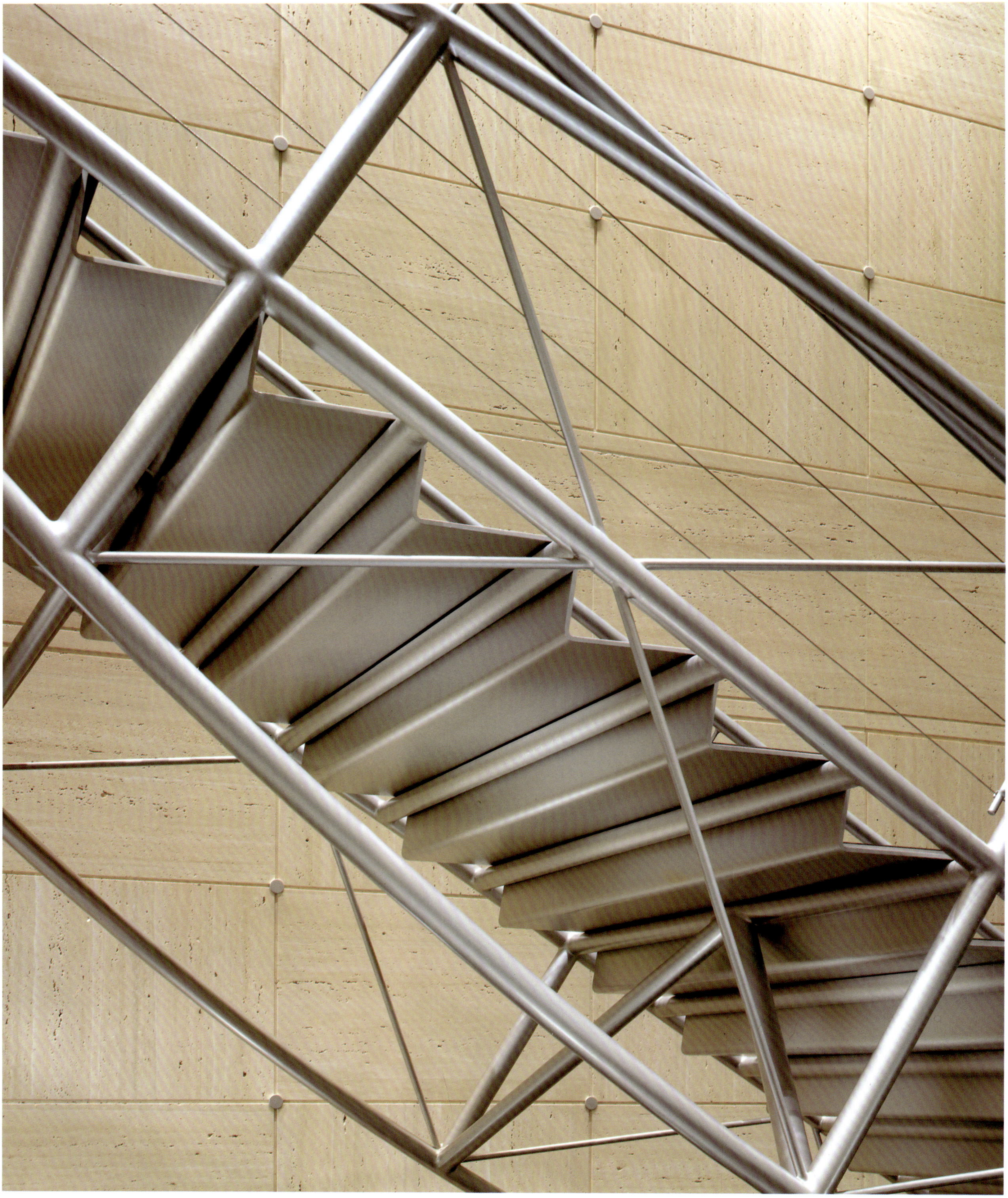

121

Dain Bosworth Tower, Minneapolis, Minnesota
1988–1991

The design for the 1.5-million-square-foot Dain Bosworth/Neiman Marcus Plaza represents the resolution of a difficult and, in some ways, contradictory program. A mixed-use building, it combines a 33-story office tower with a four-story shopping center at the base. While it was important to unify the retail and office portions of the project it was equally important to give office and retail strong identities of their own. Thus the stone base wraps the retail portion as well as the tower and extends up into the shaft of the office structure providing a needed transition.

There are relatively few high rises in Minneapolis which makes the geometric top of the Dain Bosworth prominent on the city's horizon. It stands in the company of the IDS Center by Philip Johnson and the Norwest Tower by Cesar Pelli.

This company was an influence on the tower. The massing of the Norwest Tower and the materials of the IDS Building were combined and reinterpreted in Lohan Associates' design for the Dain Bosworth Tower. The shaft and top of the building are sheathed in a taut glass curtain wall that alludes to the nearby IDS. The setbacks, which give the tower its faceted form, allude to Norwest Tower's top across the street.

The mixed-use program made the project structurally challenging. To accommodate the center atrium for the shopping center, the core for the office floors above was pushed to the far side of the tower.

The building is directly linked to Nicollet Mall, Minneapolis' main shopping street, by skyways at the second level. Three levels of parking and building services are located below ground.

1. The retail entrance.
2. General view of the tower.

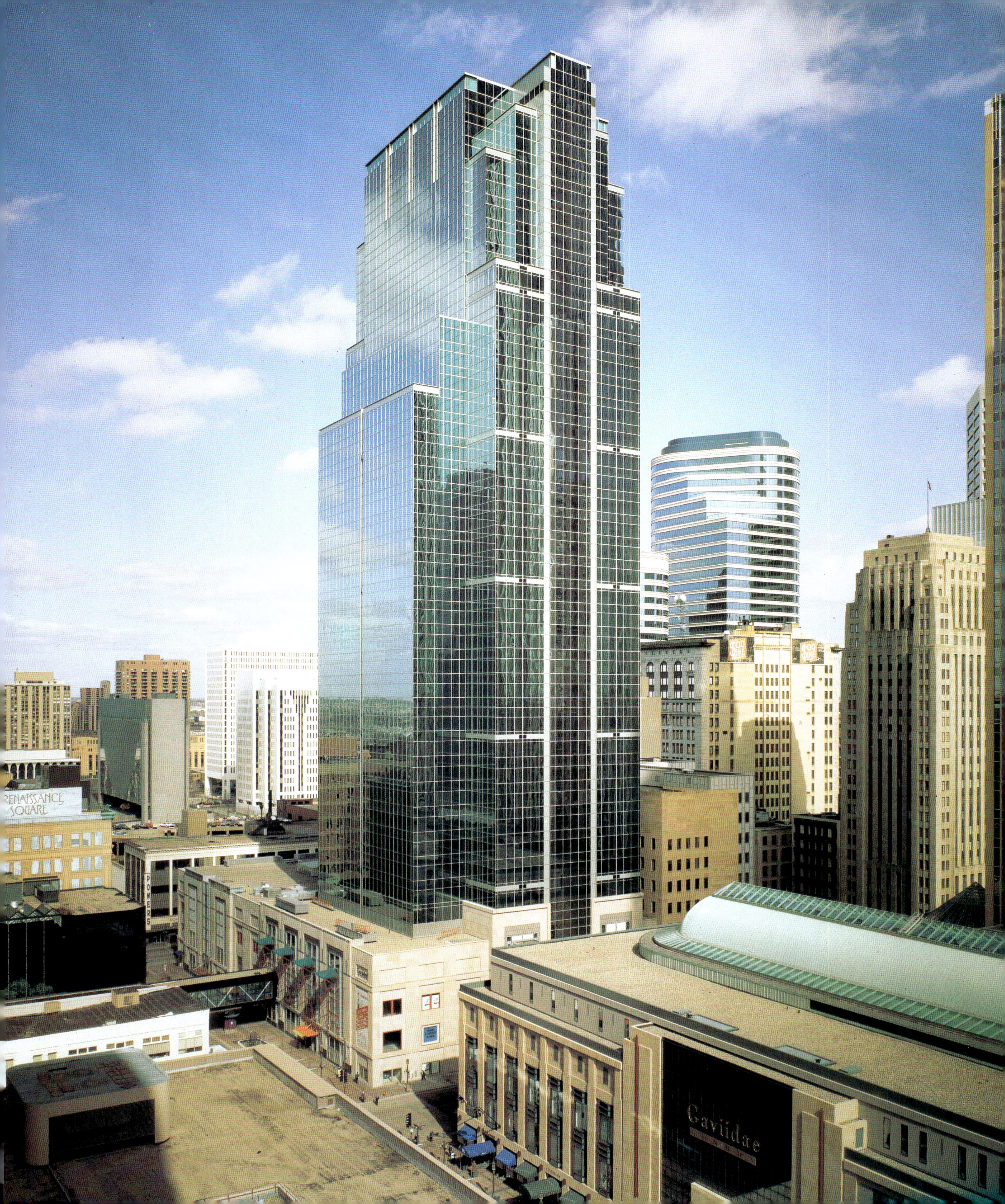
RENAISSANCE SQUARE
POWERS
Gaviidae

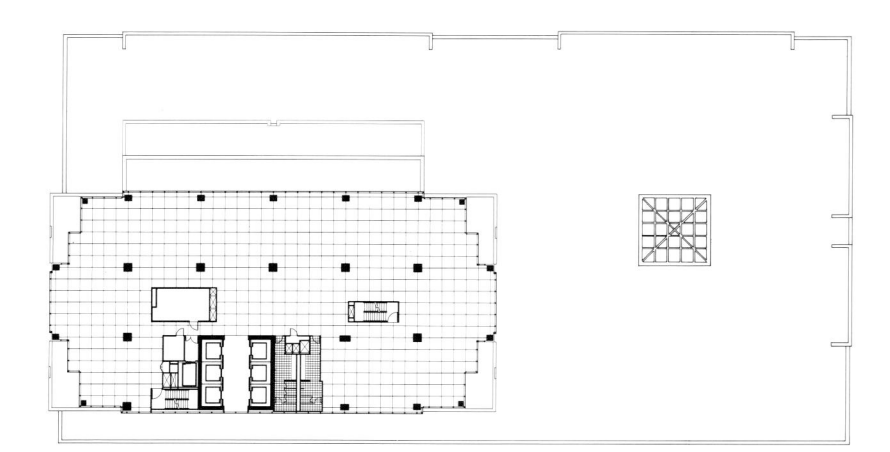

3. Plans (ground floor, 2nd floor, upper floor). Key:
1 retail atrium, 2 skyway, 3 retail, 4 retail entry,
5 office lobby.
4. The retail atrium.

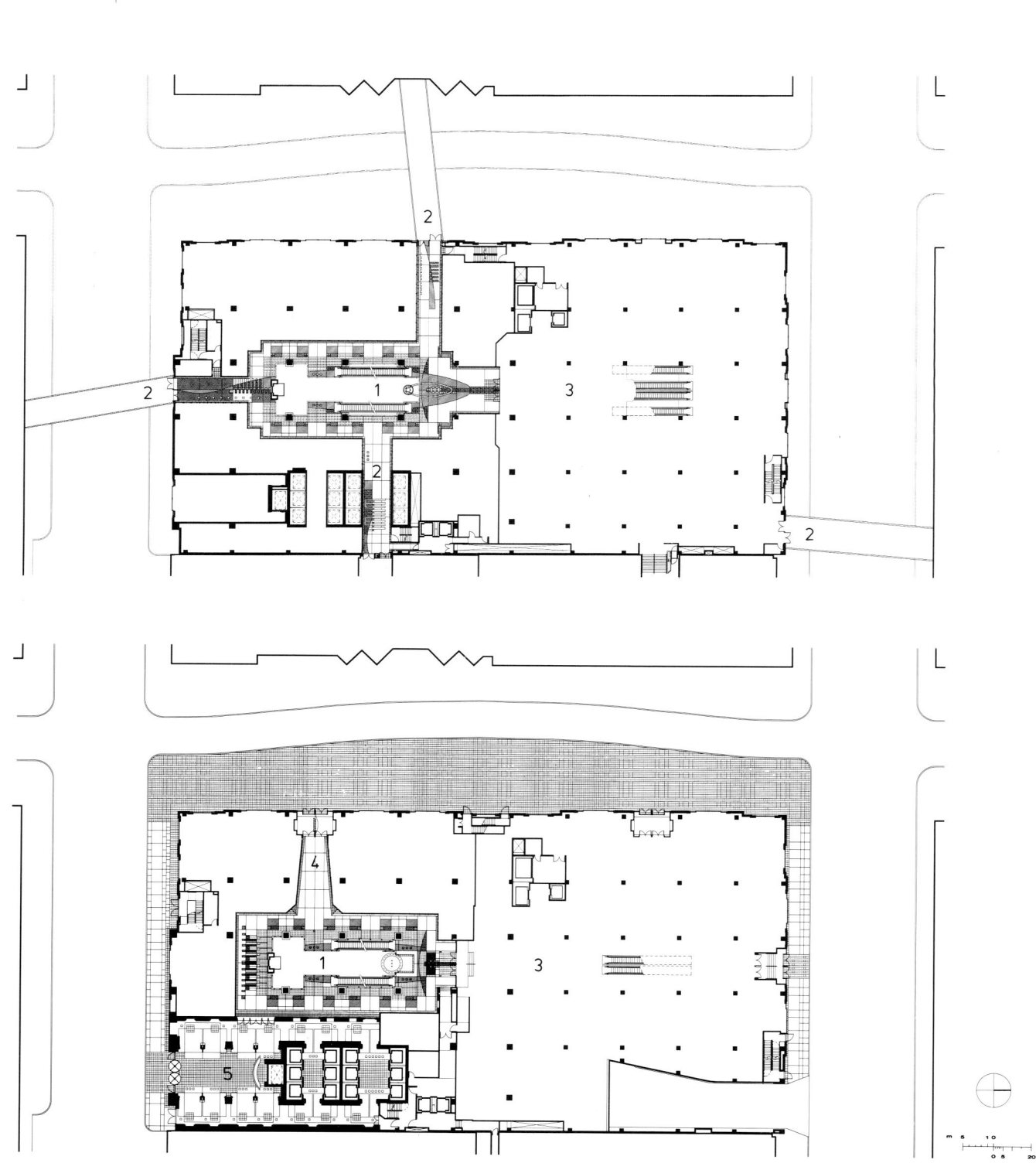

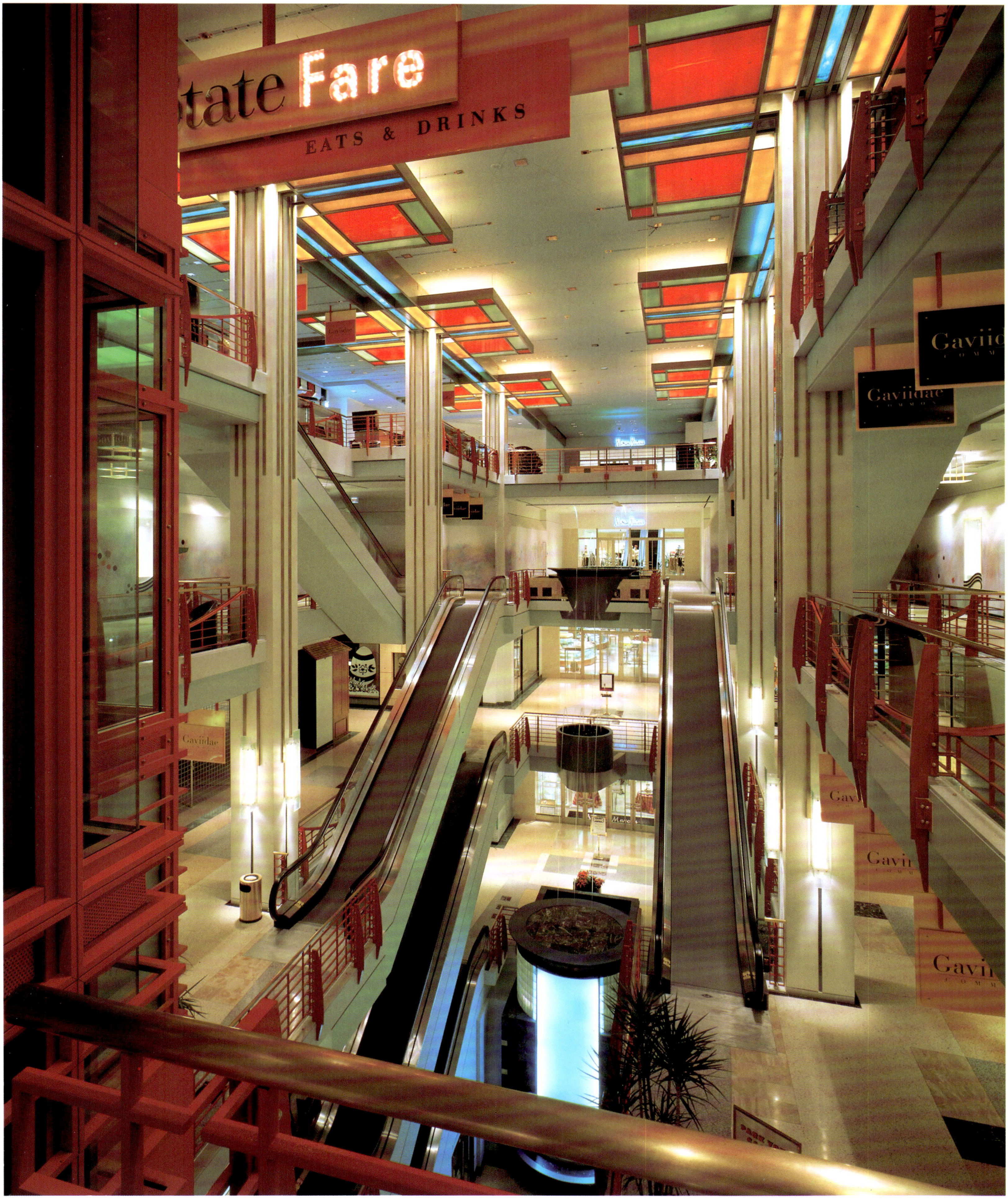
State Fare
EATS & DRINKS
Gaviidae
Gaviidae

Village of Old Mill Creek, Old Mill Creek, Illinois
1988–2008

Lohan Associates has completed a comprehensive land-use plan for an undeveloped 8,000-acre tract in northern Illinois. As the plan is implemented over the next 20 years Old Mill Creek, a self-reliant mixed-use community of approximately 15,000, will take shape. It will be anchored by existing rural structures and the Tempel horse farm which has and will continue to give the area its identity. Old Mill Creek will ultimately include residences, corporate campuses and retail centers.

The plan calls for discrete areas with defined uses. Unlike the traditional town, the plan for Old Mill Creek places low-density residential estates and a farm at its center with higher density residential and corporate campus uses in the outer areas. The corporate campus zone will be adjacent to the major highways, providing easy access by car. Support facilities will also be located in this zone, possibly including hotels, golf courses and higher-education institutions.

The Greenway is an important feature in the plan. It will extend nearly ten miles, taking a total of 2,400 acres by the time the plan is completed. Other than a few trails, it will be left in its natural state; so Mill Creek, the surrounding ponds, wetlands and flood plains will continue to function as an ecologically balanced environment.

There will be a pedestrian-scaled town center containing the customary mix of cultural, municipal, retail, office and residential uses one would expect to find in a rural Midwestern town. This diversity of uses will make the center vital and lively.

1. Aerial view of the site.
2. Master plan.

scale 0 400ft. 1200' north
April, 1990.

Safety-Kleen Corporate Headquarters, Elgin, Illinois
1989–1992

Given an exceptionally beautiful 78-acre site in suburban Chicago on which to build the corporate headquarters for Safety-Kleen, Lohan Associates designed a building that was respectful of the land.

The four-story building is sited and the approach road was mapped to leave as many mature trees undisturbed as possible. In an unusual plan, the 300,000-square-foot building envelops a structurally independent 960-car garage, thus eliminating views of parking lots from the building.

The building is clad in a beige sand-blasted precast concrete. It is trimmed with red sandstone from India and a green-painted metal. The slightly reflective glass is tinted green. The lobby is also clad in red sandstone.

Overlapping planes on the elevations give depth and shadow to the wall and express functions within the building. Stairs, for example, read as towers and the third and fourth floors are marked on the front elevation with bowed glass inserts that delineate the executive area.

The office wings have an unusually high floor-to-floor height of 15 feet. This permits offices away from the perimeter windows to be elevated 18 inches so that people in those areas will still enjoy views to the outdoors. Offices on the interior will have natural light that is admitted through light wells sandwiched between the garage and offices.

Employees who drive to the office will enter the building through a stairwell at the center of the parking lot connected to the office wings by way of bridges with ornamental railings. The building and parking lots have been designed so that employees will be no more than a half-level stair from their office after parking.

The Safety-Kleen corporate headquarters were designed as a series of repeatable units, two of which are built. In future phases the size of the building will be doubled.

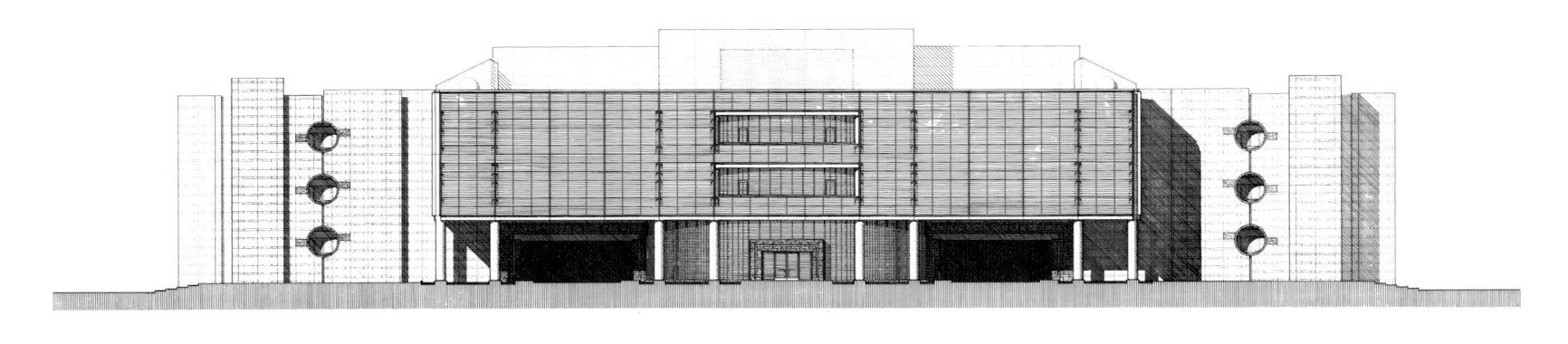

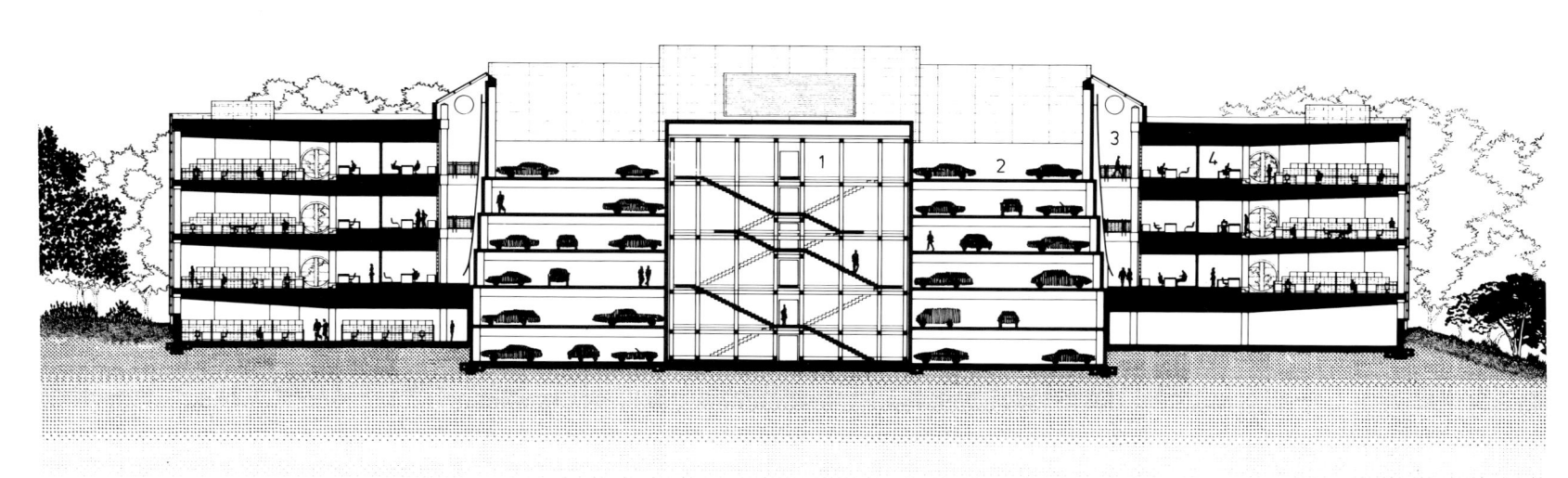

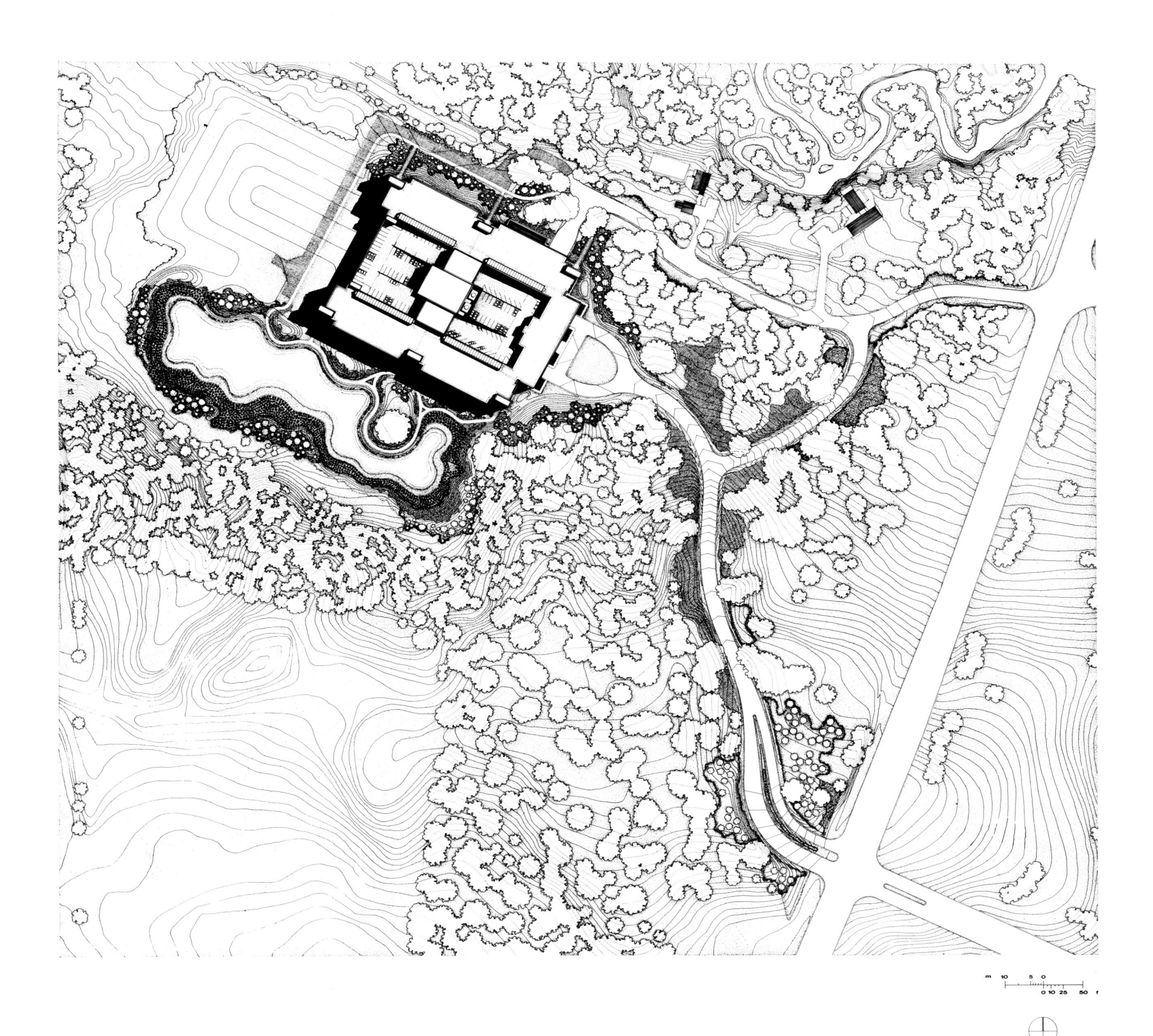

1. Elevation.
2. Section. Key: 1 stair, 2 parking, 3 light well, 4 offices.
3. Site plan.

Eli Lilly and Company Interiors, Indianapolis, Indiana
1989–1992

Eli Lilly and Company's headquarters in Indianapolis is a grouping of varied buildings acquired and commissioned over the years. Lohan Associates, in collaboration with local architects, gave the direction for a new addition to the complex and provided design services for major public interiors that included a new lobby, a concourse, and a new dining pavilion. A 12,000-square-foot training center will be completed in the second phase of work.
At the heart of the headquarters is the central dining pavilion overlooking a landscaped garden. The dining room has been broken into six areas, each offering a different mood and setting. The central dining area is raised and circumscribed by informal parklike plantings while the surrounding dining areas are lower and covered with wood trelliswork. Material selections follow this hierarchy of spaces with granite pavers used in the central area and carpet used in the surrounding areas.
The new lobby and concourse are formal, featuring satinwood paneling, high coffered ceilings, and patterned marble floors. A custom-designed desk and chandelier punctuate the entry. The concourse, which overlooks the dining pavilion and garden, connects the major new spaces with the lobby and provides a transition between the new and existing structures.

1. Plan (ground floor). Key: 1 main entry, 2 lobby, 3 dining pavilion, 4 cafeteria, 5 existing offices.
2. View from the corridor to a dining pavilion.

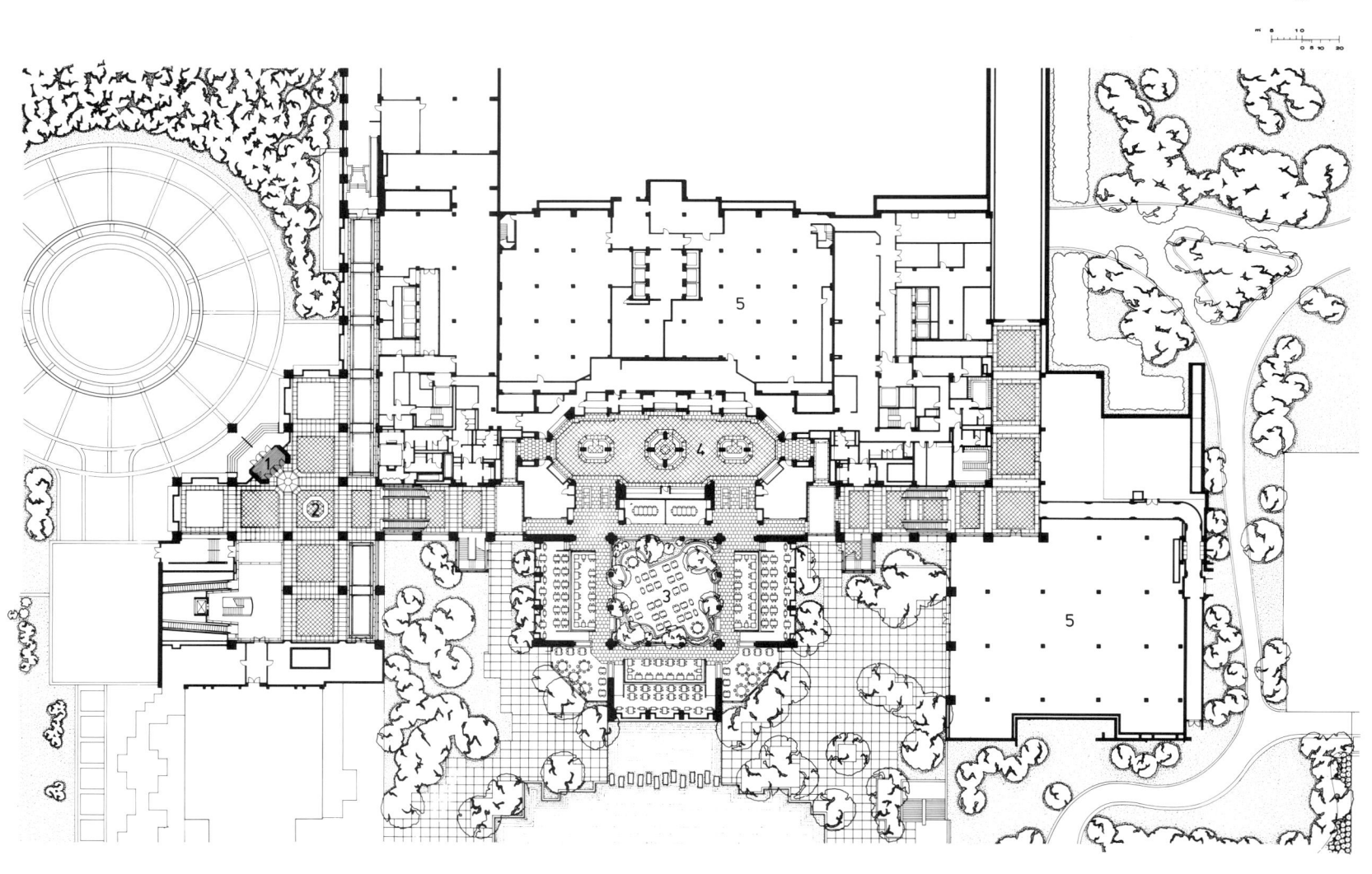

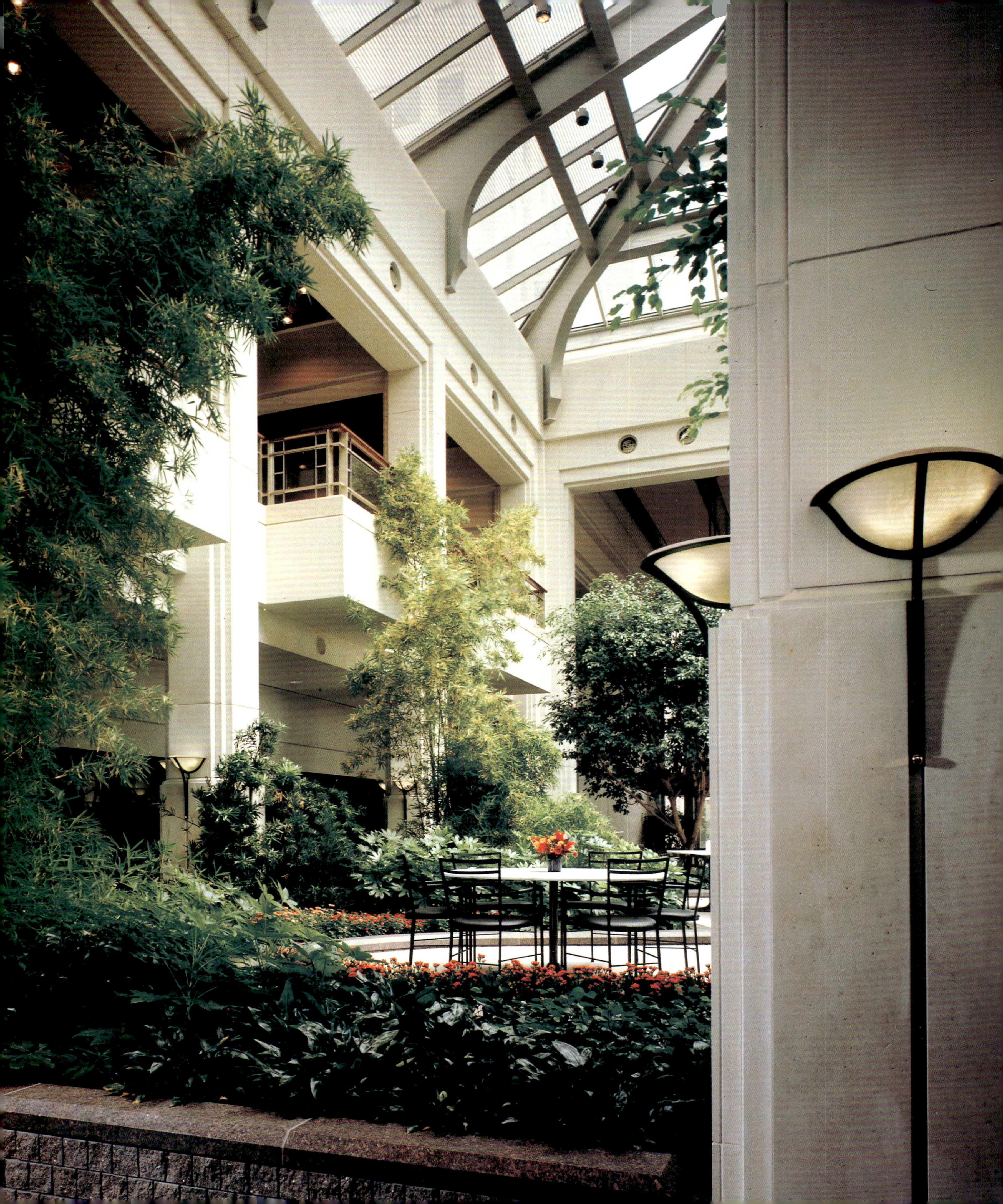

3. The lobby.
4. View of lobby seating area.

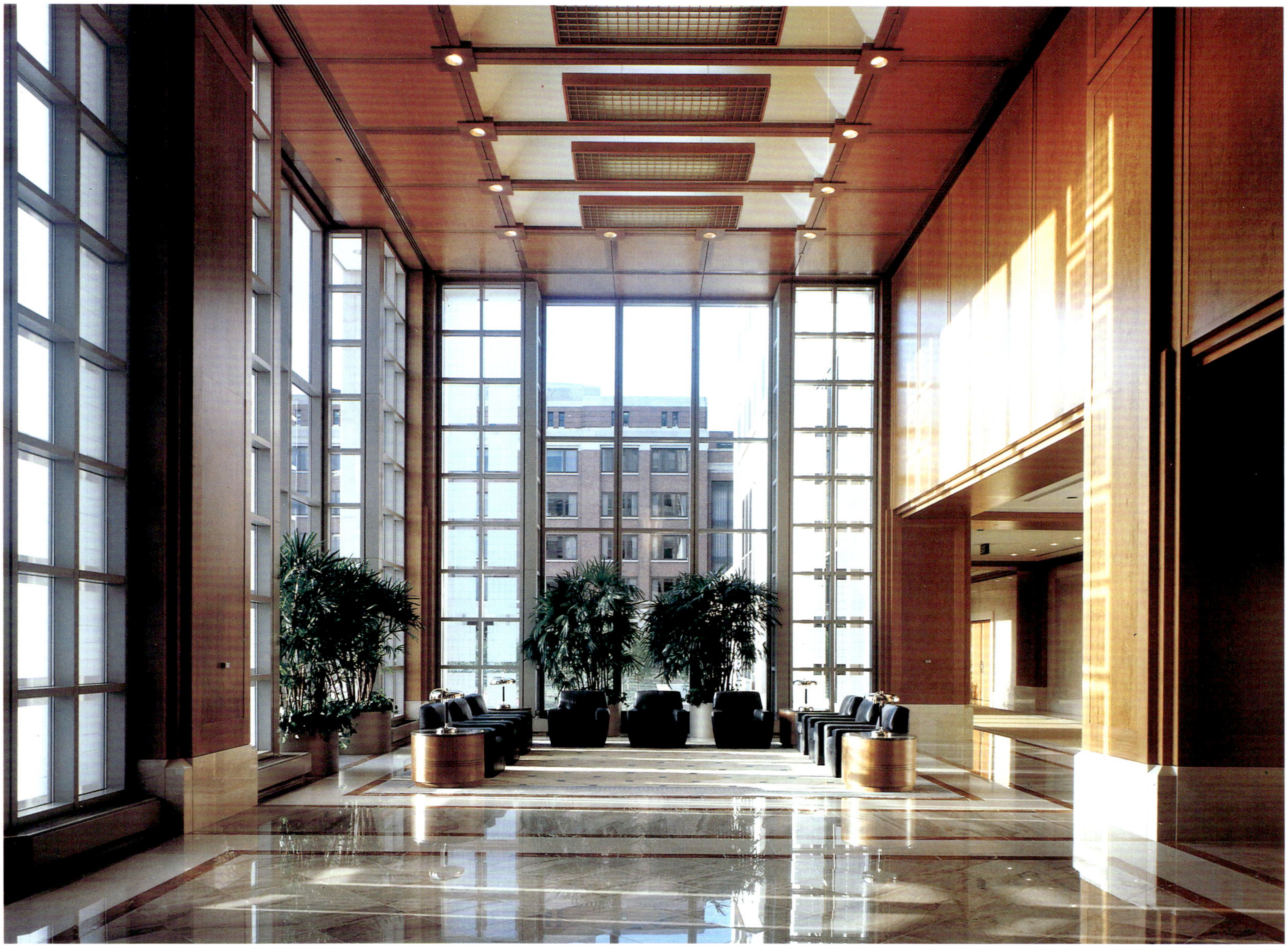

University of Chicago Graduate School of Business, Chicago, Illinois
1990–1994

Making the most of an irregular pie-shaped site, Lohan Associates has designed a distinctive new building for the University of Chicago Graduate School of Business.

The school is intended to serve adult students with full-time jobs working after hours on higher business degrees. The new 215,000-square-foot building will replace aging facilities and will be located in Cityfront Center in downtown Chicago rather than on the University of Chicago campus several miles to the south.

But the architects have formed a link between the Hyde Park campus and the new building by designing the Business School in a way that recalls the Gothic-styled campus buildings. Stone is the primary material for the Business School façade. Six shallow bays flank the entry, providing articulation and shadowing not unlike what one would see in the campus buildings. Punched windows mounted above the bays are borrowed directly from the campus where they are a recurring motif.

Glass enclosed appendages surmount and flank the stone-covered building shell. During the evening and night when the building will be used most heavily the lighted glass ends containing student lounges will call attention to the activity taking place within the building.

Near the school's site are some of the city's most prominent skyscrapers, including the Wrigley Building and Chicago Tribune Tower and, a more recent addition, the NBC Tower. The Business School will be only six stories tall and will rely on its sculptural qualities to distinguish itself in this company. The building has a roughly triangular form. Its glass ends project past the boundaries of the neighboring tower which stand between it and Michigan Avenue, so the school will be visible from the street. On the western elevation, large bays, or »saddlebags« accommodating 14 horseshoe-shaped interactive classrooms will project outwards, giving the wall an interesting high relief.

The building will also contain conventional classrooms, study rooms, lounges, a conference center with boardrooms, meeting rooms and a dining room. In addition there are to be staff offices and 42 parking spaces.

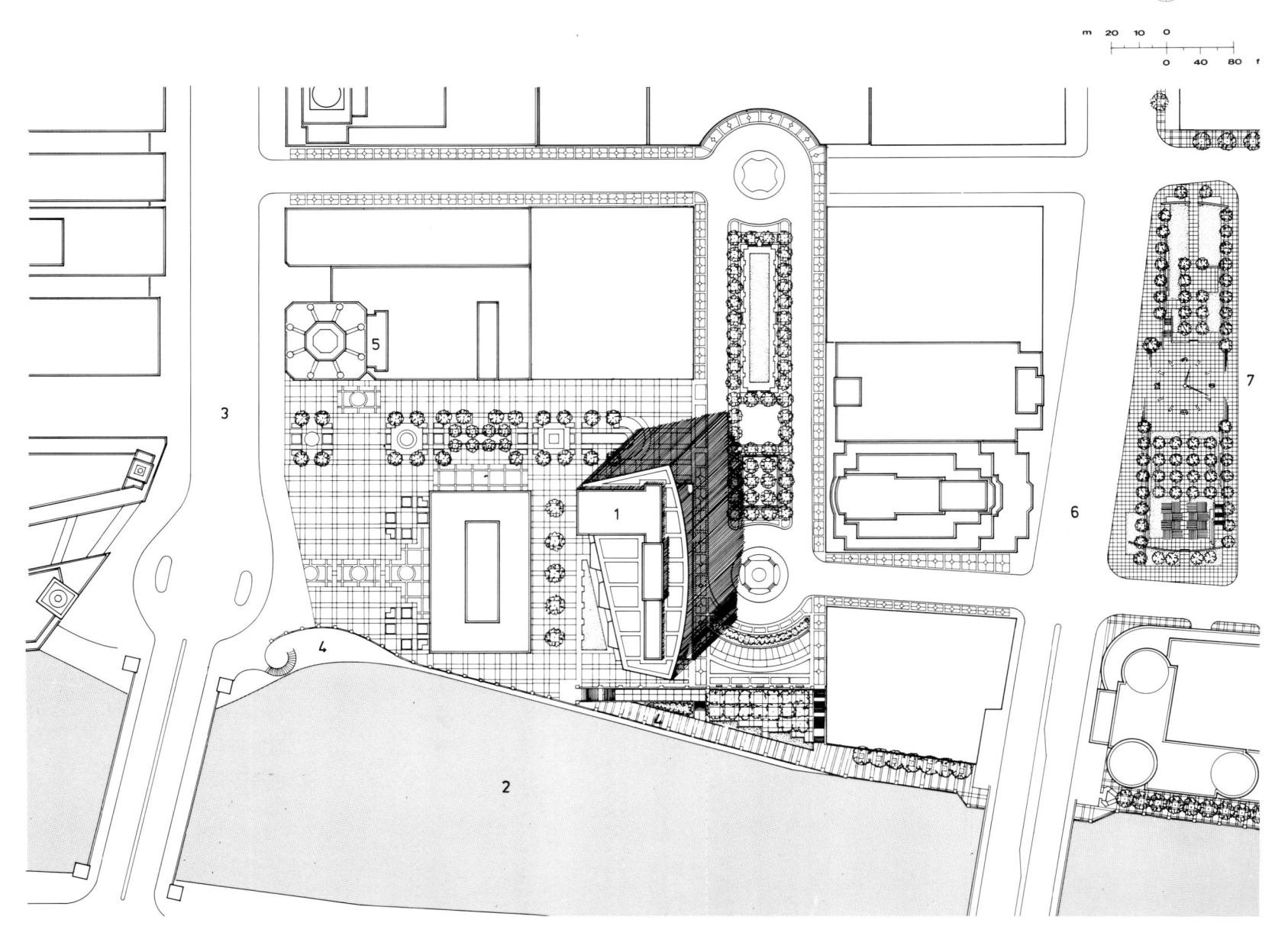

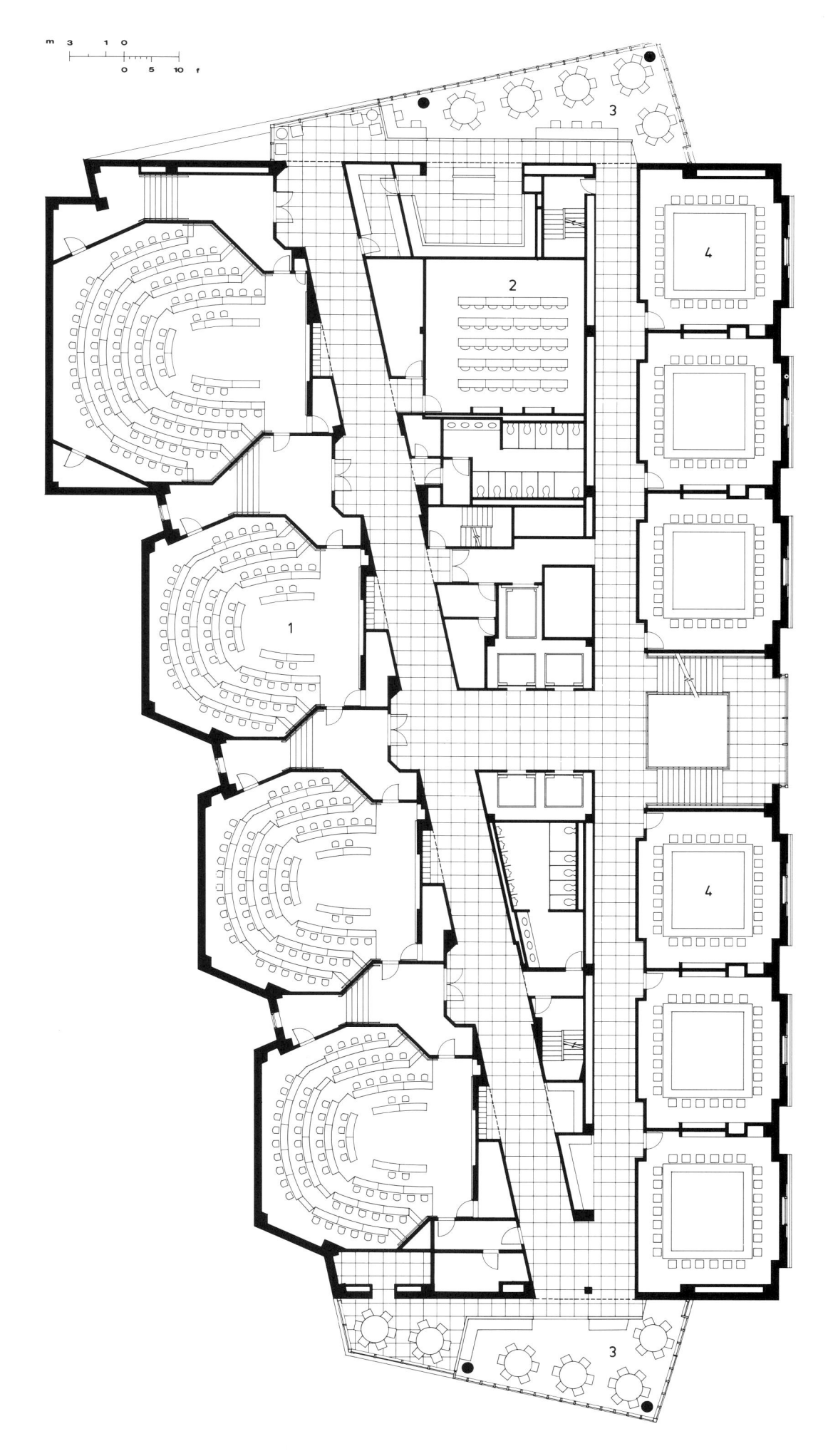

1. Site plan. Key: 1 Graduate School of Business, 2 Chicago River, 3 Michigan Avenue, 4 River Esplanade, 5 Chicago Tribune Tower, 6 Columbus Drive, 7 Mayor Ogden Park.
2. Plan. Key: 1 interactive classrooms, 2 lecture hall, 3 lounges, 4 classrooms.

p. 136/137
3. Elevation.

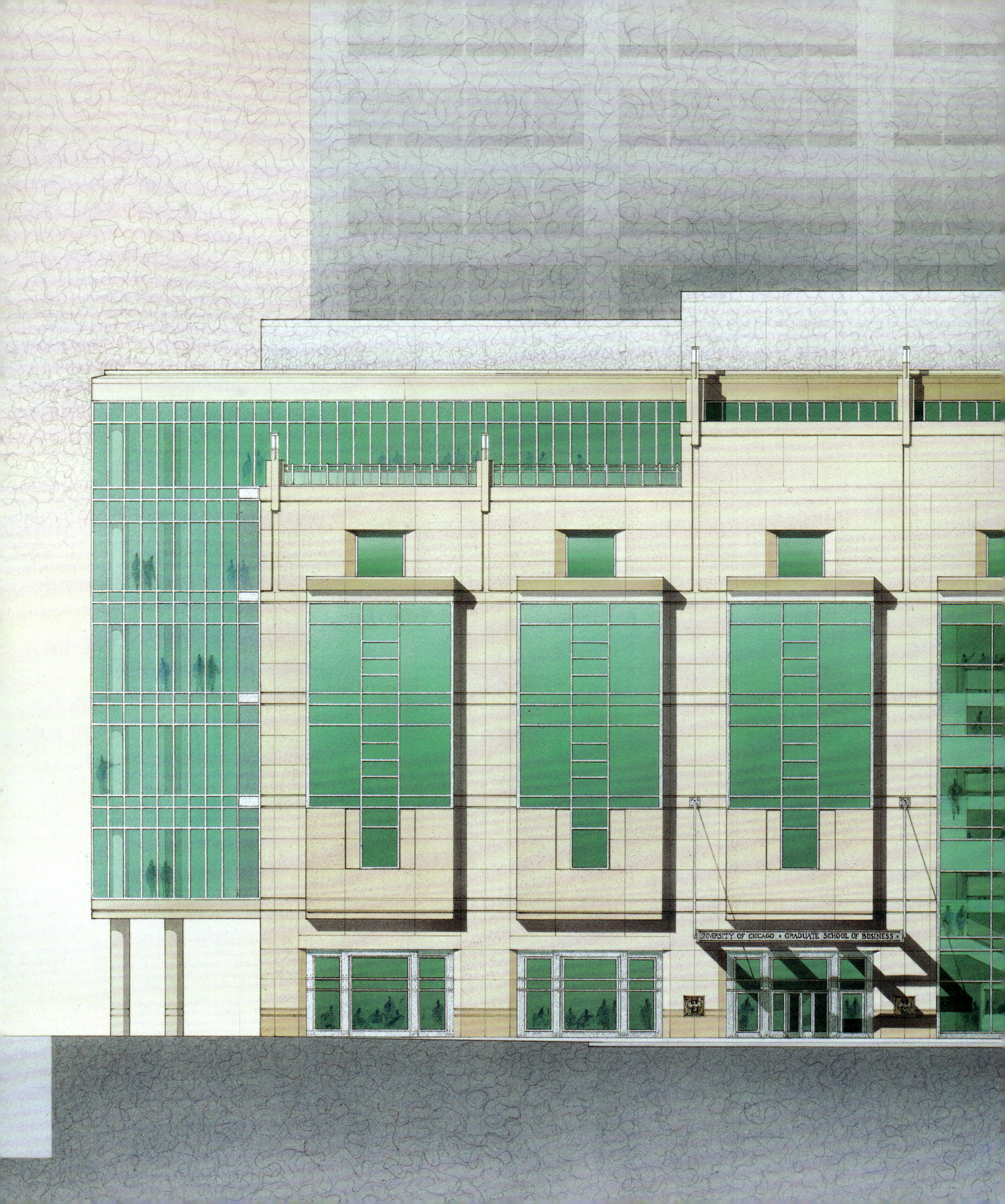

UNIVERSITY OF CHICAGO • GRADUATE SCHOOL OF BUSINESS

UNIVERSITY OF CHICAGO · GRADUATE SCHOOL OF BUSINESS

University of Illinois at Chicago Molecular Biology Research Facility, Chicago, Illinois
1990–1995

The Molecular Biology Research Facility will occupy an important site on the West Campus of the University of Illinois at Chicago. It will be the first building one sees approaching the school from the freeway; and, from the university side, the laboratory will be the terminus to a landscaped quadrangle called Academic Way. To acknowledge both approaches the architects gave equal value to the public and campus sides of the laboratory. Strictly speaking, the building has no back side.

The laboratory facility is long and thin with a total of 220,000 square feet. It is organized with offices and laboratories on the window walls and support and storage spaces on the internal spine. Aggregate precast panels form the cladding on all sides and reflect the building's organization. Mechanical and venting apparatus is exposed and divides the four bays containing laboratory and office spaces. Sun screens and reveals are cast into the panels giving the building both a highly functional and richly articulated finish. Panels with a granite aggregate will create a strong red cast that will harmonize with the existing masonry buildings in the area. Amber-tinted windows will reinforce the color scheme.

The off-center entry is distinguished by a medallion mounted above it. The architects included a reference to the subject of scientific study in the labs. A double-helix stair related to the form of DNA mounts the height of the four-story building.

1. Section.
2. Plan. Key: 1 laboratories, 2 service core, 3 double-helix stair.
3. Elevation.

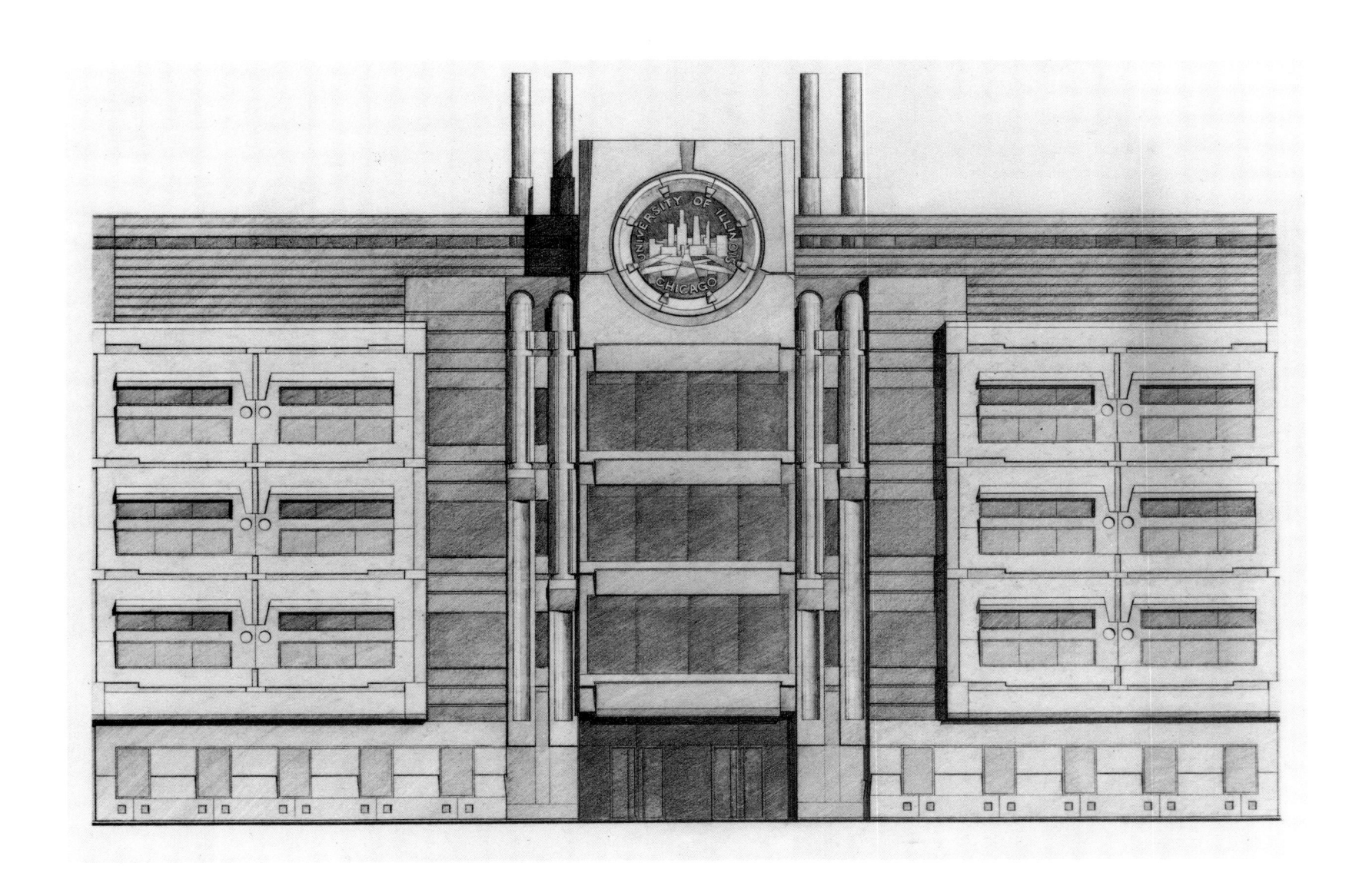

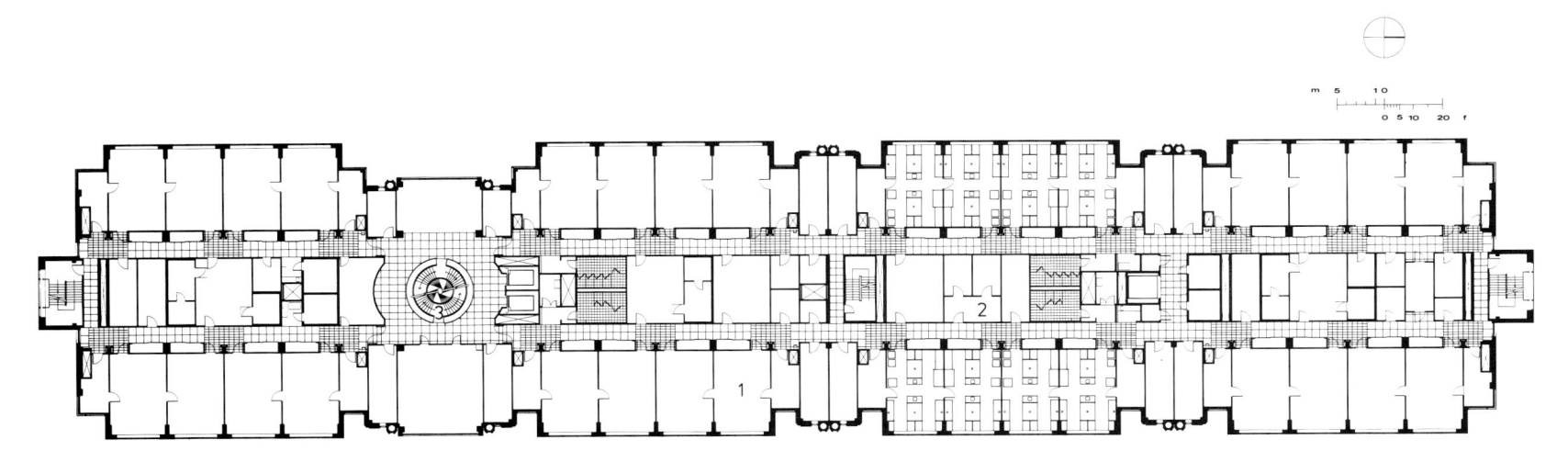

Lincoln Park Residence, Chicago, Illinois
1990–1993

A three-story house on a site across from Lincoln Park is designed to accommodate a family and their extensive art collection.

The new house mimics the height of neighboring landmark residences including, on one side, an historic mansion. But the Lincoln Park Residence establishes its independence in a quiet, assertive façade of gray granite, limestone and gray-tinted glass in varying shades.

Planes of glass and stone project asymmetrically from the angled façade. Like the mansion next door, the first story of the house is elevated above street level for the sake of privacy and for views of the park.

The interior of the 6,500-square-foot house is distinguished by its open plan where curving walls and floating ceilings flow from one space to another. A central circulation spine divides the house in two and rises the height of the building. It is surmounted by a clerestory extending the length of the house.

On the first floor, the house includes a garage, kitchen, dining room, family room, and living room; on the second floor is the master bedroom suite, a study, and a library; on the third floor are the children's bedrooms, an exercise room, and a terrace overlooking the park.

1. Section.
2. Plans (ground floor, 2nd floor, 3rd floor).

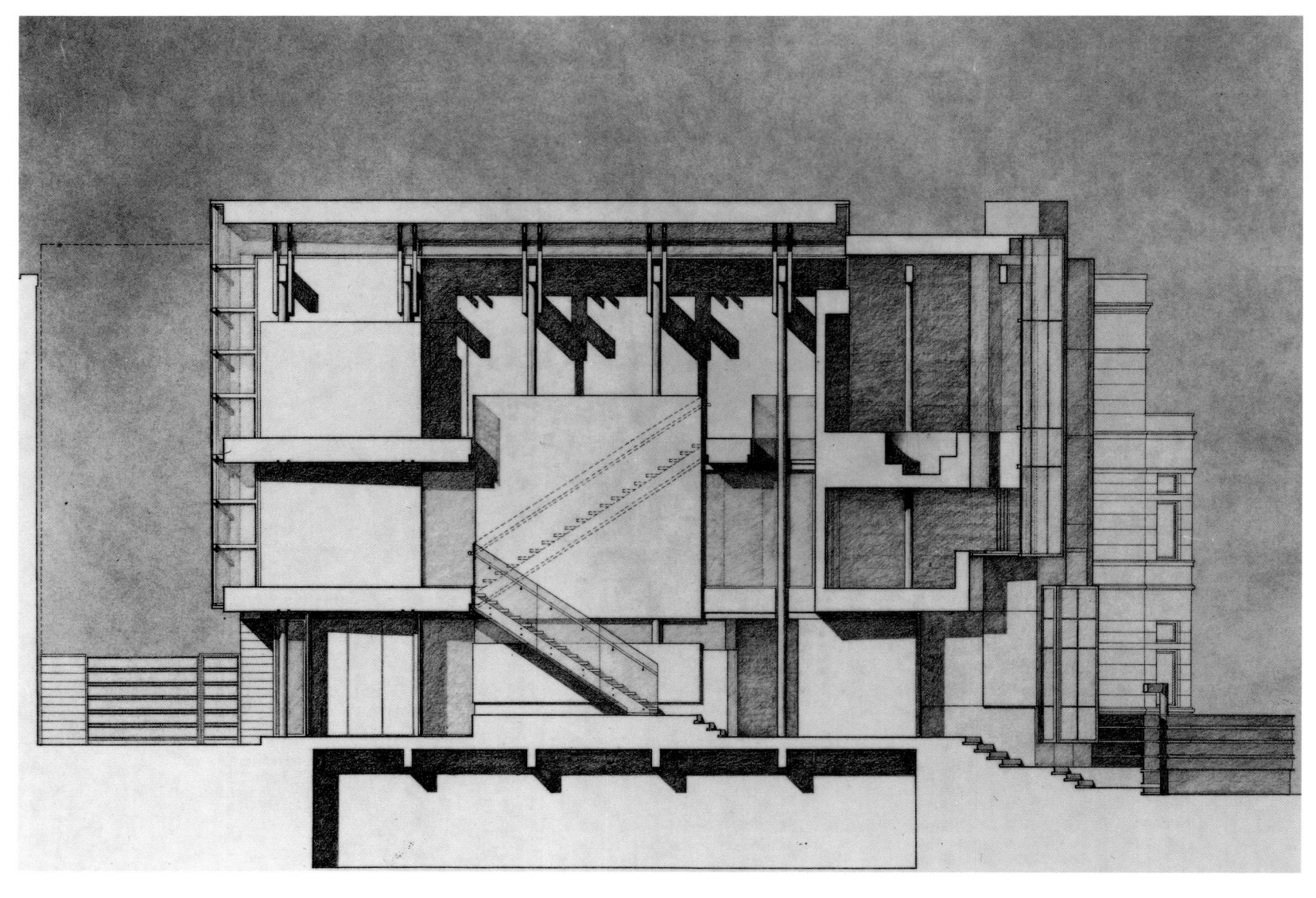

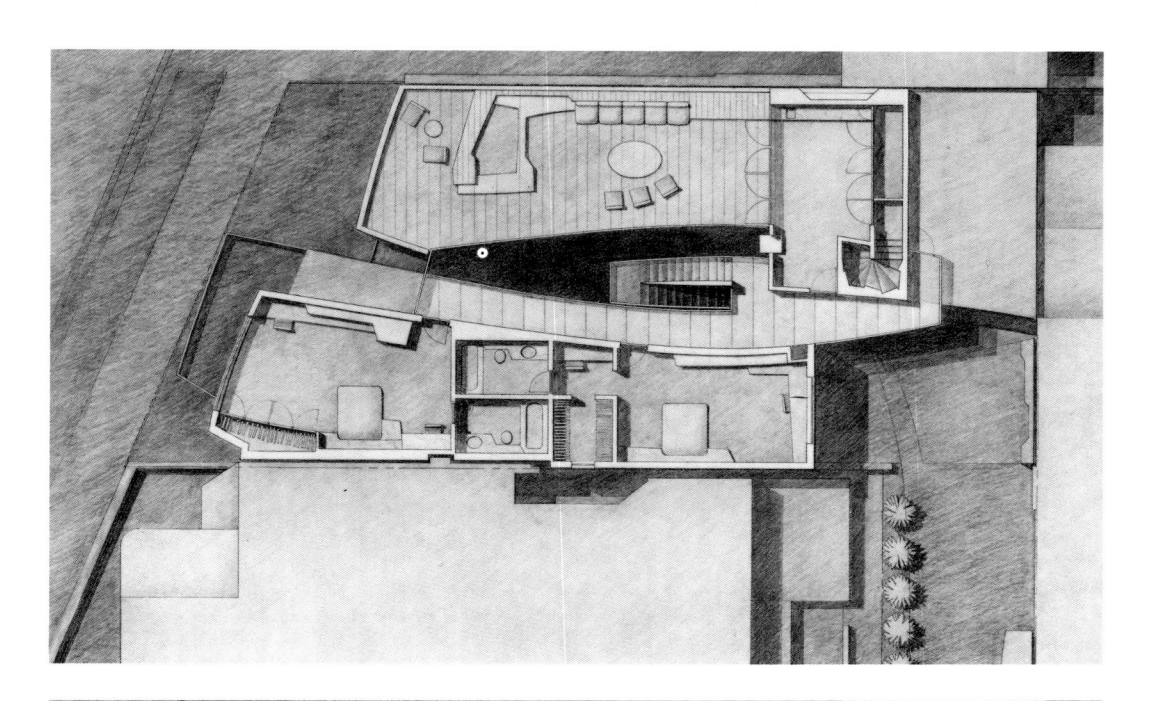

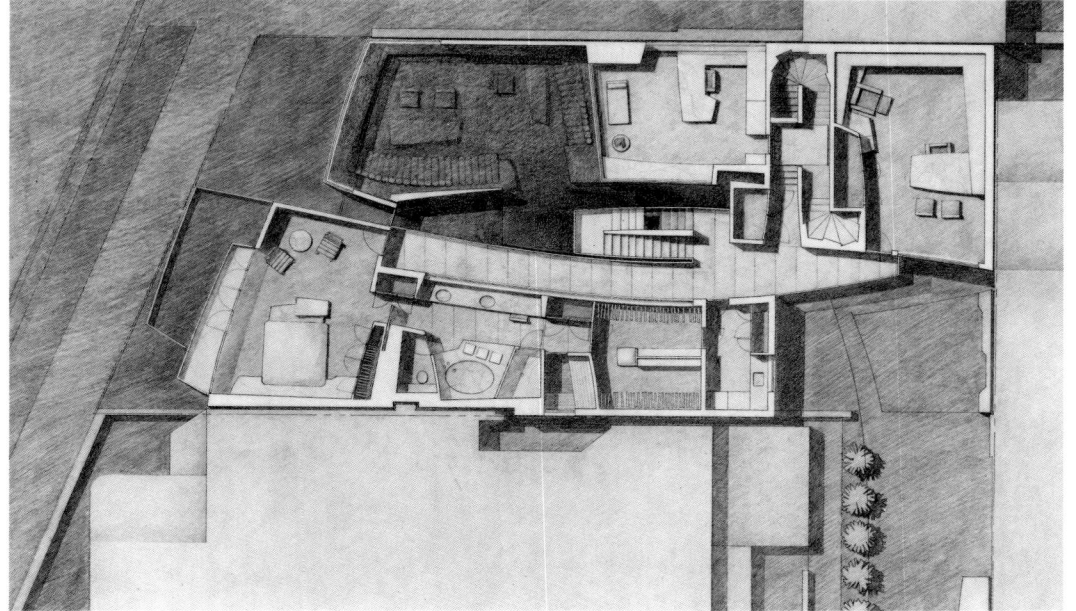

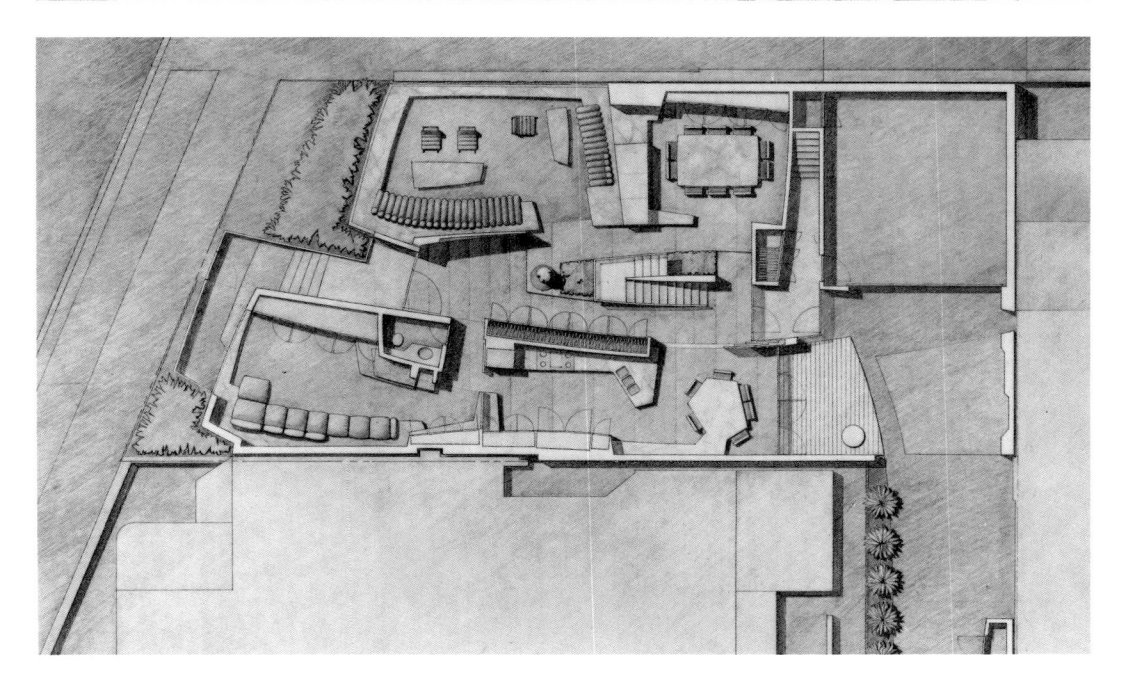

p. 142/143
3, 4. Elevations.

141

142

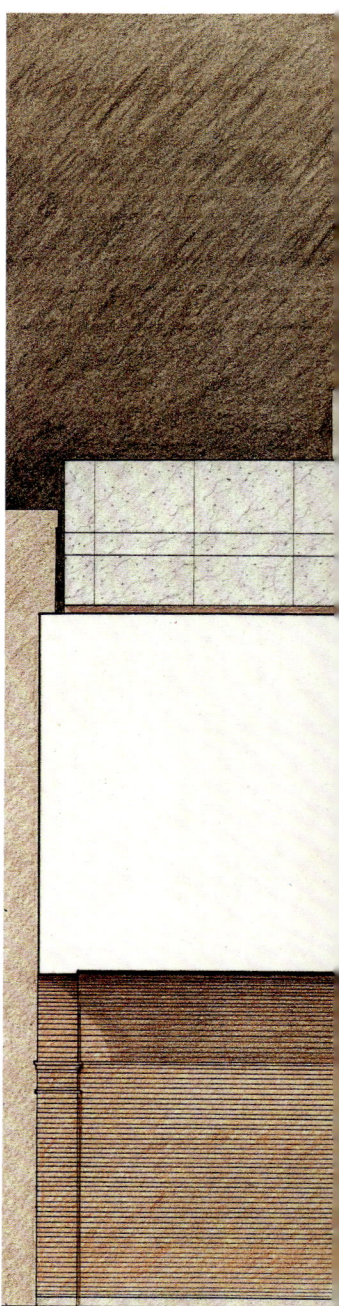

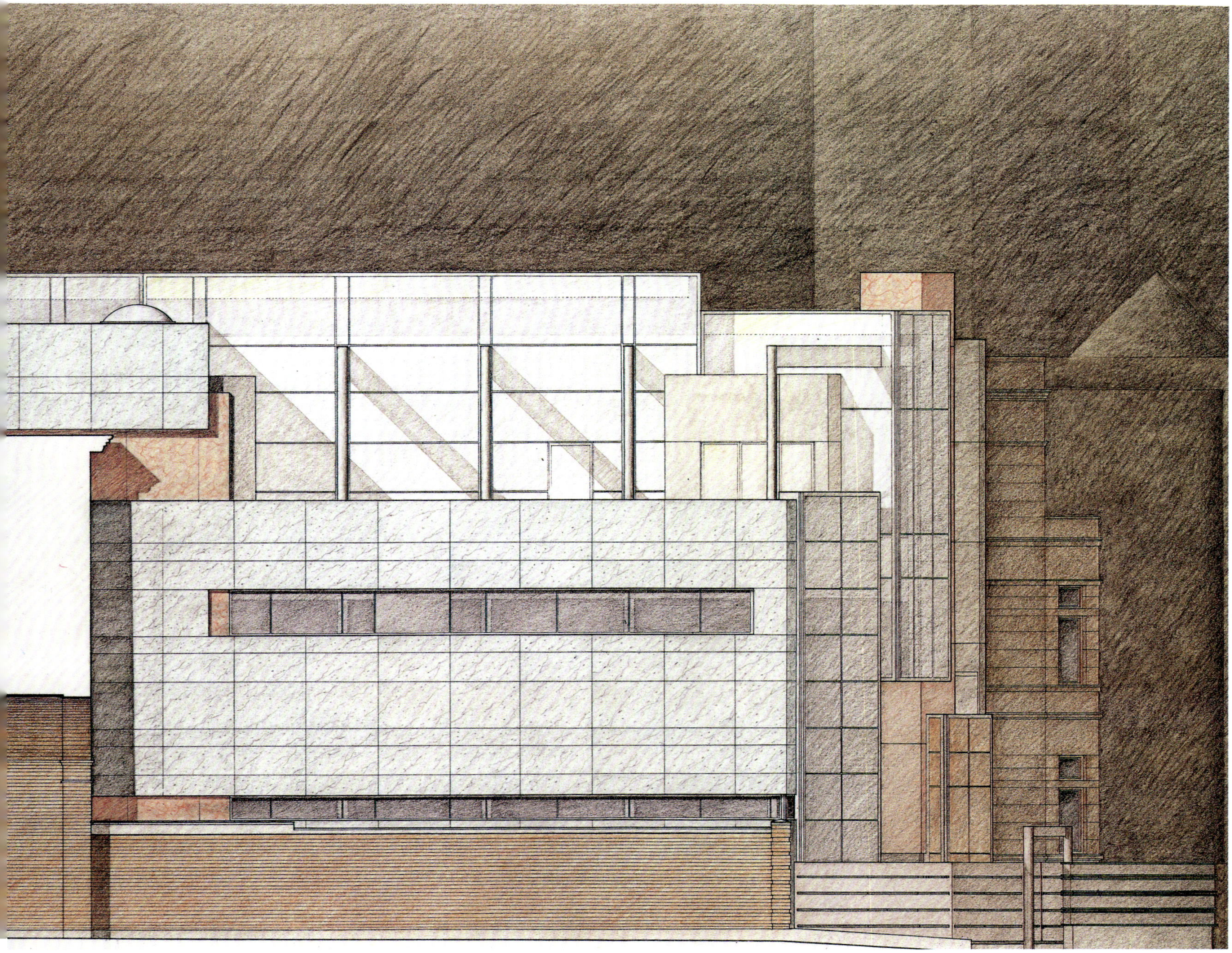

Harris Trust and Savings Bank Operations Center, Chicago, Illinois
1990–

The Harris Trust and Savings Bank Operations Center resembles a sleek efficient machine. Its imagery expresses the building's function. The 30-story, one-million-square-foot tower will be used principally as a check-processing center. As such, the building also has exacting security and technical requirements.

The tower will have a stone base with a plinth of polished black granite, and a shaft of reflective glass and metal. Metal panels form an inverted gable at the top of the building. The top's form was shaped by the power plant installed there that will permit computers to operate continuously in the event of either a general or partial power failure.

Six floors will be devoted to computer equipment. All levels are to be equipped with deep floors for the efficient delivery of computer and telephone cables. A trading floor where foreign currency will be bought and sold will be located on an upper floor. A vault meeting the toughest federal standards is to be contained in the lower level of the building. Access to the building and circulation within it is restricted.

The Harris Trust and Savings Bank Operations Center is to be erected on former rail-yard property in Franklin Point, a newly planned development on the bank of the Chicago River at the southwest edge of downtown Chicago. Bank officials are contemplating erecting another building on an adjacent site and the Operations Center has been designed with that in mind. The core is split making it possible to pass through the lobby at the ground-floor level to the adjoining site. The floors in the Operations Center are column-free with a 45-foot free span, leaving 38,000-square-foot flexible floor plates.

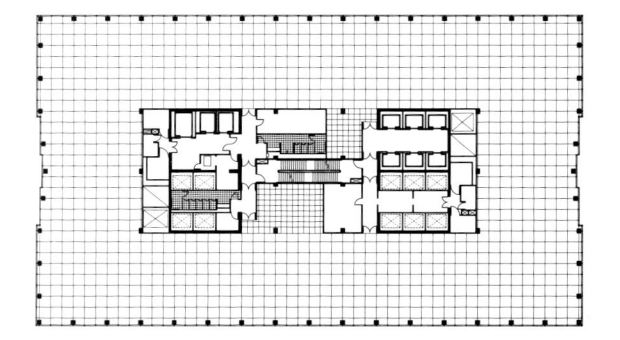

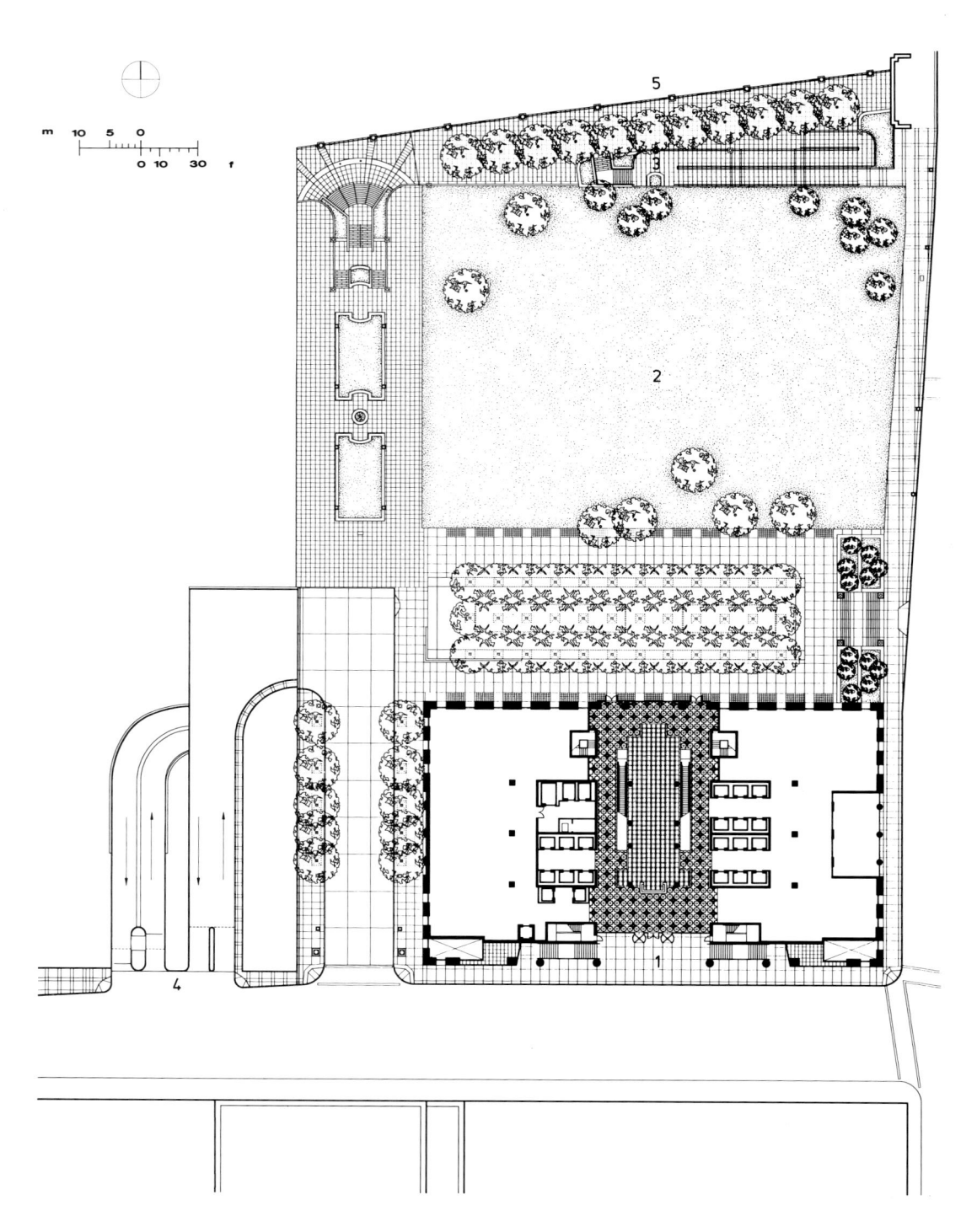

1. Plan (typical floor).
2. Site plan. Key: 1 entry, 2 future development site, 3 river walk, 4 ramps to parking and secure area, 5 Chicago River.

3. Development models.

p. 146, 147
4, 5. Elevations.

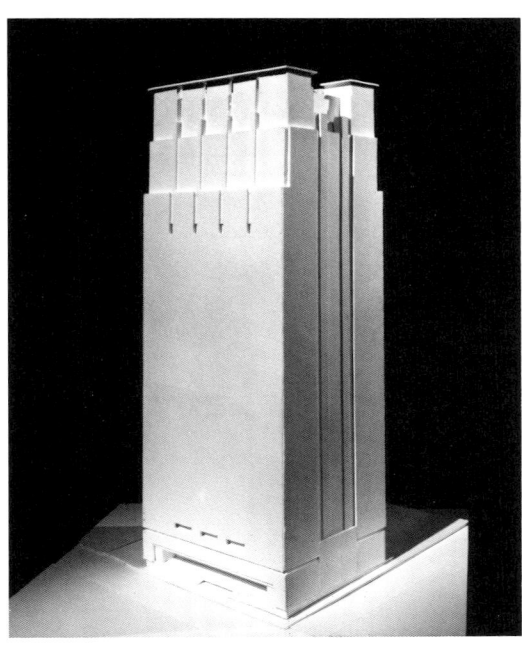

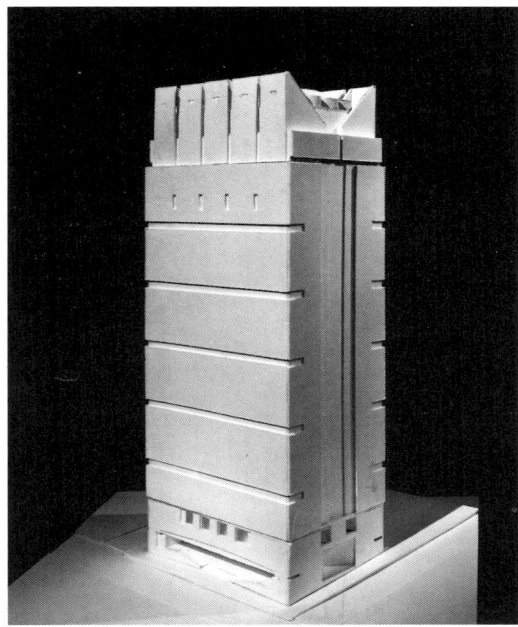

146

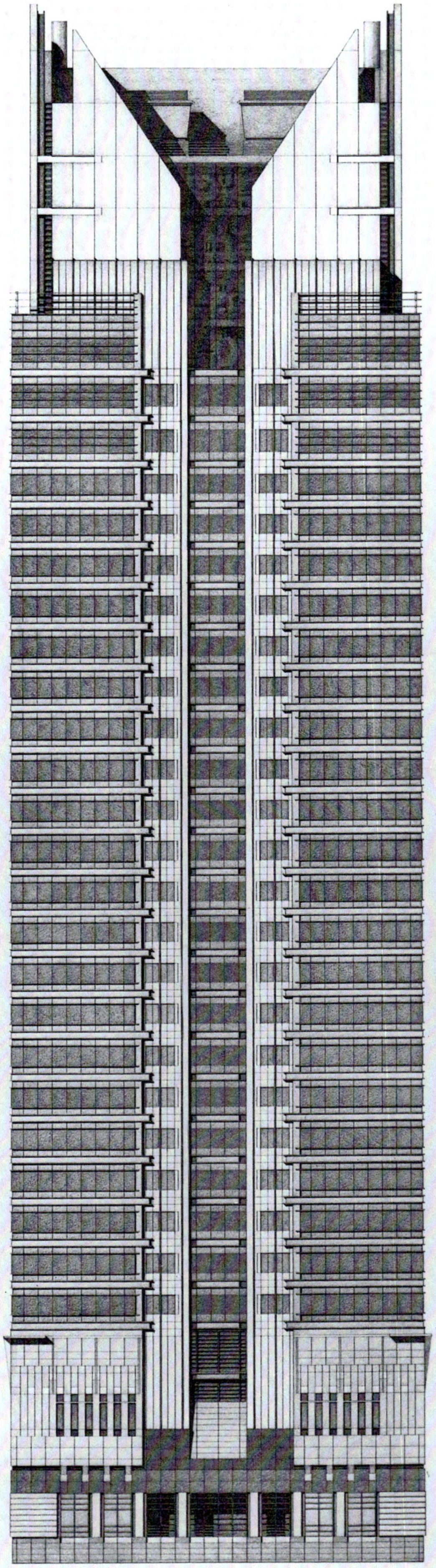

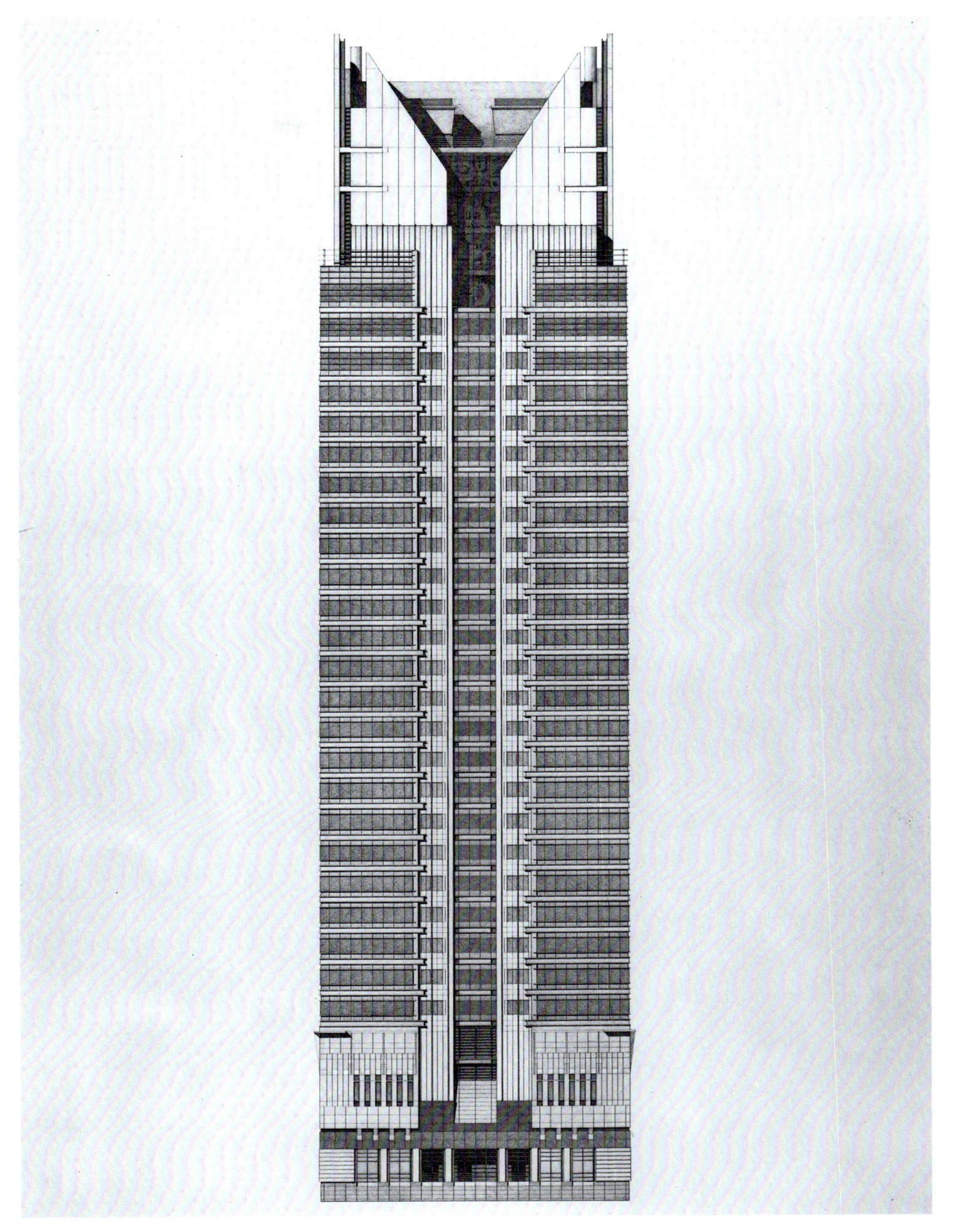

Olympiaquartier 2000, Berlin, Germany
1991. Competition entry

Since the reunification of Berlin, sites in former East Berlin – some of which have lain fallow since World War II – have become available for development.

Lohan Associates is one of two finalists in a two-stage urban design competition to conceive a mixed-use plan and design for one such 26-acre development site called Olympiaquartier 2000. A subsequent competition will be held for the development's architecture.

City leaders, who hope to demonstrate Berlin's worthiness to host the Olympics in the year 2000, are offering the site to developers provided one large stadium containing 15,000 seats and one small stadium with 4,000 seats are built as a part of the program. The stadia must have seating that can be reconfigured to accommodate different sports and cultural events.

The balance of the site is left to be used at the discretion of competing architects and developers. Aside from the stadia, Lohan's scheme includes a hotel, office space, residential and retail uses. The architects have followed the model of Berlin's urban fabric to create buildings that will preserve the scale of the city.

The Lohan scheme arrays the stadia on a new plaza connected to the Chausseestraße, the principal business street adjacent to the site. The proposed commercial office buildings are placed along this street with retail in many of the first-floor spaces. A 30-story hotel – the project's marker on the skyline and what could be one of the tallest buildings in Berlin – is to be placed across the plaza, serving as an intermediary between the public zone, and the commercial and residential zones.

The configuration of the office and residential structures in Olympiaquartier reflects Berlin's traditional block building stock. The new buildings are low – five- and six-stories – with shops at the base and apartments above. They are narrow and wrapped around generous courtyards with ample access to natural light.

The architects' plan also calls for dredging a submerged river, drawing it back to the surface and creating landscaped walks and parks along the northern edge of the site.

1. Site plan. Key: 1 large stadium, 2 small stadium, 3 hotel, 4 office and retail, 5 housing.
2. Perspective.
3. Elevations.

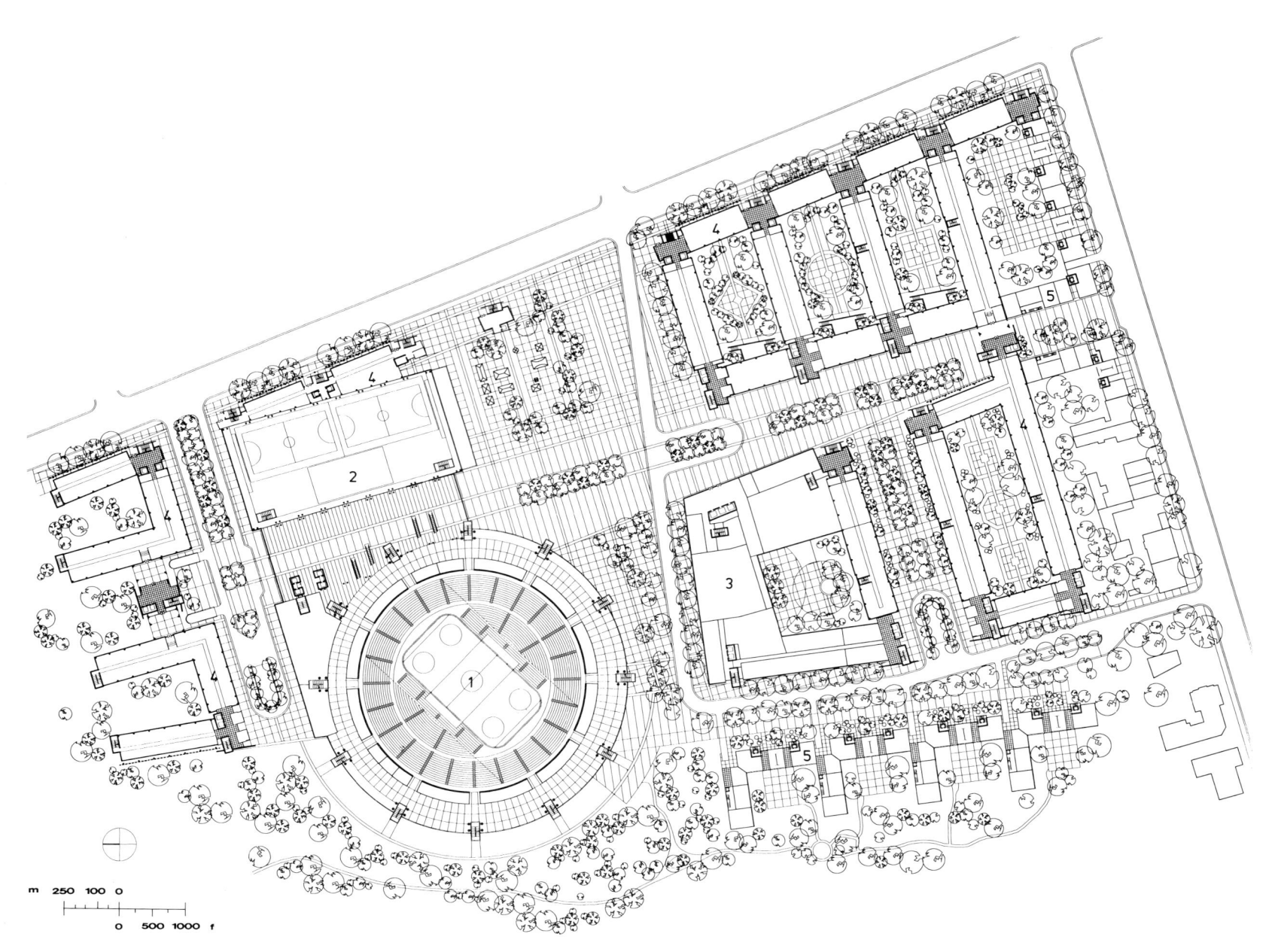

149

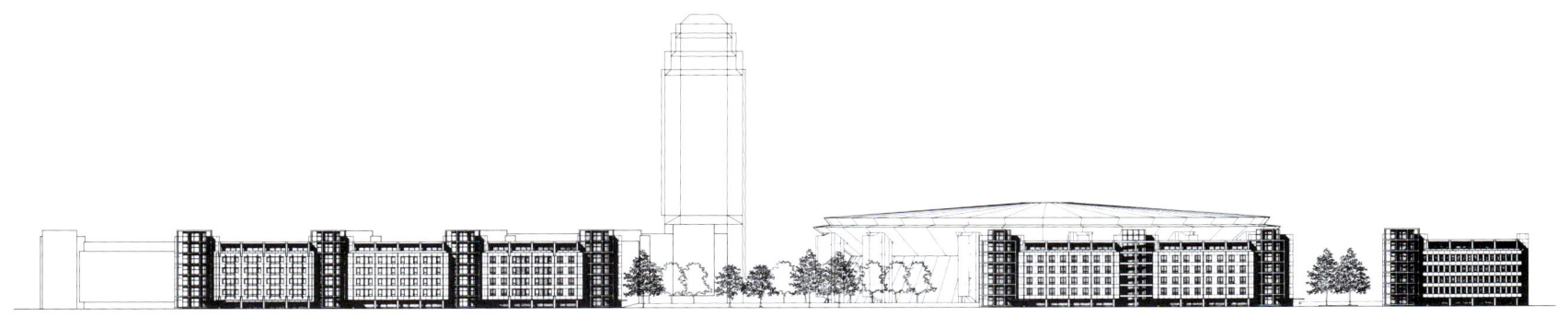

American Business Center, Berlin, Germany
1992. Competition entry

In 1992 Lohan Associates won third place in an invited design competition for a Berlin complex intended for American companies opening German offices. The designated site was challenging for its triangular shape and its historical significance as the former location of Checkpoint Charlie at the Berlin Wall.

The three-sided complex designed by Lohan Associates observes the traditional urban fabric of Berlin as it honors the importance of the site. Along its south boundary at Zimmerstraße, the structure takes on a monumental appearance, a deliberate reference to the Berlin Wall which ran along this street until recently. A bar protrudes from the top story of the complex to mark the spot where Checkpoint Charlie stood, and to suggest passage through that gate. Across the street from the new complex, fragments of the Wall have been left in place as a memorial. The Lohan scheme responds with an opening opposite the memorial, a gap that splits the complex like a street and leads to a semi-circular courtyard at the center.

The complex matches the height and scale of surrounding buildings; the incorporation of a courtyard – to be used to stage American cultural events – follows the customary model for Berlin's residential and office blocks. The new complex is six stories tall with two additional levels below ground where a convention facility and parking are located. The 400,000-square-foot complex is broken into five building units, each with a view to the courtyard and an independent core. Of these buildings, four are office structures and the fifth is residential. Where an existing building intrudes on the site on Mauerstraße, the complex steps around it, flanking it with two office buildings.

The same materials are used throughout the new complex unifying the buildings while variations on the design theme distinguish them from one another.

1. Aerial view. Model.
2. Rendering.
3. Plan (ground floor). Key: 1 jazz garden, 2 pedestrian alley, 3 lobby, 4 jazz café, 5 shops, 6 existing building, 7 parking ramp.

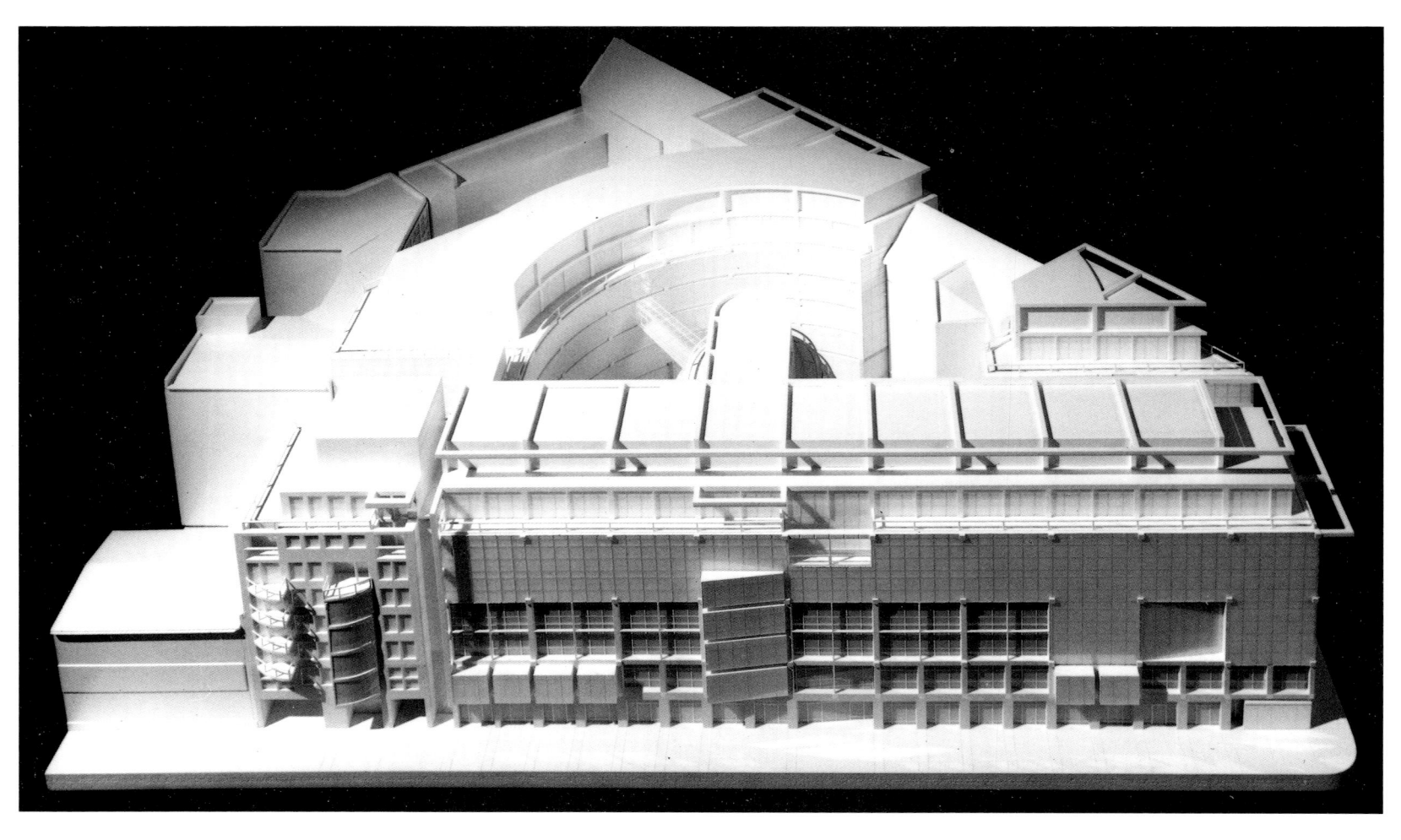

151

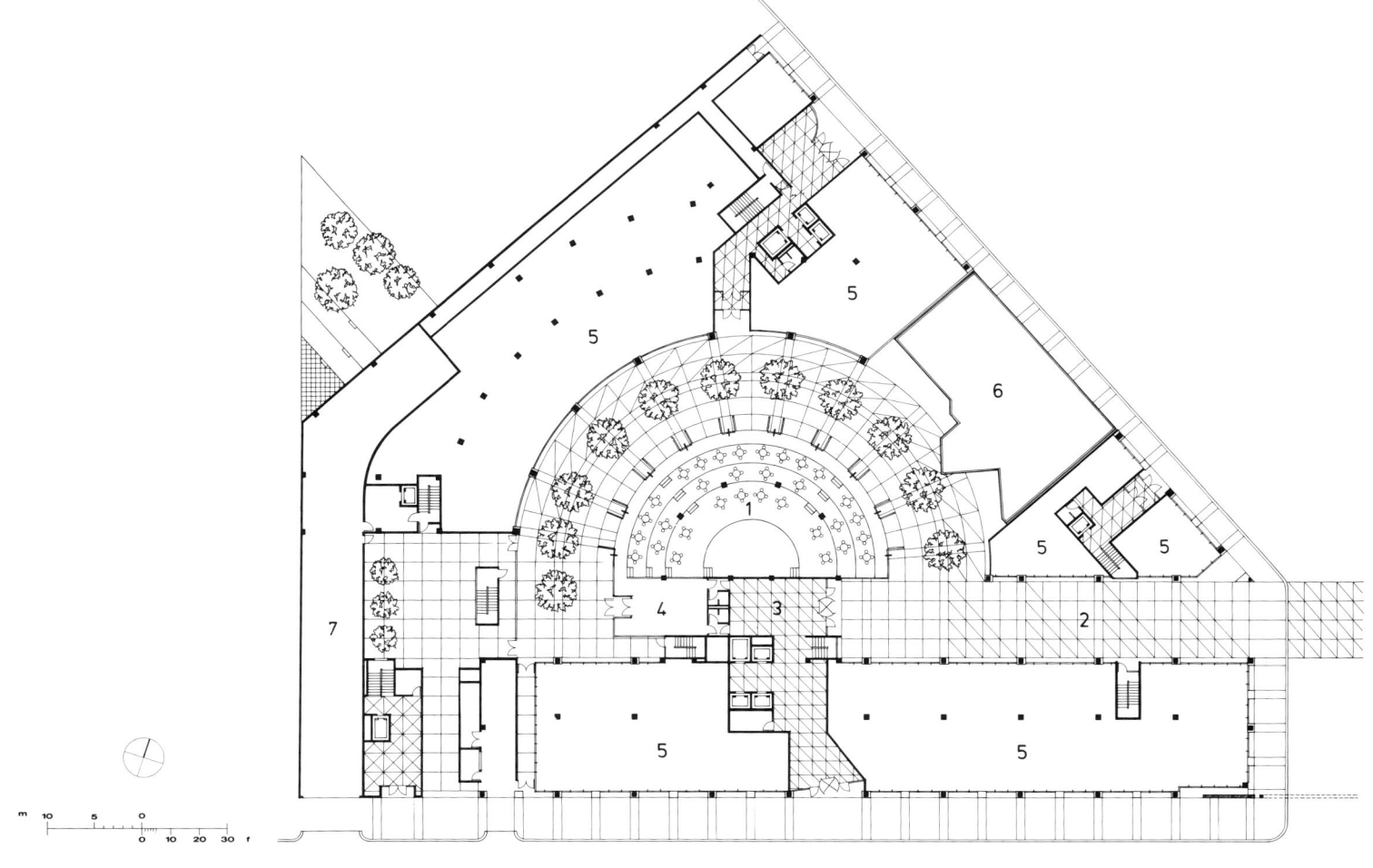

Mies van der Rohe Glass Tower at Bahnhof Friedrichstrasse, Berlin, Germany
1992/1993

In 1992 Lohan Associates was invited to submit to a competition for the redevelopment of a large area in Berlin. Aside from the Friedrichstraße train station the redevelopment area included the triangular site for which Ludwig Mies van der Rohe designed his famous glass tower in the competition of 1921/22.

Although Mies van der Rohe's entry did not even place, his design for a faceted glass skyscraper became a powerful symbol of Modernism that still resonates today. So it is that Lohan Associates transformed Mies's schematic design into a buildable tower for the same site – still standing vacant – that Mies competed for over 70 years ago. Despite the opposition of some who thought the tower should not be revived, Lohan proceeded with a proposal advancing its construction arguing that no other structure was imaginable on the site and nothing could equal Mies's vision.

Mies imagined a triangular building, conforming to the shape of the site, with three independent, angular wings projecting from a common circular core. The building was to be virtually transparent with wafer-thin floors. At the time the tower was designed the technology did not exist to realize Mies's vision. Current technology makes the building feasible, but the challenge remains: how to design the building retaining the delicacy Mies imagined while conforming to Berlin's contemporary zoning laws and life-safety codes?

Lohan's solution is double glass walls spaced roughly three feet apart. Aside from providing valuable insulation, this design will create the tower's intended transparency by separating the outer layer – which gives the tower its crystalline architectural appearance – from the functional inner building enclosure. Located between the glass walls will be a thin cantilevered plane aligned with the underside of the thicker floor construction inside the building. Glass mullions will make the outer curtain wall look seamless. Lohan's study reinterprets one of the great visions of modern architecture using contemporary technology.

To balance the tower's high density, the Lohan scheme proposed a large plaza on the south side of the railroad station. The plaza would be framed on the north by the gentle curve of the station façade, and to the south by a dramatic counter-curve of new buildings containing a circular glass winter garden. The remaining blocks would be built to the property line and match the cornice height of typical Berlin buildings. Ultimately, the Lohan scheme was not selected. Instead, a submission was chosen that contains no reference to the Mies high rise and maintains a uniform density throughout the redevelopment district.

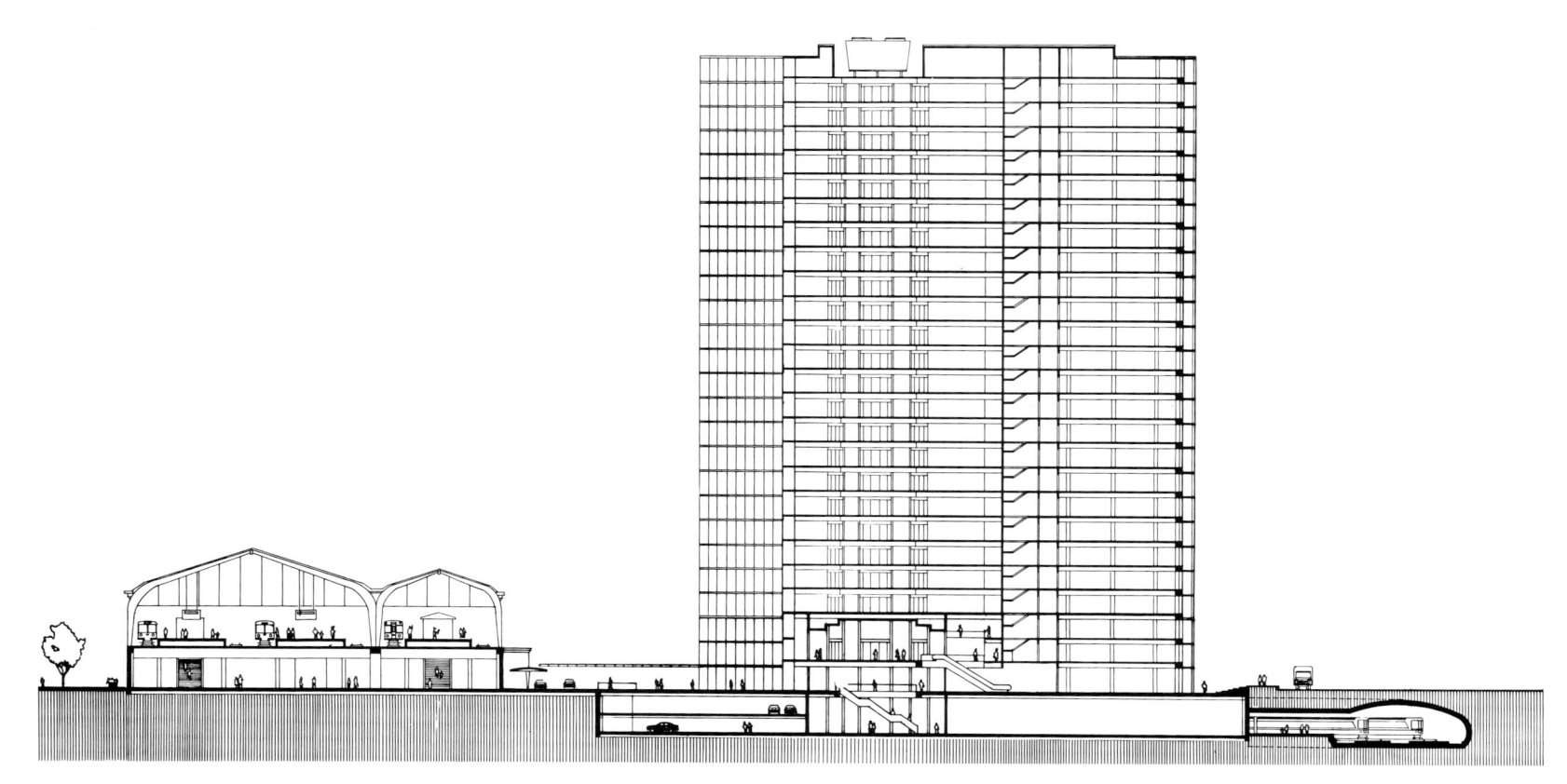

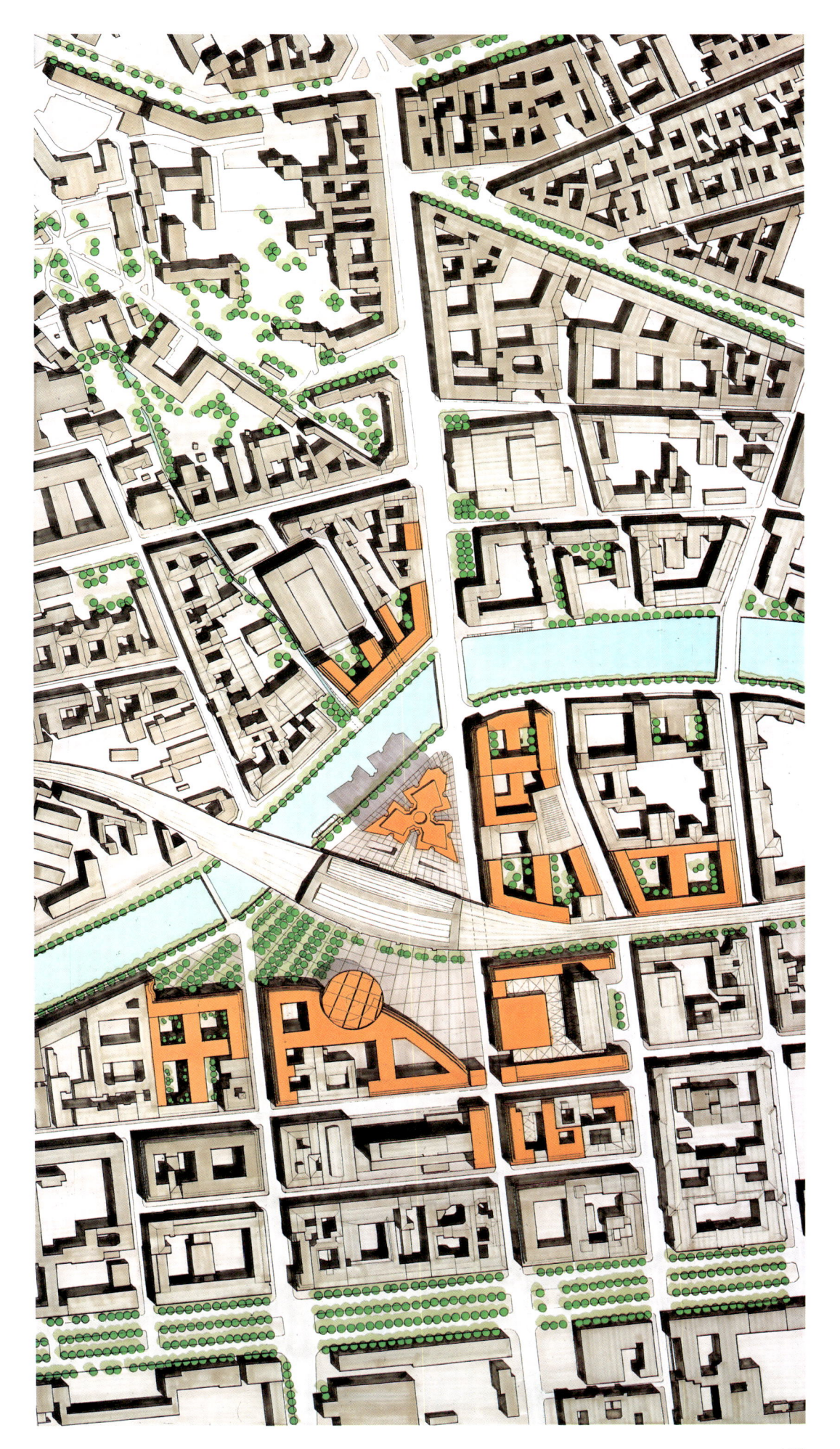

1. Rendering by Mies van der Rohe (1921/22).
2. Section showing connections to the train station and subway.
3. Site plan.

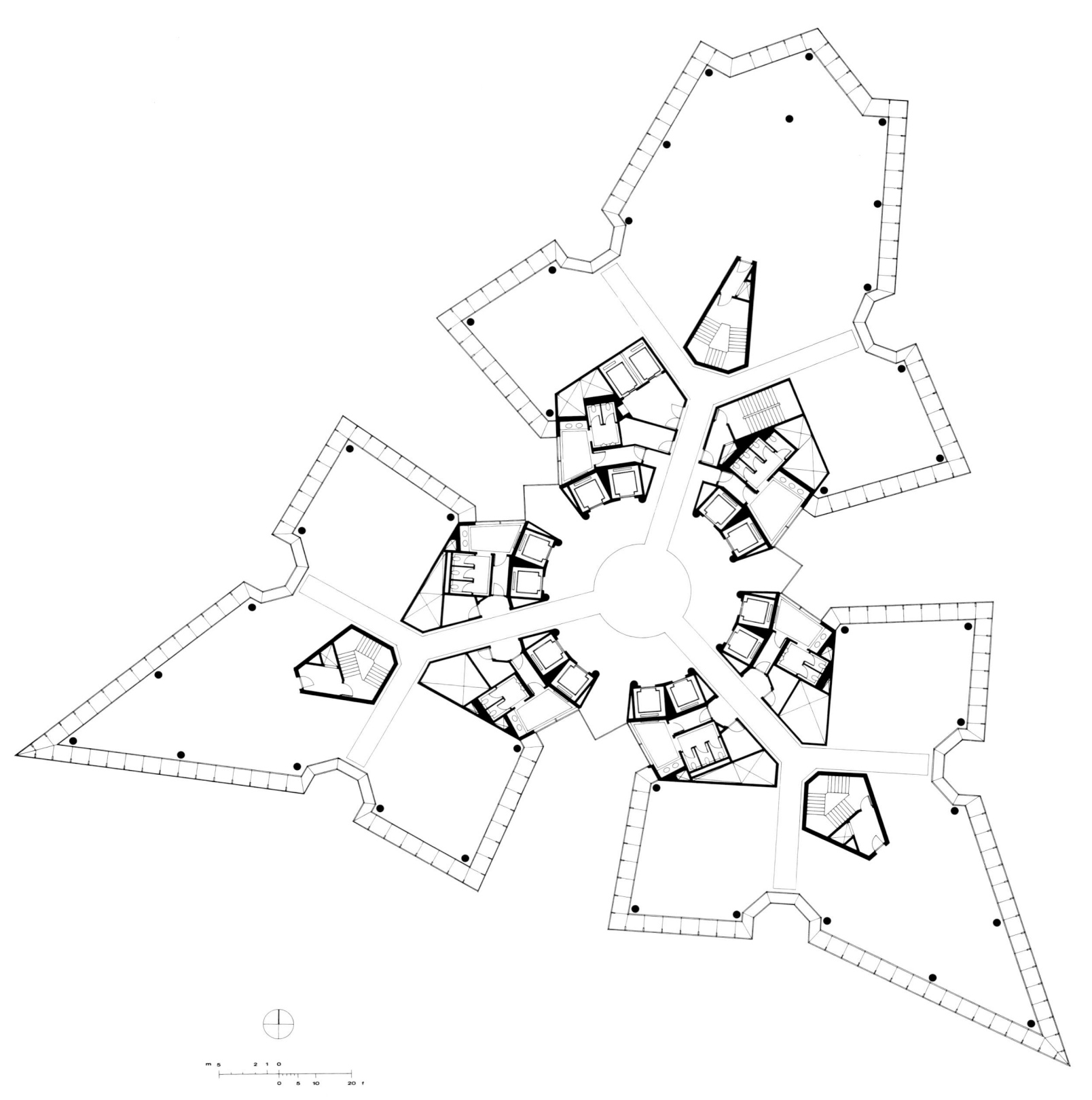

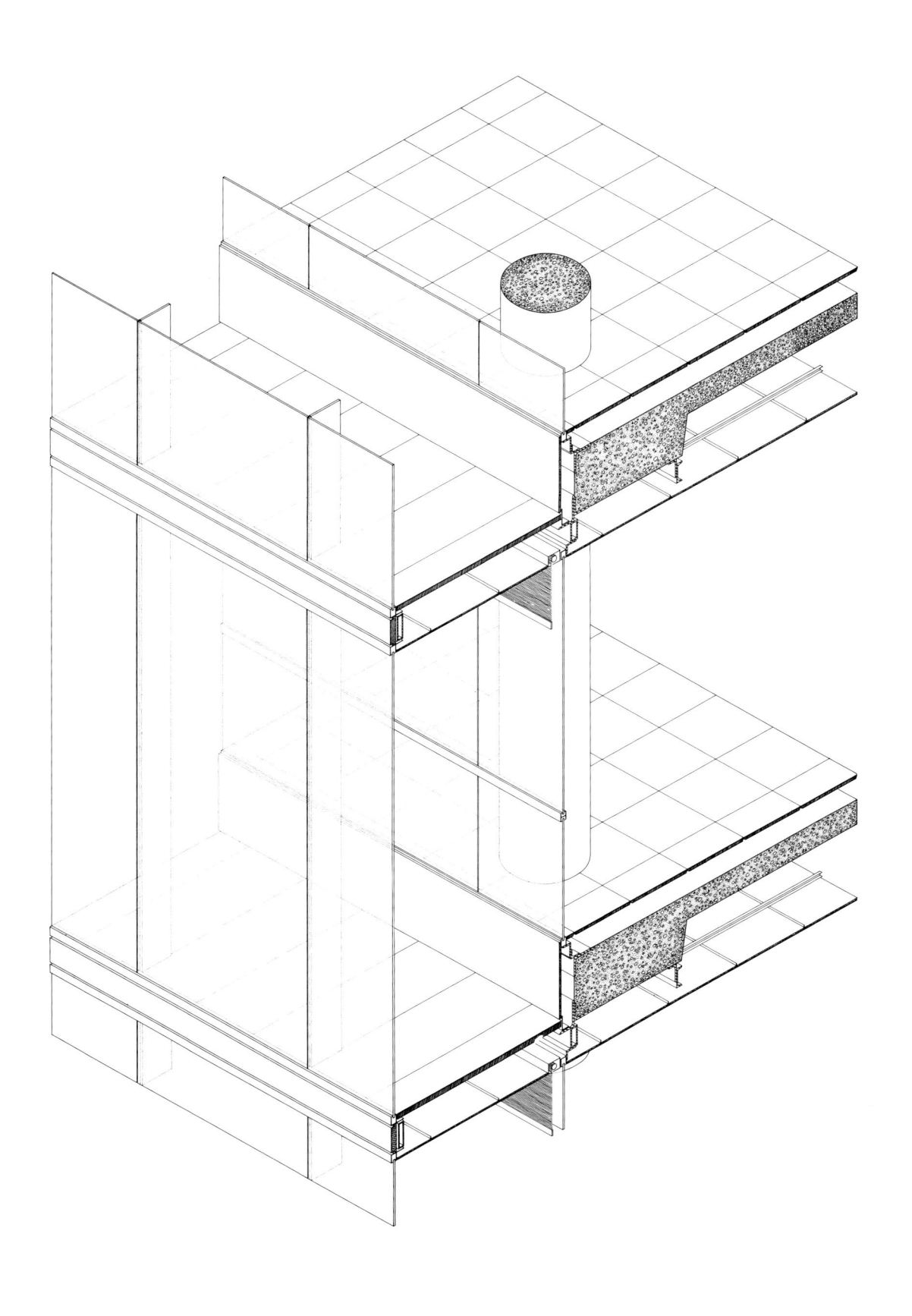

4. Typical floor.
5. Axonometric detail.

155

6, 7. The tower was conceived for a triangular site. A circular glass winter garden was proposed opposite the train station.

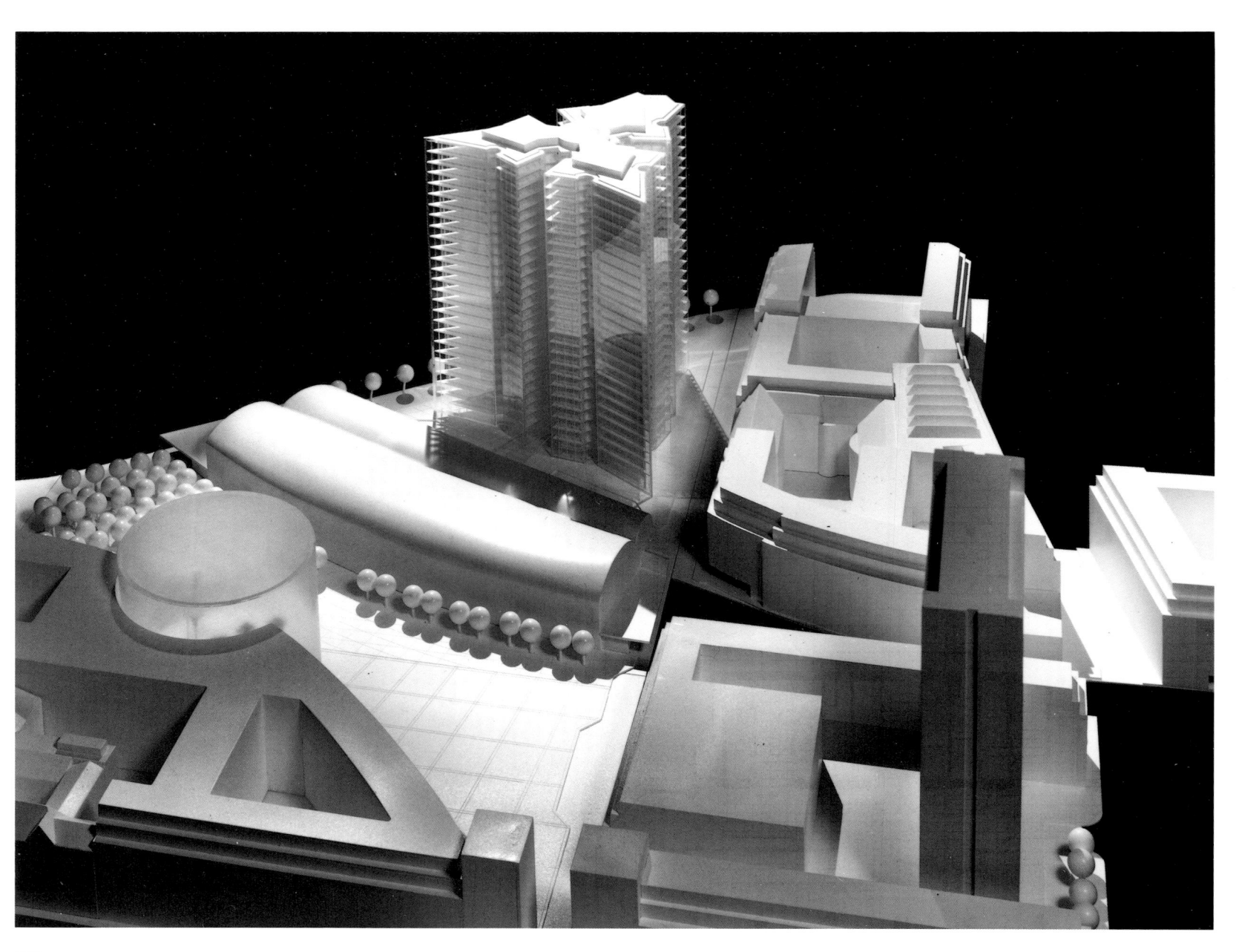

Credits for Illustrated Buildings and Projects

McDonald's Office Campus, Oak Brook, Illinois
Client: McDonald's Corporation
Principal in charge of design: Dirk Lohan
Principal in charge of management: Joseph Antunovich
Design architect: Gilbert Gorski
Project manager: Michael Vasilko
Project team: Frank Cavanaugh, Kenneth Crocco, Carl Dittburner, Joseph Dolinar, Mark Fischer, Perry Janke, William Rod Jones, Alan Lurie, Jeanne Marker, Phuong Nguyen, Jeff Pavur, Sandra Pruessner, Tracy Salvia, Carol Schmidt, William Sitton, David Swanlund, Rocco Tunzi, Timothy Vacha, Dean Walker, Theodore Witte
Interiors team: Sandra Radke, Cheryl Baughman, Michael Heider, William Mullenholz, Carol Stolt, Martha Strong Williams

TRW World Headquarters, Lyndhurst, Ohio
Client: TRW, Incorporated
Principal in charge: Dirk Lohan
Design architect: Melvin Wilson
Project manager: Joseph Caprile, Jerome Jones
Project team: John Arnold, John Birazzi, Mary DeRuntz, Joseph Dolinar, Geoff Hamburg, Leonard Koroski, Harry Kugasaki, Jeanne Marker, Nancy Novak, Arthur Salzman, Joyce Scholefield, Greg Vavra, Dean Walker, Lawrence Weldon, Stephen Yas

Frito-Lay National Headquarters, Plano, Texas
Client: Frito-Lay, Incorporated
Principal in charge: Dirk Lohan
Design architect: John Bowman
Project manager: Thomas Samuels
Project team: Kristen Andersen, Floyd Anderson, John Arnold, Thomas Bair, Michael Kaufman, Tim Meland, Algis Novickas, Arthur Salzman, Basil Souder, James Torvik, Lawrence Weldon, Gregory Williams
Interiors team: Michael Heider, Kathleen Hess, Karen Lindblad, Roger McFarland, Barbara Segal, Ann Weigand

The Oceanarium, Chicago, Illinois
Client: John G. Shedd Aquarium
Principal in charge: Dirk Lohan
Design architect: Algis Novickas
Project manager: Joseph Antunovich
Project team: Michael Barnes, Thomas Chan, Kenneth Crocco, Richard Fencl, Gilbert Gorski, Timothy Hubbard, Alan Lurie, Jeanne Marker, Phuong Nguyen, Mark Osorio, Jeffrey Pavur, Arthur Salzman, James Schubert, William Sitton, Robert Tassone, Timothy Vacha, Vytas Vepstas, Theodore Witte, Dean Walker
Interiors team: Cheryl Baughman, Karen Lindblad

Museum Campus, Chicago, Illinois
Client: Field Museum of Natural History, John G. Shedd Aquarium, The Adler Planetarium, Chicago Park District
Principal in charge: Dirk Lohan
Project planner: John LaMotte
Project team: Joel Stauber

Cityfront Center, Chicago, Illinois
Client: Chicago Dock & Canal Trust
Principal in charge of design: Dirk Lohan
Principal in charge of management: Joseph Caprile
Design architects: John Arnold, David Fleener, Stephen Yas
Project manager: Leonard Koroski
Project team: Thomas Chan, Richard Gee, Janet Krehbiel, Joel Stauber, Michael Zanco

Market Tower, Indianapolis, Indiana
Client: Mansur Development Corporation
Principal in charge: Dirk Lohan
Design architect: R. Graham Greene
Project manager: Edwin M. Denson
Project team: Edwin Davis, Roy Gunsolus, Lawrence Keen, Kellie Powers-Lawson, Stanley Schachne, Gregory Schon, Dean Walker
In association with Ratio Architects, Indianapolis

Dean Witter Financial Services Headquarters, Riverwoods, Illinois
Client: Homart Development Company
Principal in charge: Dirk Lohan
Design architect: John Bowman, Gregory Williams
Project manager: George Halik
Project team: Thomas Bair, John Birazzi, Thomas Chan, Brad Erdy, Michael Lynch, Lawrence Weldon
Interiors team: Michael Heider, Karen Lindblad

Rockwell International Graphic Systems Headquarters, Westmont, Illinois
Client: Rockwell International Graphic Systems Division
Principal in charge: Dirk Lohan
Design Architect: John Bowman
Project Manager: Floyd Anderson
Project team: Richard Caplan, Vincent Caporale, Michael Heider, Karen Lindblad, Kevin Sossong, Edwin Witkowski

Lakefront Lagoon, Chicago, Illinois
Principal in charge: Dirk Lohan
Design architect: Gilbert Gorski

One-Fifty North Dearborn Office Tower, Chicago, Illinois
Client: Miller-Klutznick-Davis-Gray Company
Principal in charge: Dirk Lohan
Design architect: Algis Novickas
Project manager: Edwin M. Denson
Project team: Paul Audrain, Michael Barnes, Susan Budinsky, Thomas Chan, Boonlert Chutkrich, Karen Kastein, James Lee, F. Jeffrey Murray, James Schubert, Brian Schutz, Timothy Vacha, Dean Walker

Ameritech Center, Hoffman Estates, Illinois
Client: Ameritech Properties Corporation
Principal in charge of design: Dirk Lohan
Principal in charge of management: Joseph Caprile
Design architect: John Bowman, David Fleener
Project planner: John LaMotte
Project manager: Basil Souder
Project team: Susan Budinski, Vincent Caporale, Stephen Carbery, Richard Fencl, William Gamble, Michael Jurick, Janet Krehbiel, Leonard Koroski, Joanne Mascaro-Baltis, Arthur Salzman, Joel Stauber, Dean Walker, Ed Witkowski

Illinois State Toll Highway Authority Headquarters, Downers Grove, Illinois
Client: State Toll Highway Authority
Principal in charge: Dirk Lohan
Design architect: Perry Janke
Project manager: Floyd Anderson
Project team: Randall Deutsch, Elizabeth Janoski, David Mann, Kevin Sossong
Interiors team: Colette Rodon, Barbara Segal, Dawn Spiewak, Carol Stolt

Devon House, Ada, Michigan
Client: Scott and Terri Devon
Principal in charge: Dirk Lohan
Design architect: John Bowman, Gilbert Gorski
Project manager: George Halik
Project team: Cathy Andrews, Paul Armstrong, William Sitton, Edwin Witkowski, Anthony Wrzosek

Harold Washington Library Center, Chicago, Illinois
Client: City of Chicago and the Chicago Public Library Board
Principal in charge: Dirk Lohan
Design architect: R. Graham Greene
Project manager: Edwin M. Denson
Interior architect: Michael Heider
Project team: Syed Ahmed, Sui-Sheng Chang, Kenneth Crocco, Randall Dolph, Mark Fischer, Mark Grasmehr, Alex Leung, Alan Lurie, F. Jeffrey Murray, Walter Myers, Donald Wetzel
In association with Johnson, Reid, Lee, Chicago

Amerika-Gedenkbibliothek, Berlin, Germany
Client: City of Berlin
Principal in charge: Dirk Lohan
Design architect: Gilbert Gorski
Project manager: George Halik
Project team: Eva Bitsch, Donald Wetzel

Steelcase/Stow & Davis Showroom, Chicago, Illinois
Client: Steelcase/Stow & Davis
Principal in charge: Dirk Lohan
Design architect: Michael Heider
Project manager: Barbara Segal
Interiors team: Cathy Andrews, Mark Fischer, Roger McFarland

Dain Bosworth Tower, Minneapolis, Minnesota
Client: Brookfield Development, Incorporated
Principal in charge: Dirk Lohan
Principal in charge of management: Joseph Antunovich
Design architect: Thomas Shafer
Project manager: Michael Kaufman, Lawrence Weldon
Project team: Paul Audrain, John Birazzi, Peter Carlson, Randall Dolph, Richard Fencl, Shirley Moy, Frank Mraz, Charles Smith, David Strandberg, Dean Walker

Village of Old Mill Creek, Old Mill Creek, Illinois
Client: Tempel Farms
Principal in charge: Dirk Lohan

Project planner: John LaMotte
Project team: Scott Freres, Joel Stauber

Safety-Kleen Corporate Headquarters, Elgin, Illinois
Client: Safety-Kleen Corporation
Principal in charge: Dirk Lohan
Design architect: John Bowman, David Fleener
Project manager: George Halik
Project team: Paul Armstrong, Brad Erdy, Richard Fencl, Kathryn Hauserman, F. Jeffrey Murray, David Swanlund, Dean Walker, Edwin Witkowski

Eli Lilly and Company Interiors, Indianapolis, Indiana
Client: Eli Lilly and Company
Principal in charge: Dirk Lohan
Design architects: Michael Heider, Timothy Vacha
Project manager: George Halik
Interiors team: Cathy Andrews, Paul Armstrong, Cheryl Baughman, Howard Dorf, Kathryn Hauserman, Robert Leady, Karen Lindblad
Building architect: Browning Day Mullins Dierdorf Inc.

University of Chicago Graduate School of Business, Chicago, Illinois
Client: University of Chicago Graduate School of Business
Principal in charge: Dirk Lohan
Design architect: Algis Novickas
Project manager: Edwin M. Denson
Project team: Cathy Andrews, Dawn Brightfield, Michael Barnes, Frank Cavanaugh, Boonlert Chutkrich, Brad Erdy, William Gamble, Michael Heider, Karen Lindblad, James Lee, F. Jeffrey Murray, Phuong Nguyen, Dean Walker, Donald Wetzel

University of Illinois at Chicago Molecular Biology Research Facility, Chicago, Illinois
Client: University of Illinois at Chicago
Principal in charge: Dirk Lohan
Design architect: Perry Janke
Project manager: Floyd Anderson
Project team: Stephen Carbery, Thomas Chan, Randall Deutsch, Nevin Hedlund, Shirley Moy, Donald Wetzel

Lincoln Park Residence, Chicago, Illinois
Client: Name withheld at the owner's request
Design architect: Perry Janke
Project manager: Floyd Anderson
Project team: Randall Deutsch, Elizabeth Janoski, William Sitton

Harris Trust and Savings Bank Operations Center, Chicago, Illinois
Client: Harris Trust & Savings Bank
Principal in charge of design: Dirk Lohan
Principal in charge of management: Joseph Caprile
Design architect: Thomas Shafer
Project manager: Michael Kaufman
Project team: Boonlert Chutkrich, Randall Dolph, Brad Erdy, Amy Jordan, Joanne Mascaro-Baltis, David Strandberg, Donald Wetzel, Michael Zanco
Interiors team: Michael Heider, Karen Lindblad

Olympiaquartier 2000, Berlin, Germany
Client: DG Immobilien Management GmbH, SIAB International, PAN Immobilien GmbH
Principal in charge: Dirk Lohan
Design architects: David Fleener, Perry Janke
Project team: Eva Bitsch, Frank Cavanaugh, Elizabeth Janoski, Frank Mraz, Martin Newton, Phuong Nguyen
In association with Albert Speer & Partner, Frankfurt am Main

American Business Center, Berlin, Germany
Client: Central European Development Corporation GmbH & Co. Checkpoint Charlie KG
Principal in charge: Dirk Lohan
Design architect: Matthias Royal-Hedinger
Project team: John Bowman, Martin Newton, Norberto Rosenstein, Edwin Witkowski

Mies van der Rohe Glass Tower at Bahnhof Friedrichstrasse, Berlin, Germany
Competition entry for the urban design of the district around the Bahnhof Friedrichstrasse
Principal in charge: Dirk Lohan
Project team: John Bowman, Stefan Bräuning, Matthias Royal-Hedinger, Michael Heider, Martin Newton, Michael Patten